TOEFL
READING AND
VOCABULARY WORKBOOK

The directions to the sample questions were reprinted by permission of The Educational Testing Service. However, the sample test questions were neither provided nor approved by The Educational Testing Service.

Second Edition

Macmillan General Reference
A Prentice Hall/Macmillan Company
15 Columbus Circle
New York, NY 10023

An Arco Book

MACMILLAN is a registered trademark of Macmillan, Inc.
ARCO is a registered trademark of Prentice-Hall, Inc.

Library of Congress Cataloging-in-Publication Data

Davy, Elizabeth.
TOEFL reading and vocabulary workbook /
[Elizabeth Davy, Karen Davy].
Previously published as TOEFL reading comprehension and
vocabulary workbook.
    p.   cm.
ISBN 0-13-926965-7
1. English language—Textbooks for foreign speakers.
2. English language—Examinations—Study guides.
3. Reading comprehension. 4. Vocabulary. I. Davy, Karen, 1951-
II. Title.
PE1128.D354   1992   92-24199
428.2'421—dc20   CIP

Manufactured in the United States of America

10 9 8 7 6 5 4

CONTENTS

Preface v
   General Information v
   Why Use This Book? v
   Tips for Taking Tests vi

International Students' Guide to College Admissions 1

Reading Comprehension and Vocabulary Pretest 5

Part I.   Developing Reading Comprehension Skills 13
      Finding Main Ideas and Supporting Details 13
      Skimming for Specific Information 16
      Defining Words from Context 22
      Making Inferences 25
      Understanding Advertisements 46

Part II.   How Thoughts Are Related 69

Part III. Understanding Contemporary Reading Passages 105

Part IV. Tactics for Reading from History Textbooks 130

Part V.   Interpretation of Scientific Reading Materials 159

Answer Sheets for Practice Tests 181

Reading Comprehension and Vocabulary Practice Test A 185

Reading Comprehension and Vocabulary Practice Test B 198

Reading Comprehension and Vocabulary Practice Test C 211

Word List 224

Answer Key 228

PREFACE

General Information

The Test of English as a Foreign Language (TOEFL) measures the English ability of people whose native language is not English. The test, which takes about three and one-half hours to administer, consists of three separately timed sections of multiple-choice questions:

1. Listening Comprehension, which evaluates proficiency in understanding spoken English
2. Structure and Written Expression, which evaluates proficiency in recognizing language appropriate for standard written English
3. Reading Comprehension and Vocabulary, which evaluates comprehension of non-technical reading material and knowledge of the meanings and uses of words and idiomatic phrases

The TOEFL is required for admission to more than 2,300 colleges and universities in the United States, Canada, and other places where English is the language of instruction. Government agencies, scholarship programs, and other institutions require the test. According to the *TOEFL Bulletin of Information*, last year more than 787,000 people applied to take the TOEFL. The TOEFL office does not decide what scores are acceptable; each institution or agency makes its own decision.

The *TOEFL Bulletin* describes the test and provides information you need about registering for and taking the test. All candidates should read the *TOEFL Bulletin of Information* for the most up-to-date information about the test. To obtain a copy, write to TOEFL, Box 6151, Princeton, New Jersey 08541, United States.

Why Use This Book?

This workbook will prepare you for the Reading Comprehension and Vocabulary section of the TOEFL. This section, one of the three parts that make up the exam, consists of multiple-choice questions testing your knowledge of word meanings and your ability to comprehend a variety of reading materials.

Start your preparation for the TOEFL Reading and Vocabulary Test by taking the Pretest on page 5. This test is shorter than the actual TOEFL section, but the instructions are exactly as you will find them on the TOEFL, and the questions are very similar to those on the exam. Thus you may familiarize yourself with the TOEFL instructions and the kinds of questions you will face. After taking the Pretest, check your answers with the explanations that follow each type of question to see where you need to concentrate your efforts in order to improve your score.

This book has been designed to teach reading skills and increase vocabulary by means of reading passages with both comprehension and vocabulary exercises. The reading passages progress from relatively simple to relatively difficult as you continue through the book. Various skills, such as finding the main idea and supporting details, are taught. Following the reading and vocabulary lessons you will find three complete Comprehension and Vocabulary Tests. These tests consist of ninety questions similar to those on the TOEFL. They will show you how well you have mastered the reading and vocabulary skills presented in this book. Should you score well on these tests, you may face the TOEFL with high expectations of a good score. If your score is lower than you would like it to be, isolate the types of material on which you scored badly and go back to the sections of this book that provide instruction in those areas.

Tips for Taking Tests

1. Review before the test, but do *not* cram the night before the test. Get a good night's sleep and try to feel confident and calm as you go to the test location.

2. Arrive at the test center with your registration confirmation ticket and proper identification—your passport if you take the test outside your country or either your passport or whatever identification requirements are printed on your reservation confirmation ticket if you take the test within your country. *Without acceptable identification you will not be admitted to the test center.*

3. Listen carefully to all verbal instructions.

4. Read all written instructions carefully. Do *not* rush to the questions. Be sure you understand the instructions before you begin the test. Look at the examples given on the test.

5. You are given either 45 or 65 minutes to complete the Reading Comprehension and Vocabulary section of the test depending on whether or not the TWE, Test of Written English, is being given on the same day. Answer the easy questions first; then go back to the more difficult questions. Avoid hurrying to finish.

6. Stop and rest a few times during the allotted time.

7. On your answer sheet, blacken the circle for the answer completely. A partially filled circle may not record on the computer that scores your test.

8. If you are not sure of an answer, try an intelligent guess. You are scored on the basis of the number of correct answers, so you should answer every question.

9. You should choose the *best answer*. Vocabulary is presented in context. The best answer, therefore, is the meaning of the word as it is used in the sentence given in the test. Words may have several meanings, but only the meaning in the context of the given sentence is correct.

10. Work quickly but carefully. Keep your eye on the time as you work.

International Students' Guide to College Admissions

By Anna Leider, President, Octameron Associates

Getting into an American College

Students making plans to study abroad often choose to study in the United States. The reason is clear. The U.S. education system has developed in response to the needs of a diverse population, and is therefore adaptable to many career and personal goals. At the same time, students should keep in mind that college-level study in the U.S. is both serious and demanding, especially for international students who come without family or cultural support. Accordingly, before students decide to study in the U.S., they should ask themselves the following:

1. Why do I want to study in the U.S.? Is the program of study I plan to pursue not available in my own country? Am I truly committed to education, or am I just trying to avoid an unpleasant home situation?

2. What do I want to study? Am I studying something relevant to my country's needs? What will my degree be worth when I return home?

3. How well prepared am I? Have I completed the equivalent of a high school education? How proficient am I in English?

4. What is my financial status? Will I be able to support myself if I am unable to work while in the U.S.?

5. Am I mature enough to live in a different culture? Am I accepting of different customs, food and climate? Am I ready to be looked on as "a foreigner?"

If, after thinking about all these questions, a student still wants to pursue a U.S. education, he or she should begin the application process.

International Student Characteristics

Nearly 356,000 international students currently study in the U.S. The largest group (approximately 180,540) comes from South or East Asia. Sixty-eight percent of international students are male. Eighty–eight percent attend four-year colleges and universities. Sixty-five percent attend public institutions. Twenty-one percent of international students study engineering. Twenty percent study business or management. Thirty-eight and a half percent are working toward a four-year undergraduate degree. Forty-four percent are working toward a graduate degree. Eleven percent are working toward a two-year associate degree. The remaining six-and-a-half percent are in non-degree programs, or English language programs.

Choosing a College

Choosing a college from among 3,000 options is not easy for anyone, but the process is especially difficult for students unfamiliar with the U.S. This section is intended to supplement the general chapter on college selection. It focuses on ways to begin researching colleges, and lists additional criteria for international students to consider as they read through brochures and college catalogs.

Overseas Educational Advising Centers. These agencies are the best places for students to begin their research. Trained counselors are available to answer questions and provide guidance. The centers usually have books and catalogs with detailed information on study programs, application procedures, attendance costs and freshman class profiles. Overseas Counseling Centers sometimes contain videotapes of college campuses, so students can "visit" a variety of schools. A list of Overseas Educational Advising Centers is available from the College Board, Office of International Education, 1717 Massachusetts Avenue NW, Washington DC 20036, U.S.A.

Foreign Student Information Clearinghouse (FSIC). Many overseas counseling centers use this computer program to help students identify suitable colleges. The student answers a series of questions about school preferences and in return, receives a computer printout of schools meeting his or her requirements. A small fee is charged for this service. Students should discuss the institutions named on the printout with a college advisor, and write the schools directly for more current information. Please note: Use of the Clearinghouse does not mean students have been admitted to the colleges listed on their printout! More information on FSIC may be obtained from the College Board (address above).

Field of Study. Unless students know exactly what they want to study, they should select a school that offers a wide range of subjects.

Location. In selecting a college, students must consider geography, climate, and demographics. No matter what their preference, they will discover a school. Colleges are found near beaches, mountains, and deserts; in regions that have freezing temperatures for nearly half the year, and in regions that are always warm; in densely populated cities and in thinly populated rural areas. Note: Large cities are generally more ethnically diverse and offer a greater variety of cultural activities.

Size of School. Students must also choose between a large university and a small college. A large university generally has better international student support services; a small school is often less intimidating.

Accreditation. Unlike many countries, the U.S. has no centralized authority for educational matters. Instead, it uses a system of accreditation to verify the quality of institutions. Accreditation covers admission and graduation requirements, curriculum, and academic facilities. To enroll in a non-accredited program is usually a waste of time and money. All of the schools listed in this book are accredited.

Inquiry Process

After students have narrowed their choice of schools to ten or twelve, they should write to the schools directly to obtain application forms, current catalogs, and information on international student services.

Letter of Inquiry. The inquiry letter should include the following:

1. Full name, age, marital status, and mailing address.
2. Education to date (include the location of the school, subjects studied, dates of attendance, class rank, and grades received).
3. Total amount and source of funds (in U.S. dollars) which will be available to contribute to education each year.
4. Planned course of study.
5. Estimate of English proficiency (written and spoken).

International Student Advisor. Almost all schools with international students have at least one designated international student advisor. This person helps students make cultural, academic, and social adjustments. He or she can answer questions about visas, financial assistance, student employment, and U.S. government regulations specific to the international student community. Finally, the advisor can help students find places to stay during semester breaks (small schools, especially, close down between semesters and often will not allow any students to remain on campus).

English as a Second Language (ESL). This program is designed to help students improve their written and spoken English. Many schools will accept students not fluent in English with the understanding they will complete an ESL program before they begin their official program of study. *English Language and Orientation Programs in the United States* contains a list of ESL programs (the book is available from the Institute of International Education (I.I.E.), 809 United Nations Plaza, New York, NY 10017, U.S.A.). Note: These are not degree programs, so it does not matter if they are accredited. In fact, very few are.

International Student Orientation. Some schools have a special orientation for international students before the start of the fall semester. This is a good time for students to become familiar with the school and the surrounding community, to meet the international student advisor, and to meet each other.

Community Support Programs. Large cities, especially, will have non-profit organizations that sponsor activities for international students. Activities include tours of the city and surrounding areas, museum visits, travel seminars, "ethnic" dinners, and visits with American families.

Mailing Instructions. Although it is expensive, students should use air mail for all their correspondence. Students should also send colleges the correct international air postage (which may be purchased in local post offices) so their requests are answered using air mail. Why is this so important? Surface mail takes months to reach a location abroad and students may miss deadlines while waiting for their ship to come in.

Applying to Colleges

In filling out the college application, students should be completely honest and not omit anything. An incomplete application, or one with deliberate falsehoods, will be returned and the student may miss application deadlines or be denied admission altogether. If students must leave something unanswered, they should attach a note which explains the reason. Students may be asked to do any or all of the following.

Complete an Application Form. The application form is used to collect basic information about the applicant, including country of citizenship, community or scholastic awards, future goals, employment history, and statement of personal objectives.

Pay an Application Fee. In countries with a currency restriction in effect, this fee (usually between U.S.$10 and U.S.$50) may be waived.

Submit a Transcript. Students must provide an official English language transcript (a detailed list of subjects studied, examination results, and an explanation of the school's grading system). Official transcripts are those sent directly by one school to another, and are stamped with an official school seal.

Submit Letters of Recommendation. Letters must be from teachers or employers and should discuss the applicant's strengths and weaknesses as a candidate for admission to a U.S. college.

Take Standardized Tests. Many schools require students to take the SAT or the ACT. Test scores must be submitted by the testing agency directly to the schools designated by the applicant.

Demonstrate English Language Proficiency. Students must submit satisfactory test results from an examination such as the Test of English as a Foreign Language (TOEFL). The TOEFL is a timed examination consisting of listening comprehension, written expression, and reading comprehension. The TOEFL Bulletin of Information contains registration forms, a list of test centers, test dates, and sample questions. To obtain a bulletin, write TOEFL, Box 6151, Princeton, New Jersey 08541–6151, U.S.A. Reminder: The TOEFL is not an application for admission to any institution. Two other English language proficiency tests are the American Language Institute of Georgetown University (ALIGU) exam which is given by American Embassies overseas, and the Michigan Test (English Language Institute, University of Michigan, Ann Arbor, Michigan 48104, U.S.A.) Students should check with the schools to which they are applying to learn which tests to take. Many schools recognize only TOEFL scores.

Submit Detailed Financial Information. Students must fill out the College Scholarship Service's "Declaration and Certification of Finances" (or its equivalent) to prove they will have adequate financial support for the intended period of study. All sources of support must be documented. Savings accounts must be verified with financial statements signed by a bank official. Sponsors, whether they be employers, relatives, or friends, must sign an affidavit of support witnessed by a Notary Public or Legal Official. If the student lives in a country that restricts funds sent abroad, the student must submit bank approval for currency exchange (a guarantee that funds will be transferred to the U.S. college or university).

Certification of Health. Students must fill out a medical history form. In addition, students are often given a brief medical examination upon arrival at the school. Note: Health care in the U.S. is very expensive. As students are likely to require health care at some point during their college years, they are strongly encouraged to protect themselves by enrolling in the school's health insurance plan.

Paying for College

Employment. Strict regulations govern the employment of international students in the U.S., therefore, students should not assume they will have a salary to assist them in paying their educational expenses. International students are eligible for fellowships and assistantships but, returning students and graduate students are given preference for these positions.

Grants and Loans. Students should not expect to receive money from U.S. government student aid programs. This money is reserved for U.S. citizens or permanent residents. Private banks may extend personal loans to students with the necessary collateral.

Scholarships. Some institutions offer scholarships to entering international students. They want to attract outstanding students from all across the world, to diversify their student body and enhance their reputation. For a list of scholarships, get *Scholarships for International Students: A Guide to U.S.A. Colleges and Universities* from Scholarship Research Group, 16600 Sprague Road, Ste. 110, Middleburg Heights, Ohio 44130.

Private Sources. Many private awards are available for study and research. For information on these awards, write to the I.I.E. (address above) and ask for *Financial Resources for International Study.* Information on Fulbright Hayes awards (a large scholarship program) is available from Binational Education Centers.

Visa and Immigration Requirements

Visa and immigration requirements are complex. A brief summary of the most common travel documents follows. For additional information, or clarification, students should contact a U.S. consulate.

Passport. Students must have a passport! This document is issued to students by their home government to identify them for the purpose of traveling to other countries. Passports are official documents and may be used only by the person to whom they are issued. Passports should never be lent to anyone. They should never be used as a form of collateral, nor should they ever be altered, except by authorized government agents.

Visa. This is a stamp on a passport that gives people permission to enter a country other than their own. Issuance of a student visa requires a valid passport, proof of English language proficiency, and proof of financial support. More specific requirements are listed for each visa type.

F-1. Nonimmigrant Student Visa. This is the most common visa granted to students. An F-1 visa permits students to enter the U.S. temporarily to pursue a full-time program of study. An F-1 visa is issued only after receipt of a Form I-20A, Certificate of Eligibility for Nonimmigrant Student Status. Form I-20A is sent to students by a school after they have been accepted. It indicates the program name and cost, the expected term of study, verification of English proficiency, and the student's means of financial support. Students must apply for their visa using the I-20A issued by the school they plan to attend, and no other. U.S. Government regulations require attendance for at least one semester at the school whose I-20 is used to obtain a visa. Form I-20A (like Forms I-20M and IAP-66 described below) will be returned to the student after the visa has been issued. Students should be careful not to lose it, as they must present the form at the port of entry when they arrive in the U.S.

M-1. New Student Visa. This classification of student visa is granted to students who wish to pursue a vocational program of study. The visa requirements are similar to F-1 visas, except the visa is issued for a shorter period of time and form I-20A is replaced by Form I-20M.

J-1. Exchange Visitor Visa. This visa is granted to students or teachers participating in an educational exchange program recognized by the U.S. Department of State. Generally, these are people engaged in research, consultation, teaching, or specialized training. A visa is issued only after receipt of Form IAP-66, Certificate of Eligibility for Exchange Visitor Status. This form is similar to the I-20A, except it is issued by the U.S. organization or government agency sponsoring the student.

F-2, M-2, J-2 Dependent Visas. These visas are granted to the spouse and children of F-1, M-1, and J-1 visa recipients, respectively.

Form I-94, Arrival-Departure Record. This is a U.S. Immigration form that indicates the purpose of the student's admission to the U.S., and the length of time the student may remain. Form I-94 should remain with the student's passport.

Form I-20 ID. This yellow card describes the entitlements F-1 or M-1 students may receive, such as whether they may accept employment or transfer schools. It also bears an 11-digit identification number assigned to the student (for life) by the INS. Students should keep this card separate from their passport, and carry it with them at all times. Thy should also memorize their ID number in case the card is lost or stolen. Replacement will be much easier.

Employment. An F-1 student may accept part-time (less than 20 hours per week) on-campus employment while school is in session, but these jobs are generally low-paying ($3.00 to $6.00 per hour) relative to student expenses. Full-time work is permitted only during vacations. Off-campus employment is permitted only with approval of the Immigration and Naturalization Service (INS), and that approval is extremely difficult to obtain. The spouse of an F-1 student is not eligible to work under any conditions. Neither M-1 students nor their spouses may accept employment of any kind. J-1 students may work either on- or off-campus provided they can show financial need and they obtain the approval of their program sponsor. Spouses of J-1 students may receive permission to work from the INS if they can prove employment is needed for their own support (or the support of a child). The spouse may not work if the wages are for the support of a J-1 student.

Change of Schools. F-1 students may transfer from one school to another to begin a new educational program only with INS permission. F-1 students may transfer from one school to another to pursue the same educational program just by notifying the INS a transfer has occurred. M-1 students may not change their educational objectives. They may not transfer between schools after six months. And they may not switch their student status to F-1. J-1 students may transfer between schools or programs as long as they have approval from their program sponsor.

Intent to Return Home. Students should not expect their student status to lead to an immigrant visa. In fact, students who do not intend to return home after finishing their studies are legally barred from even obtaining a student visa. In the visa interview, the U.S. consul will want to hear about close family ties and job options available at home upon completion of studies.

Tourist (B-2) Visas. Students should not come to the U.S. on a tourist visa and expect to change their classification after arrival. The INS is strict about this. Students who want to visit the United States before their student visa can be processed should prove to the U.S. consul their intent (and financial ability) to attend one of the schools to which they've applied. The consul realizes some students may want to look at schools before deciding which one to attend, and can stamp "prospective student" on a B-2 visa. This will eliminate later problems with the INS.

Arrival in the United States

Students should plan to arrive on a weekday when college and university offices are open and staff is available to assist them. Some schools (those located near ports of entry) may send representatives to the airport to assist students with immigration procedures.

Welcome, and best of luck!

Some of the material contained in these pages has been condensed from *Scholarships for International Students: A Guide to U.S.A. Colleges and Universities.* It is used by permission of Octameron Press.

Anna Leider is the owner and president of Octameron Associates, a publishing firm in the Washington, D.C. area that specializes in books on the topic of financial aid. Their publications cover the full range of financial aid available, from government grants to loans to private subsidies and scholarships.

READING COMPREHENSION AND VOCABULARY PRETEST

This test is designed to measure your ability to understand various kinds of reading materials, as well as your ability to understand the meaning and use of words. There are two types of questions in this section, with special directions for each type.

PART A. VOCABULARY

Directions: In Questions 1–15 each sentence has a word or phrase underlined. Below each sentence there are four other words or phrases, marked (A), (B), (C), and (D). You are to choose the *one* word or phrase that *best keeps the meaning* of the original sentence if it is substituted for the underlined word or phrase. On this pretest, circle the letter of the answer you have chosen.

Example:
His students think he is odd.
(A) dangerous   (C) strange
(B) friendly   (D) humorous

The best answer is (C) because the sentence, "His students think he is strange," is closest in meaning to, "His students think he is odd."
As soon as you understand the directions, begin work on the problems.

1. Oil is one of the principal sources of energy.
   (A) most expensive   (C) most difficult
   (B) most important   (D) most popular

2. No one can survive for very long without water.
   (A) reproduce   (C) transcend
   (B) prosper   (D) exist

3. The assignment was to write a synopsis of our favorite novel.
   (A) evaluation   (C) critique
   (B) summary   (D) dramatization

4. It is futile to go shopping when you don't have any money.
   (A) useless   (C) idiotic
   (B) brilliant   (D) challenging

5

5. The actress had to raise her voice in order to be <u>audible</u> in the balcony.
   - (A) musical
   - (B) dramatic
   - (C) heard
   - (D) appreciated

6. Dictators do not <u>tolerate</u> opposition of any kind.
   - (A) understand
   - (B) permit
   - (C) justify
   - (D) execute

7. Earthquakes occur <u>frequently</u> in parts of California.
   - (A) instantly
   - (B) annually
   - (C) spontaneously
   - (D) often

8. Martin Luther King fought to put an end to racial <u>segregation</u> in the United States.
   - (A) integration
   - (B) education
   - (C) separation
   - (D) torture

9. The number of <u>illiterates</u> in this country continues to rise.
   - (A) people who cannot read and write
   - (B) people without children
   - (C) people who participate in sports
   - (D) people who purchase more than they can afford

10. Since his wound was <u>superficial</u>, only a Band-Aid was required.
    - (A) frivolous
    - (B) on the surface
    - (C) deep
    - (D) supercilious

11. The main road will be closed until the <u>blizzard</u> ends.
    - (A) snowstorm
    - (B) hurricane
    - (C) tornado
    - (D) thunderstorm

12. Tennis wear has become a very <u>lucrative</u> business for both manufacturers and tennis stars.
    - (A) illegal
    - (B) circumstantial
    - (C) expansive
    - (D) profitable

13. A familiar <u>adage</u> says that the early bird gets the worm.
    - (A) proverb
    - (B) lady
    - (C) gentleman
    - (D) book

14. A television ad shows a busy baker with a new computer that the advertiser claims will help him "make <u>dough</u>."
    - (A) a baking mixture
    - (B) more customers
    - (C) money
    - (D) bread

15. At every faculty meeting, Ms. Volatile always manages to <u>put her foot in her mouth</u>.
    - (A) trip over her big feet
    - (B) say the wrong thing
    - (C) move rapidly
    - (D) fall asleep

   If you thought the fifteen vocabulary items in this Pretest were simple, don't think the TOEFL will be as easy. Check your answers against the following Explanation of Answers to see how well you did.

EXPLANATION OF ANSWERS

1. The answer is (B), *most important*. If your answer is wrong, write the word on a 3 x 5-inch card. Include the synonyms *main*, *chief*, and *major*. As you continue to study in this book, add to your file all words that you discover you do not know. Keep the cards in alphabetical order for easy reference.

2. All four choices can be used to make a meaningful sentence. Therefore, you had to know that *survive* is the same as (D), *exist*. If you do not know the meaning of the words given as alternatives, add them to your card list.

3. The answer to this item is (B), *summary*. If you know that *critique* and *evaluation* have approximately the same meaning, *critical writing*, then you can assume that neither is the correct answer. *Dramatization* of a novel would certainly not be an assignment a teacher would give. By elimination and using your good sense, you get the correct answer.

4. In the context of this sentence, there is only one sensible answer, (A), *useless*. Neither *brilliant* nor *challenging* would describe the experience of shopping with no money. *Idiotic* might be a description of the shopper, but it is not a word used to describe the shopping experience.

5. All of the alternatives relate to an actress's experience on stage. The key word in this sentence is *balcony*. What would be necessary for an actress if there are people in the balcony? She would have to be (C), *heard*, not *musical*, *dramatic*, or *appreciated*.

6. The key words in this sentence are *dictators* and *opposition*. You know that dictators by nature do not (B), *permit* opposition, so the other three alternatives will not fit in with what you know about dictators.

7. The answer is (D), *often*. The word *frequently* is commonly used, so you should know its meaning.

8. The correct answer is (C), *separation*. Your knowing about Martin Luther King will help you answer this item correctly. The fact that *segregation* and *separation* both begin with *se* may lead you to the correct answer here. However, there is no guarantee that all words that begin with the same syllable will mean the same thing.

9. The word *illiterate* is composed of two parts—*il*, which is a prefix meaning *not*, and *literate*, which means *able to read and write*. Therefore, the answer is obviously (A), *people who cannot read and write*.

10. The prefix *super* means *above*, so the answer must be (B), *on the surface*. Another clue is that only a Band-Aid is needed, so the wound must not be *deep*. It is true that a *frivolous* person is *superficial*, but the word applies to people, not to inanimate things. *Supercilious* might be the correct answer, since it begins with the same prefix. You would have to know that *supercilious* means *haughty* and therefore applies only to people.

11. All four alternatives relate to a serious weather disturbance. You would have to know that only a *blizzard* creates the hazard of snow, so the answer is (A), *snowstorm*.

12. The only word that makes any sense as a synonym for *lucrative* is (D), *profitable*.

13. Familiarity with old sayings such as the one given in this sentence—the early bird gets the worm—will give you answer (A). *proverb*. The other alternatives are senseless in the context of this sentence.

14. This is a difficult item because the word *dough* is a slang expression for (C), *money*. The advertiser is making a play on words to get a humorous effect, since a baker necessarily makes dough, a mixture of flour and water. The computer will help the baker make more money, not more baking mix.

15. *To put your foot in your mouth* is an idiomatic expression that means (B), *to say the wrong thing*. Like most such expressions, this would be impossible to translate literally into another language. It has simply become a frequently used expression that is generally understood by native speakers. Another such expression is *to have a heart*, which means *to be sympathetic*. Can you think of more idioms?

PART B. READING COMPREHENSION

Directions: The rest of this test is based on a variety of reading materials (single sentences, paragraphs, and the like) followed by questions about the meaning of the material. For questions 16–30, you choose the *one* best answer, (A), (B), (C), or (D), to each question. Answer all questions following a passage on the basis of what is *stated* or *implied* in that passage.

Nat Turner was born in Virginia in 1800. As a young man, he organized a group of fellow slaves in a violent uprising in which eighty-five whites were killed. Turner said that he had heard a voice in 1828 that told him "the last shall be first." He considered this experience and a solar eclipse three years later as signs to begin the insurrection for which he was tried, convicted, and hanged.

Example 1:
Nat Turner was
(A) a politician
(B) an astronomer
(C) a slave
(D) a farmer

Example 2:
What happened to Turner in 1828?
(A) He heard a voice.
(B) He saw a solar eclipse.
(C) He organized an uprising.
(D) He was convicted and hanged.

Example 3:
You can infer from this passage that Nat Turner was
(A) intelligent
(B) popular
(C) superstitious
(D) creative

EXPLANATION OF ANSWERS

For Example 1, the answer is (C), *slave*. The passage says *fellow* slaves.
For Example 2, the answer is (A), *He heard a voice*. The event given for 1828 is that one.
The answer to Example 3 is (C), *superstitious*. While it is possible that Turner was intelligent, popular, and/or creative, the passage emphasizes only the solar eclipse and the voice he heard, both indicating that he was guided by superstition.
When you understand the instructions, continue with the next problems.

Questions 16 and 17 relate to this passage.

Despite predictions that the Twenty-sixth Amendment to the United States Constitution would bring on radical changes in American politics, very little effect was felt, as few young people between the ages of 18 and 21 actually want to vote, and those who do vote show voting patterns similar to those of older voters.

16. It can be inferred from this passage that the Twenty-sixth Amendment
    (A) was ratified recently
    (B) greatly affected politics
    (C) gave young people the right to vote
    (D) doubled the number of voters

17. The Twenty-sixth Amendment did not greatly affect American politics because large numbers of young people
    (A) vote differently from older people
    (B) do not know how to vote
    (C) do not understand the Constitution
    (D) do not want to vote

Questions 18–21 relate to this passage.

The United States developed from a predominantly rural nation at the end of the Civil War in 1865 to the world's largest and wealthiest industrial power by the time it entered World War I in 1917. Among the key factors for this major transformation were a huge population increase, discovery and exploitation of enormous mineral resources, consolidation of the vast Great Plains and Western settlements, and the construction of the extensive railroad networks to service industrial, agricultural, and population growth.

18. This passage is mainly about
    (A) why the United States entered World War I
    (B) how the United States became an industrial power
    (C) how the Great Plains and the West were settled
    (D) why the railroads were built

19. In 1917 the United States
    (A) became involved in a war
    (B) discovered minerals in the Southwest
    (C) ended its Civil War
    (D) became a wealthy country

20. You can infer from this passage that between 1865 and 1917, many people
    (A) left the cities   (C) died in the war
    (B) went to work by train   (D) moved to the cities

21. Which of the following words does *not* refer to size?
    (A) huge   (C) enormous
    (B) key   (D) extensive

Questions 22–24 relate to this passage.

There is fear that short-term interest rates could rise in the next month as the Federal Reserve attempts to reduce growth in the money supply by reducing reserves in the banks. A crucial issue is whether money supply increases forecasted for September will be temporary or part of a fundamental increase in the public's demand for money. The former would improve the chances for renewed interest rate declines, whereas the latter would indicate stable or higher interest rates.

22. You may infer that this item appeared in
    (A) the entertainment section of a newspaper
    (B) the business section of a newspaper
    (C) a television newscast
    (D) a current textbook

23. Money supply increases will be temporary and would
    (A) indicate higher interest rates
    (B) improve the chances for interest rate declines
    (C) create fear in the market
    (D) increase public demand for money

24. The Federal Reserve reduces the money reserves in order to
    (A) reduce money supply
    (B) reduce interest rates
    (C) forecast future events in the stock market
    (D) increase public demand for money

Questions 25–27 refer to the following item.
    The wild turkey existed in great numbers when the settlers first arrived in America. During the first half of this century, however, their numbers decreased so rapidly that they can no longer be found in some states. The ax, the plow, and the gun are blamed for the decline of the wild turkey. Recent game propagation laws prohibit the shooting of anything but the bearded birds, usually males, to protect the brooding hens.

25. The passage says that at present wild turkeys are
    (A) decreasing in number   (C) bearded birds
    (B) easy to shoot   (D) increasing in number

26. The decline of the wild turkey was a result of
    (A) lumberjacks   (C) hunters
    (B) farmers   (D) all of the above

27. The law allows hunters to kill
    (A) brooding hens   (C) wild turkeys
    (B) bearded birds   (D) anything they want

Questions 28–30 refer to the following passage.
    I am convinced that we stand on the edge of a great intellectual period of history comparable to the epoch of the great mathematicians who formulated the laws of the universe. Explorations in the last twenty years pushed back the frontiers of human knowledge. New concepts have completely changed our ways of seeing the universe. I envisage space travel far beyond earth orbit and mastery of the solar system before 2061. Whole families will work on orbital stations in space.

28. When the author uses the expression *pushed back the frontiers of human knowledge,* the meaning is
    (A) human knowledge expanded
    (B) there are borders beyond which human knowledge cannot go
    (C) human knowledge was pushed beyond its frontiers
    (D) frontiers pushed back human knowledge

29. The author foresees
    (A) families living in space
    (B) a complete understanding of the solar system
    (C) great intellectual development in the world
    (D) all of the above

30. You can infer that the author is referring to explorations
    (A) in space   (C) to the sun
    (B) over the frontier   (D) of the mind

EXPLANATION OF ANSWERS

16. The passage does not state explicitly that the Twenty-sixth Amendment (C) *gave young people the right to vote.* You can infer that (C) is the correct answer because of the supporting details—"people between the ages of 18 and 21," "little effect" because young people vote like older voters.

17. The answer is (D), *do not want to vote.* The passage says that "few young people . . . actually want to vote."

18. The answer is (B), *how the United States became an industrial power.* The main idea is given in the first sentence; supporting details follow in the second sentence.

19. The answer is (A), *became involved in a war.* You get this answer by skimming, that is, by looking for *1917* in the passage to see what occurred on that date. You do not have to read the whole passage to answer this type of question.

20. To arrive at the correct answer, (D), *moved to the cities,* you need to use your good sense. Industrialization by its nature would cause people to move to cities to find work or would create big cities from small towns.

21. The answer is (B), *key. Huge, enormous,* and *extensive* refer to size, whereas *key* in this context means *important.*

22. The answer is (B), *the business section of a newspaper.* This is obviously a news item, and it discusses current business matters, interest rates, and money supply. The matter is not suitable for a television report or the entertainment section of a newspaper. A current textbook would not include this type of daily report but would be more general about the state of the economy over a long period of time.

23. The answer, (B), *improve the chances for interest rate declines,* is in the last sentence. The word *former* refers to the previous sentence, which has two important facts. The *former* fact is the first, "money supply increases . . . will be temporary," and so you can connect the two items of information.

24. The answer to this item is in the first sentence. It says that "the Federal Reserve attempts to reduce growth in the money supply by reducing reserves in the banks." This sentence turned around to give cause and effect would give you the correct answer, (A), *reduce money supply.*

25. To get the answer, (D), *increasing in number*, you have to understand that *propagation laws* protect female wild turkeys so that the number of birds is increasing. They decreased in the past because both male and female birds were killed by hunters.

26. The answer is (D), *all of the above*. The ax, the plow, and the gun represent lumberjacks, farmers, and hunters.

27. The passage states clearly that hunters may shoot only at (B), *bearded birds*, usually males. Hens are protected so that the wild turkey numbers may increase. *Wild turkeys* is too general an answer since only some birds may be shot.

28. This type of expression relies on figurative language. There are no visible *frontiers* of human knowledge. The idea is answer (A), *human knowledge expanded*.

29. The supporting details in this passage state that the author envisages (A), (B), and (C), so the answer is (D), *all of the above*.

30. Since the author's emphasis is upon the universe and space travel, you may reasonably infer that explorations (A), *in space*, are what he refers to.

PART I. DEVELOPING READING COMPREHENSION SKILLS

Finding Main Ideas and Supporting Details

The most valuable reading comprehension skill is probably the ability to determine the most important thing an author is saying. Read the following paragraph to see if you can distinguish between essential and non-essential information and between the *main idea* and the *supporting details*. (Answers for all these questions are provided at the end of the book.)

Reading 1

Left-handed people suffer more from stress than their right-handed peers, according to a study of 1,100 adults by University of Michigan researchers. As a result, they smoke and drink more. Fifty-five percent of the lefties smoked, whereas fewer than half of the righties smoked. Furthermore, the lefties consumed more alcohol per year than their right-handed counterparts.

The main idea is_____

_____

Notice that in this paragraph, it was the first sentence that told you the main idea. This sentence, called a "topic sentence," usually appears at the beginning. Sometimes, however, the paragraph's main idea is expressed in the last sentence, and sometimes readers must determine the main idea of a paragraph by summarizing the author's message themselves.

Underline the main idea and circle the supporting details as you read the paragraph below. Then write them in note form in the space provided (page 14).

Reading 2

You ought to know what to do to help a person who is choking. First, you stand behind the choking victim and put your arms around his or her waist. Second, you make a fist and place the thumb side against the person's stomach just above the navel, but below the ribs. Third, grasp your fist with your other hand and press into the victim's abdomen with a quick upward thrust. Repeat this action if necessary.

Main idea:_____

_____

Supporting details:

(A) _____

(B) _____

(C) _____

(D) _____

Now read this passage and answer the questions.

Reading 3

What's the best way for you, as an employer, to deliver bad news to an employee? First of all, you have to break the news yourself, face to face with the recipient. You can't write memos to tell people they will not get raises this year or that they have made an error or are not performing as well as expected. You have to show them how you feel about the matter and that you are personally sorry and sympathize with them. If you indicate that you are ready to listen to their reactions to your bad news, you will undoubtedly save yourself from their wrath. Above all, you must be ready for an emotional reaction from the recipient of bad news. Give people time to digest your news and to control the emotion they invariably feel. Although it is never easy to break bad news, if you follow these steps, you will at least soften the blow.

1. The author's main idea is that
   (A) bad news is hard to impart
   (B) all employers have to criticize their employees
   (C) there are ways of softening the impact of bad news
   (D) people respond emotionally to bad news

2. Where is the main idea expressed?
   (A) in the first sentence
   (B) in the last sentence
   (C) in the middle of the paragraph
   (D) nowhere

3. The main idea is supported by
   (A) examples of employers giving bad news
   (B) a list of reasons for having to break bad news
   (C) sympathy for both the employer and employee
   (D) instructions on how to soften the blow of bad news

In addition to finding the main idea and supporting details in a reading passage, it is also important to understand an author's intent or purpose. When you read *critically,* you must
- Understand what the author is saying
- Distinguish fact from opinion
- Determine the author's attitude toward the topic

Read the paragraph that follows. Then answer the questions about the author's intent and attitude.

Reading 4

Yogurt has as much nutritional value as a glass of milk, yet dieters and health food fanatics claim that yogurt will prolong your life and reduce your girth. Their claims are backed by reports that yogurt eaters over the years have lived longer and healthier lives than non-yogurt eaters. However, what proof is there that rural life and its ensuing greater physical activity rather than consumption of yogurt are not the cause of these persons' longevity?

1. The author's intent is to show that
   (A) yogurt is good for your health
   (B) eating yogurt will prolong your life
   (C) yogurt is the same as milk
   (D) there is no proof that yogurt increases longevity

2. The paragraph advises the reader that
   (A) yogurt will help a person to live to be 100
   (B) the author has little faith in yogurt lovers' claims
   (C) yogurt may be harmful to dieters and health food lovers
   (D) people in rural areas eat a lot of yogurt

Now go back to Readings 1 and 2 and answer these questions.

Reading 1

1. The author's intent is
   (A) to show the effects of smoking and drinking on left-handed people
   (B) to encourage people to stop drinking and smoking, especially if they're left-handed
   (C) to show that left-handed people suffer more from stress than right-handed people
   (D) unclear

2. The author's attitude toward the subject is
   (A) favorable
   (B) unfavorable
   (C) unclear

3. After reading this paragraph, the reader would
   (A) have a favorable opinion
   (B) have an unfavorable opinion
   (C) need more information to form an opinion

Reading 2

1. The author's intent is
   (A) to describe a choking person
   (B) to instruct a person taking a first-aid course

(C) to give advice to a choking person
(D) unclear

2. This type of paragraph is considered to be
   (A) frightening
   (B) difficult to understand
   (C) a "how-to" item
   (D) a reading exercise

Now try this one.

Reading 5

Most of us believe that the death of a spouse often leads to the premature death of the bereft partner. After twelve years of study involving 4,000 widows and widowers, Johns Hopkins University researchers have perceived that it is the husbands, and not the wives, whose lives are shortened by the loss of their spouses. However, the study indicates that widowers who remarry enjoy greater longevity than men the same age who continue to live with their first wives.

1. The main idea is that
   (A) men live longer than their wives
   (B) widowers live longer than single men
   (C) remarriage after a spouse's death prolongs men's lives
   (D) the death of a spouse shortens the life of the surviving partner

2. The author's intent is to
   (A) discuss a medical discovery
   (B) make a conjecture regarding death
   (C) correct a generally held misconception
   (D) advise widowers to live alone

Skimming for Specific Information

It is not always necessary to read every word of a passage. Your purpose for reading something determines how closely you should read it. Once you know what your purpose is, *skimming* is a valuable procedure. Skimming through a passage involves reading very fast in order to recognize main ideas and supporting details while skipping (not reading) parts that are not relevant to your reading purpose. Although skimming should never replace careful reading, it can save you time in deciding what or what not to read, in getting the general content of a passage, and in finding the author's main point without having to deal with details. You read the morning newspaper, for example, quite differently from the way you read a detective story, an assignment for a class, or a letter from a friend. Skimming to find a specific piece of information such as a number or the answer to a question is often called *scanning*.

The readings you will encounter in the next few pages are the kinds of things you are likely to find in a newspaper. News items are usually set up in such a way that each sentence is its own paragraph; they normally follow the pattern *who, what, where, when, why*.

Here are the opening paragraphs of some news items. Scan them for information about who, what, where, when, and why.

Reading 6

A. Mexican conservationists are wondering how to get rid of killer piranhas that were found yesterday in a lake near Puebla.

Who _____

What _____

Where _____

When _____

Why _____

B. The Commodities Futures Trading Commission today designated four commodities exchanges to trade options on futures contracts, as part of a three-year pilot program beginning October 1.

Who _____

What _____

Where _____

When _____

Why _____

C. On October 14, workers at the Lenin shipyard in the Baltic seaport of Gdansk put down their tools in protest against poor working conditions.

Who _____

What _____

Where _____

When _____

Why _____

When you have found the who, what, where, when, and why information in the beginning of a news story, decide whether or not to continue reading. If you do read the rest of the article, skim it by skipping to places where words are capitalized or where there are numbers, or to any points that particularly interest you. Most importantly, don't get lost in all the words; practice reading only what you need to read within a selection. Titles are often useful indicators of what the article is about. In a longer passage, it is sometimes enough to read only the first sentence of each paragraph. Then read the last paragraph in its entirety. Authors frequently provide a summary or conclusion in the last paragraph.

Reading 7

1) Finding a suitable place to live is always difficult. However, there are various methods of going about the search. One source of information is the classified

advertising sections of local newspapers; another is rental brokers, whose fees you must pay. Occasionally friends might lead you to a place they've heard about. In relatively small communities, you might find a bulletin board in a local store with listings of rentals or sales.

2)   A single person might look for a studio apartment, a one-room unit complete with sleeping and cooking facilities. Ads for studios generally read like these.

(A)
```
45TH ST (330W)
New 12 story bldg. Furnished.
Studio apt & exec suite. $430–
$600 Terr apt. Short term lse's
avail. 407-4445
```

(B)
```
RIVERSIDE DRIVE (100s)
River view apt. Doorman bldg.
lg. L-shaped studio with dressing
rm. eat-in kitch. garage avail.
6mo to 1yr sublet. $500/mo incl.
util. 735-0607
```

(C)
```
79 St. E. nr. 1st Av. Sunny stu-
dio, sep. kitchen, a/c, beaut.
furn. $600mo. 278-1234
```

Can you guess what these abbreviations mean?

bldg. _____   mo _____

exec _____   yr _____

terr _____   incl. util. _____

lse _____   nr. _____

lg. _____   sep. _____

rm. _____   a/c _____

kitch. _____   beaut. _____

avail. _____   furn. _____

3)   A single person with a small income may decide that the only way to rent a comfortable apartment is to share with one or more people. By sharing, two or more people can divide the cost of a house or apartment. Naturally, such people must be relatively compatible. Each person must have a private bedroom. Newspaper ads for apartments or houses to share look like these.

(A)
```
FOR THE HARD TO PLEASE:
ROOMMATE REFERRALS
LARGEST   SELECTION   OF
SHARES   ALL   WITH   OWN
BDRM: CPW 70'S-E 30s-$375. E
50s $400. E 70s Own Studio $550.
W 70s $400. W 80s $350. E 80s
$350.
    MANY MORE AVAILABLE
           362-6262
    153 Main St. Open 7 Days
NO FEE TO LIST YOUR APT
```

(B)
```
CHELSEA-Female 28 looking
for same to share 2 BR $375/mo
+ sec. Call Sue 681-2412
```

(C)
```
1AV        All Areas, Ages & Rents
1st AV/83 St-Own Sunny rm  .. $140
1st AV/80s-Own rm. elev  ..... $175
76St/Columb Av-Own rm/lg apt  . $200
Upper East-Own rm & bth  .... $400
50s E/Own rm. river view  ..... $230
VILLAGE-Renov blk  ........ $230
75 ST E/Own rm & bth. lux  .... $400
E.Side-Twnhse  ..... $450 incl G&E
      ROOMMATE SERVICE
           758-4208
```

4)   Couples with children will necessarily require more extensive living quarters, schools, and recreation areas. Homes in the suburbs like those in the *for sale* ads below appeal to families.

(A)
> LA JOLLA $77,500
> Activities all year 'round available near this artist's delight on one acre with 3 bedrooms, 2 baths and yet close to everything. 666-6661.

(B)
> OSSINING
> Natural shingle 3 bdrm Village Colonial, lge liv rm/deck, din rm, eat in kit, fam rm. Conv loc.
> $104,000

(C)
> NASHUA
> A Spacious Family Colonial Owner offers 1st mtge to qualified buyer! On a cul-de-sac w/ lovely wooded acre. Liv rm, din rm,eat-in kitch opening to family rm w/sliding glass doors, fplc, views, Master BR/bath + 3 family BR/3 bath. Super lower level playroom too.
> Exclusive Agent $175,000

(D)
> SEASIDE
> COUNTRY LIVING IN TOWN
> Convenience to town, village colonial, 3 BR, 2½ BTH, den, LR, formal DR. Pretty and level property, $132,000 238-9033.

5)   However, with high interest rates on mortgages causing absurdly high monthly payments that few buyers can afford, many families are turning to rental ads such as these.

HOUSES—NEW JERSEY
RENTALS—NEW JERSEY

(A)
> HOBOKEN
> 4BR, 2bth, grdn. Newly renov. $1350/mo. 867-2468

(B)
> ELIZABETH
> 4BR Rnch, cntry. kit, LR/DR w/ fpl., rec. rm.htd bsmt, close to Metro Pk. $900/mo 832-8904.

(C)
> BERLIN
> 4BR Col, all appliances. $950/mo. furn./unfurn. central air condit'g. 753-6209.

6)   No matter what your requirements are, the best place to go for help is your newspaper or a real estate broker. If you're lucky, you may find what you want through a friend.

A. COMPREHENSION CHECK

Respond to each question according to the nature of the item.

1. The main idea of paragraph 1 is
   (A) finding a place to live is difficult because of the housing shortage
   (B) a broker will find you a house quickly
   (C) brokers charge for their services; you have to pay fees
   (D) there are several sources of aid in finding a place to live

2. Imagine that you are a single person with a good job, a salary of $2500 a month, and many friends you enjoy entertaining. Which of the three studios advertised in paragraph 2 would be most likely to suit you?
   (A) ad A   (C) ad C
   (B) ad B   (D) none of the above

3. Explain why you answered question 2 as you did. _____

   _____

4. If you share a house or an apartment,
   (A) you will have to share a bedroom
   (B) the other tenants will disturb your sleep
   (C) you will probably eat better than you would if you had to pay the rent alone
   (D) you will get your room and board for a monthly sum

5. In paragraph 4, which of the houses for sale gives the size of the property?
   (A) ad A only   (C) ad C only
   (B) ad B only   (D) ads A and C

6. Which of the houses for sale has the largest number of bathrooms?
   (A) ad A   (C) ad C
   (B) ad B   (D) ad D

7. The houses-for-rent ads in paragraph 5 include one house with fireplaces.

   Where is the house?_____

   _____

8. What do all of the houses for rent have in common? _____

   _____

9. What do you suppose a "cntry. kit." is?
   (A) a center kitchen   (C) a carpentry kit
   (B) a tame kitten   (D) a (country) large kitchen

10. What would a "rec. rm." (paragraph 5, ad B) be good for?
    (A) watching television   (C) reading a detective story
    (B) playing ping-pong   (D) all of the above

11. According to the ads in paragraph 3, where is the cheapest apartment for sharing?
    (A) 76th Street   (C) the East 50s
    (B) 83rd Street   (D) in the Village

12. What might you use a "den" for?
    (A) studying   (C) bathing
    (B) cooking   (D) housing your pets

13. The author of this selection intends to
    (A) explain why it is difficult to find a home
    (B) instruct the reader regarding high interest rates
    (C) describe alternative ways of finding a home
    (D) influence your lifestyle

14. It is possible to find brokers for
   (A) rentals
   (B) sales
   (C) sharing
   (D) all of the above

B. VOCABULARY WORK

Choose the word that best completes the sentence.

1. You should look in the _____ ads for an apartment to share.
   (A) fashion
   (B) country
   (C) classified
   (D) studio

2. When Mary rented her apartment through a broker, she didn't have enough money to pay both rent and broker _____.
   (A) rentals
   (B) reductions
   (C) fees
   (D) listings

3. You will definitely have to sign a _____ for a year.
   (A) bulletin
   (B) rental
   (C) check
   (D) lease

4. You and the person with whom you share an apartment must be _____ _____.
   (A) compatible
   (B) similar
   (C) generous
   (D) neat

5. Middle-income families cannot pay _____ high monthly interest charges.
   (A) standard
   (B) absurdly
   (C) intensely
   (D) fashionably

6. The cheapest apartment I could find was a _____.
   (A) studio
   (B) river view
   (C) terrace
   (D) den

7. Newspaper _____ show a wide variety of available housing.
   (A) columns
   (B) editorials
   (C) headlines
   (D) ads

C. VOCABULARY BUILDING

Compound Words

Many words are formed by joining two words already in use. The following list gives some of these words. New compound words are constantly added to the English language.

Find the separate parts of each of the following words. Then look up any you do not understand.

1. landlord	15. shipyard	29. nowhere
2. weekend	16. houseboat	30. wildlife
3. screwdriver	17. moonshine	31. earthquake
4. nevertheless	18. crestfallen	32. worthwhile
5. furthermore	19. mastermind	33. classroom
6. sometimes	20. hilltop	34. fireplace
7. roommate	21. spacecraft	35. bathroom
8. newspaper	22. godparent	36. typewriter
9. bedroom	23. longtime	37. doorman
10. airport	24. keystone	38. commonwealth
11. Thanksgiving	25. grandparent	39. handcuff
12. something	26. widespread	40. footloose
13. someone	27. easygoing	41. deadlock
14. birthday	28. drugstore	42. landmark

Defining Words from Context

As you probably know, the best way to improve your vocabulary is to read—as often and as much as possible. You sometimes learn a word you don't know by looking at how it is used in a sentence, that is, by looking at its *context*.

As you read, see if you can get the meaning of the underlined words from the context in which they appear. Then do the vocabulary and comprehension work that follows.

Reading 8

To the Editor:

Your article on plans for aiding the elderly to pay their housing costs was not quite clear in several aspects. I would like to clarify the requirements and exemptions available for those who qualify.

In the first place, a tenant 62 years old or older must live in a rent-controlled or rent-stabilized dwelling, pay more than one-third of his or her income for rent, and have a yearly income of $8,000 or less. Such a tenant must apply for exemption from rent increases and must reapply each year thereafter. Once is not enough. It is understood, however, that should the landlord make a major improvement, a new furnace for example, all tenants must accept rent raises to pay for increased comfort. The elderly, poor tenant is not excluded from such a rent increase.

Landlords receive tax exemptions as reimbursement for the money they lose in not increasing rent for the elderly. In New York City the cost of these tax reductions is $41 million a year, a tremendous figure, but likely to be higher if more of the poor elderly learn they may apply for exemptions. The city is so slow in processing applications that some tenants have paid the full rent. They ought not to have done so. They are fully protected by the law and, once they have applied for exemption, they do not have to pay rent increases.

I appeal to you to clarify this issue so that the elderly poor of our city may become aware of the housing benefits for which they qualify.

Clara Torres
Office of Housing for the Elderly

A. DETAILED COMPREHENSION

Answer the questions according to the information given in the reading.

1. This letter was written to
   (A) a friend
   (B) the elderly
   (C) a newspaper or magazine
   (D) the Office of Housing

2. We can probably believe in the authenticity of this information because
   (A) once something is in print, it has to be true
   (B) the information is common knowledge
   (C) the elderly deserve to be relieved from the burden of rent increases
   (D) the writer is an employee of a government housing agency

3. List the requirements to qualify for exemption from rent increases:

   (A) _____

   (B) _____

   (C) _____

   (D) _____

4. True or false? Once a person qualifies for the exemption, he or she will continue to be exempt if the application is renewed annually. _____

5. Would an unemployed woman, 65 years old, with an income of $6,000 in Social Security and $3,000 in aid from her children qualify for exemption from rent increases?
   (A) Possibly, but more information is needed.
   (B) Definitely.
   (C) Never.
   (D) Maybe next year she would qualify, but not this year.

6. When a landlord air conditions an apartment building
   (A) he can then raise the tenants' rent
   (B) he has improved his property and must bear the expense himself
   (C) he can take the cost off his income tax
   (D) his tenants are poor and elderly

7. New York City provides the following to landlords who do not increase rent for the elderly:
   (A) a list of restrictions
   (B) $41 million a year in cash refunds
   (C) an amount equal to the rent increases in tax exemptions
   (D) higher prices for improving their buildings

8. Elderly tenants who qualify for exemptions from rent increases have nevertheless paid rent increases because
   (A) they have the necessary income
   (B) they are old and ignorant
   (C) their applications are not processed quickly
   (D) the law does not protect them

9. Wider knowledge of this plan to help the elderly will
   - (A) raise rents
   - (B) lower taxes
   - (C) cost the city less
   - (D) none of the above

10. The author of this letter is
    - (A) poor and elderly herself
    - (B) concerned for the elderly
    - (C) a very callous person
    - (D) not very sympathetic toward landlords

11. The word *clarify* is related to the word
    - (A) classic
    - (B) classify
    - (C) clash
    - (D) clear

12. The word *ought* is the same as
    - (A) may
    - (B) can
    - (C) should
    - (D) might

13. A furnace is considered a major improvement because
    - (A) it is hot
    - (B) landlords have to provide heat
    - (C) it is expensive to buy
    - (D) it increases the rent

B. VOCABULARY WORK

Getting the Meaning from Context

Choose the correct meaning of the underlined word.

1. Tenants over 62 can apply for benefits at the Office of Housing for the Elderly.
   - (A) poor
   - (B) people over 62
   - (C) people who need aid
   - (D) people who need housing

2. If you don't get that furnace repaired before winter, we will freeze to death.
   - (A) fire escape
   - (B) heater
   - (C) water container
   - (D) staircase

3. Since landlords get reimbursements for rent raises for the elderly, they shouldn't complain about losing money.
   - (A) bills
   - (B) increases
   - (C) payments
   - (D) housing benefits

4. The elderly are not excluded from rent raises that all tenants have to pay when the landlord makes a major improvement.
   - (A) obliged
   - (B) included
   - (C) excited
   - (D) eliminated

5. When their rent increased from $200 to $400 a month, they protested against such a tremendous increase.
   - (A) light
   - (B) difficult
   - (C) huge
   - (D) tiring

6. Because the city is slow in <u>processing</u> applications, many of the elderly do not get housing benefits.
   - (A) providing
   - (B) working on
   - (C) raising
   - (D) trying

7. The landlord notified his <u>tenants</u> that their rent would be increased the following month.
   - (A) janitors
   - (B) friends
   - (C) occupants
   - (D) poor people

8. Reading a daily newspaper will make you <u>aware</u> of what is going on in the world.
   - (A) knowledgeable
   - (B) ignorant
   - (C) alike
   - (D) dependent

Making Inferences

There are two basic kinds of reading comprehension. When you are able to use the author's words to answer a comprehension question, it is your *factual comprehension* that is being tested. Sometimes, however, the information is not directly stated, so you must infer a meaning using your own reasoning and logic. This type of understanding is sometimes referred to as *inferential comprehension*. Imagine that you are at a friend's house. It is 11:00 P.M. and your host starts to look at his watch and yawn out loud. Although he never actually tells you to leave, he *implies* and you *infer* that it is time for you to go home.

Astrologers think that the sun, moon, and other planets play an important role in our lives on Earth. Do you believe in astrology?

Many newspapers and magazines publish daily, weekly, and monthly horoscopes. What is your sign?

Do you follow your horoscope? Do the predictions ever come true?

This horoscope column appeared in a daily newspaper. Read it; then answer the questions.

Reading 9

Your Horoscope

AQUARIUS   January 20–February 18
After last month's frantic partying, you begin to recuperate. A new job is opening for you. Take no one's advice, but use your own judgment. Try a restful weekend in the country.

PISCES   February 19–March 20
Beware of quack doctors who offer nebulous cures. Watch your weight. Expect to meet a debonair companion.

ARIES March 21–April 19

You incur new expenses this month and find unexpected problems in paying your bills. After the 15th take a look at your budget and try to cut your expenses. Be more submissive to your employer.

TAURUS April 20–May 20

Rest and exercise should rejuvenate you this month. You cope with tension and put a little frivolity into your life. Watch for friends who are too glib in their professions of love.

GEMINI May 21–June 20

Don't be seen in public places with gauche companions. Try a change of scene, perhaps a trip to far-flung places. Use a new stratagem to advance your career.

CANCER June 21–July 22

This month starts out with a multitude of problems. Expect a shift around the middle of the month to new and exciting social events. Remember to control your tendency to overeat.

LEO July 23–August 22

Don't overlook your relatives; they need your loving attention. Your efforts to lose weight will be futile unless you stop now and take a good look at yourself.

VIRGO August 23–September 22

You are too bossy. Try to develop more compliance in your relations with the other sex. Look for an influx of visitors at the beginning of the month.

LIBRA September 23–October 22

You'll need extra money to pay your bills this month. Too much stress will ruin your health. Try to enlist your friends' help.

SCORPIO October 23–November 21

You summon the energy this month to achieve a lifelong goal. You are at the zenith of your career. You make new friends and live harmoniously with the old.

SAGITTARIUS November 22–December 21

Intrigue at the office surrounds you. Discuss your dilemma with a Leo. Unexpected money comes to you this month and clears up your financial worries.

CAPRICORN December 22–January 19

Accept the inevitable. Stop smoking this month. Plan a change from your regular routine. See a show or a movie and relax.

A. DETAILED COMPREHENSION

Respond to the following according to the nature of the item. Note that you will often have to infer the answer if the information is not stated in the reading.

1. This horoscope column relates to the following matters:
    (A) future events, past mistakes, and current tensions
    (B) money, moods, and careers

   (C) lovers, jobs, and income
   (D) all of the above

2. People turn to their horoscope for
   (A) predictions   (C) encouragement
   (B) bad news   (D) all of the above

3. It can be inferred from the horoscope that an Aries
   (A) has a lot of money
   (B) cannot live within his or her income
   (C) is a rebellious person
   (D) is very mercenary

4. It can be suggested to a Virgo that he or she should
   (A) speak more quietly to the boss
   (B) leave the office early
   (C) find a roommate to share expenses
   (D) stock up on groceries and clean the house

5. Leo deserves our sympathy because he or she
   (A) has too many relatives   (C) ought to look in the mirror
   (B) can't lose weight easily   (D) has trouble with the budget

6. If Gemini takes the advice given, he or she will
   (A) go to the grocery store after work
   (B) give up his or her job
   (C) try to save money on clothes
   (D) call a travel agent

7. Apparently Gemini's friends include people who
   (A) lack social polish   (C) break the law
   (B) are left-handed   (D) seldom bathe

8. Aquarius is exhausted from
   (A) too much work at the office   (C) a serious illness
   (B) too much house cleaning   (D) too much social activity

9. Scorpio this month can expect
   (A) friends to be disappointing
   (B) to gain weight
   (C) to have a very rewarding time
   (D) to be on a magazine cover

10. Cancer's month begins badly and ends with
   (A) overeating
   (B) the need for some new party clothes
   (C) a restful vacation
   (D) a depressing feeling of loneliness

B. VOCABULARY WORK

Getting the Meaning from Context

Try to get the meaning of the underlined word from its context in the following sentences. Choose the correct synonym. If you cannot understand the word, go back to the reading where it was used in a different context. If you still cannot figure it out, look the word up in your dictionary.

1. It is inevitable that smoking will damage your health.
   (A) invading
   (B) unhealthy
   (C) unavoidable
   (D) intriguing

2. What you need after a hard week's work is a little frivolity over the weekend.
   (A) luxury
   (B) harmony
   (C) fireworks
   (D) triviality

3. The general planned a new stratagem to conquer the rebel forces.
   (A) strafing
   (B) scheme
   (C) bomb
   (D) headquarters

4. Only a quack would recommend a lettuce diet to an athlete.
   (A) charlatan
   (B) duck
   (C) coach
   (D) doctor

5. The expression "out of the frying pan and into the fire" means to go from one dilemma to a worse one.
   (A) situation
   (B) predicament
   (C) embarrassment
   (D) aura

6. He made one last futile effort to convince her and left the house.
   (A) difficult
   (B) favorable
   (C) firm
   (D) ineffectual

7. After climbing to the zenith, he slowly worked his way down the mountain.
   (A) zero
   (B) top
   (C) cabin
   (D) mountain

8. A glib answer will not serve for a serious question.
   (A) gross
   (B) capable
   (C) facile
   (D) ignorant

9. Mary set off on her vacation with the intention of finding a tall, dark, handsome, debonair companion.
   (A) doleful
   (B) decent
   (C) gay
   (D) mercenary

10. Ponce de Leon searched in vain for a means of rejuvenating the aged.
    (A) making young again
    (B) making weary again
    (C) making wealthy again
    (D) making merry again

C. VOCABULARY BUILDING

Many English words are made up of a combination of word elements. A *root* is a word element, often taken from Latin or Greek, that serves as a base to which other elements are added to modify the root itself. A *prefix* is a word element placed at the beginning of a root, and a *suffix* is attached to the end of a root or word. Both prefixes and suffixes change the meaning of the root and form a new word.

Recognizing and understanding word elements provide a valuable system of analyzing words, figuring out their meaning, and comparing them to find relationships with words you already know. Using this system, you will also be able to organize and learn words in groups rather than individually.

Here are some common Latin and Greek prefixes. Study them and look up the meanings of the words you do not know in the Example column.

Prefix	Meaning	Example
ab, a	away from	abduct, amoral
ad, ac, ag, at	to	advent, accrue, aggressive, attracts
ante	before	antedated
anti	against	antipathy
bene	well	benefit
circum	around	circumnavigate
com, con, col	together	compliant, conducive, collate
contra	against	contrary
de	from, down	delete, descend
dis, di	apart	disperse, dilate
ex, e	out	exit, elicit
extra	beyond	extracurricular
hyper	excessively	hypertension, hyperactive
in, im, il, ir, un	not	intrepid, impossible, illicit, irreparable, unlikely
inter	between	interrupt
intra, intro, in	within	intramural, introduction, inside
mal	bad	malediction
per	through	permeate
peri	around	perimeter
post	after	postoperative
pre	before	precedence, predecessor
pro	forward, for	propose, proponents
re	again	review
semi	half	semicolon
sub	under	submarine
super	above	supervisor
trans	across	transport

Use the words in the Example column to complete these sentences.

1. The men had to _____ their canoe through the woods to the river's
   carry across

   edge.

2. That sentence requires a(n) _____.
   half colon

3. His _____ condition was excellent.
   after the operation

4. The law requires that there be a(n) _____ from the second floor
   way out

   apartment.

5. Magellan _____ the world.
   sailed around

6. Our new president is much more popular than his _____.
   one who came before

7. After the protest march, the crowd _____.
   split apart

8. In the evolution of animals, plants _____ insects.
   came before

9. We never agree; his opinions are always _____ to mine.
   against

10. There seems to be a natural _____ between cats and dogs.
    feeling against

11. Workmen at the refinery find that the smell of oil _____ their
    goes through

    clothing.

12. Students engage in many _____ activities.
    beyond the curriculum

13. The unceasing ring of the telephone _____ my work.
    came between

14. It is _____ for him to see you today.
    not possible

15. Living in a(n) _____ is most confining.
    underwater vehicle

16. He got a job as a(n) _____ in a dress manufacturing company.
    person above

17. The chairman of the board takes _____ over the other
    right to come before

    board members.

18. The _____ of conservation protested against strip-mining.
       people for

19. Cutting your salt consumption will _____ your health.
                                        do well for

20. The professor has to _____ his test papers.
                          put together

21. Let's _____ our algebra for the exam tomorrow.
            go over again

22. The terrorists planned to _____ the American general.
                                take away

23. Some students give more of their time to _____ sports than to
                                                within the school
    their assignments.

24. What is the _____ of this triangle?
                 distance around

25. A magnet _____ iron and its alloys.
              draws to itself

Daily newspapers publish advice columns for everything from successful vegetable gardening to curing yourself of high blood pressure. This one answers readers' questions about car problems.

Read the selection and answer the questions that follow.

Reading 10

Q. My engine cranks all right. But why won't it start up?

A. Think twice. Are you following the exact starting procedure given in your owner's manual? Next, pin down the trouble area by checking these possibilities: (1)gasoline, (2)spark, and (3) air–gasoline ratio.

1. First make sure you have gasoline in the tank. If that's not the problem, maybe you have flooded the engine. Hold the gas pedal to the floor for 10 seconds (do not pump it) as you crank the engine.

Still no start? Maybe the problem is a stuck needle valve. Tap the carburetor bowl lightly near the gas line, using pliers or a screwdriver handle. This should free the valve so you can start. But if nothing has done the trick so far, move to the next step.

2. Check to see if the engine is getting the spark it needs to start. First look for loose or broken spark plug wires. Fix what you can.

If the wires look all right, make a detailed check for a spark. Twist one spark plug boot away from its plug. Push an insulated screwdriver into the boot. Hold the shank of the screwdriver about ⅛ inch away from a metal engine part. Have someone crank the engine. (Be sure you keep your hands away from the screwdriver shank and the wire to avoid shock.) You'll see a small spark if the ignition system is working. No spark? Get help. (Caution: If there is any gasoline *on* the engine, be sure you let it evaporate before you try this test.) If you see a spark, you have eliminated that as a possibility. Move on to the next step.

3. Finally, find out if the carburetor is feeding sufficient air and gasoline to the

engine. Remove the top of the air cleaner so you can see the choke plate. If the plate is stuck open, push it shut (only if the engine is cold) and try to start again.

Still no start? Hold the choke wide open and peer deep inside as someone else pumps the gas pedal. (Make sure they don't crank the engine.) If you can't see gas squirting, you need professional help.

Courtesy of the Shell Oil Company

A. DETAILED COMPREHENSION

Answer the questions according to the nature of the item.

1. This type of selection is
   - (A) scientific reading
   - (B) a "how-to" article
   - (C) editorial writing
   - (D) automobile advertising

2. The author's intent in this article is to
   - (A) explain why cars break down
   - (B) warn you about the dangers involved in do-it-yourself car repairs
   - (C) describe the method of checking spark plugs
   - (D) instruct you how to deal with a car problem

3. From the context of the word *crank*, it must mean
   - (A) complain
   - (B) start
   - (C) turn over
   - (D) shut off

4. List briefly the steps involved in checking the starting mechanism.

   (A) _____

   (B) _____

   (C) _____

   (D) _____

5. If you check for a spark and don't get one, what should you do?
   - (A) Check the carburetor next.
   - (B) Get an auto mechanic.
   - (C) Clean the gas off the motor.
   - (D) Get a shock.

6. What is the first thing to do when your car doesn't start?
   - (A) Check your gas.
   - (B) Flood the engine.
   - (C) Contact your automobile salesman.
   - (D) Be sure you're following the rules for starting the car.

7. If you are testing for a spark, gas on the engine is dangerous
   - (A) because it might start the car
   - (B) when it has evaporated
   - (C) after it leaks out of the carburetor
   - (D) because the spark might ignite the gas

8. You should use an insulated screwdriver to
   (A) protect the engine
   (B) avoid scratching the metal
   (C) avoid getting a shock
   (D) twist the spark plug boot

9. You can unstick a valve by
   (A) taking it out
   (B) hitting it
   (C) loosening it
   (D) twisting it

10. You have to hold the screwdriver shank away from metal to
    (A) prevent fire
    (B) avoid cutting yourself
    (C) avoid getting a shock
    (D) check for a bad spark plug

11. Presumably a spark plug *boot* is a
    (A) covering
    (B) shoe
    (C) trunk
    (D) plug

12. It can be inferred that a carburetor
    (A) is connected to the spark plugs
    (B) cranks the engine
    (C) regulates gas and air flow
    (D) has an open plate

13. If the engine is cold, it is all right to
    (A) try to start the car
    (B) close the choke plate
    (C) take off the air cleaner
    (D) pump the gas pedal

14. The choke plate is
    (A) next to the gas tank
    (B) above the air cleaner
    (C) beneath the air cleaner
    (D) inside the spark plugs

15. Do you think a person with no understanding of the mechanism of a car could follow these instructions?

    Why or why not? _____

    _____

B. VOCABULARY BUILDING

Study these suffixes. Be sure that you understand what each of the words in the Example column means before you do the exercise.

Suffix	Meaning	Example
able, ible	capable of being	expendable, comprehendible
al	relating to	traditional
ance	relating to	alliance
ary	relating to	aviary
ation	action	provocation
cy	quality	potency
ence	relating to	complacence

Suffix	Meaning	Example
er	one who	worker
fy	make	beautify
ic	pertaining to	atmospheric
ious	full of	gracious
ist	person who practices	psychiatrist
ity	condition	complexity
ize	to make like	stabilize
less	without	penniless
ment	result, state	contentment

From the Example column above, choose a word that best fits the following definitions.

1. A person with no money is _____.

2. Something that is potent has _____.

3. The state of being content is called _____.

4. Something capable of being comprehended is _____.

5. A person full of grace is _____.

6. A celebration that has become a tradition is considered _____.

7. Two countries that are allied form a(n) _____.

8. The area where birds (avi) are kept is called a(n) _____.

9. Something capable of being expended is considered _____.

10. When weather forecasters talk about the pressure of the atmosphere, they refer to _____ pressure.

11. A person who practices psychiatry is a(n) _____.

12. Someone who works is a(n) _____.

13. If something is described as complex, we can say it has _____.

14. When someone provokes you, we can say he or she has given you _____.

15. When you make something stable, you _____ it.

16. A complacent person is noted for his or her _____.

17. To make a house beautiful is to _____ it.

Now see if you can use the suffixes given above to form new words. When you have finished, check your dictionary to make sure you spelled all the words correctly.

1. Someone who employs others is a(n) _____.

2. A person who favors conservation is a(n) _____.

3. The condition of being sane is _____.

4. Something giving comfort is _____.

5. Something full of infection is _____.

6. The result of adjusting is _____.

7. A person without sense is _____.

8. A person with ideals is a(n) _____. We can say he or she is _____.

9. A lenient judge is noted for his _____.

10. To commit something to memory is to _____ it.

11. A turbulent sea is characterized by its _____.

12. To excite intensely as if by an electric shock is to _____ another person.

You are probably familiar with another kind of advice column that appears in newspapers throughout the country. Read these letters about personal problems. Are the suggestions offered in the answers good ones? Think about what you would tell these two women.

Reading 11

Dear Sandy,

I wrote to you last year about my suspicions of my husband and our next-door neighbor, the widow Talbot. You never answered, and now I really need help.

My husband and I have been married for ten years. We have three beautiful children, a house with a pool in a lovely suburban development, and I don't go out to work because I think children need their mother; don't you? Two years ago the widow Talbot moved into the house next door, and our children and hers became the best of friends. Feeling sorry for the lonely widow, I invited her and her family over for barbecues and other social events. All was proceeding well until the widow began to ask my husband to do little home-repair jobs, like fixing the air conditioning, the leaky faucets, and the furnace.

Now I have found out that her house has been in perfect condition. She and my husband have been carrying on at her house. I wondered why she always sent her children over to play with my children when he was "making repairs." Well, now I know. Our phone was out of order one day while he was there, and I went over to use her phone and found my husband in her arms. I am frantic. I am sure he loves me and the little ones. What should I do? Should I get a divorce?

Distraught in Detroit

Dear Distraught,

You sound like a devoted mother. We all know that divorce is very hard on everyone, especially the kids. I recommend that you talk over the situation with your husband. After ten years of marriage, surely you can reach an understanding about the widow Talbot. Try cooking his favorite food and pampering him a bit more than usual to woo him back to you. If your own efforts fail, you should make an appointment with a professional marriage counselor to discuss the situation.

A. DETAILED COMPREHENSION

Answer the following questions according to the nature of the item.

1. The author of this letter is writing to
   (A) a marriage counselor
   (B) her mother
   (C) an advice-to-the-lovelorn columnist
   (D) her lawyer

2. The reply to the letter is based upon the writer's
   (A) dislike of flirtatious widows
   (B) desire to protect the children
   (C) wide experience with such marital problems
   (D) impatience with a silly wife

3. According to the letter from "Distraught," the widow
   (A) was lying about needing home repairs
   (B) bought a run-down house
   (C) was monogamous
   (D) had a telephone that worked

4. "Distraught" is advised to
   (A) prepare the children for the divorce
   (B) pamper the widow
   (C) see her lawyer
   (D) give her husband special care and attention

5. How did you get your answer to question 4?
   (A) It was stated in the reading.
   (B) It was implied in the reading.
   (C) The reading did not give the necessary information.

6. You can infer that "Distraught" and her husband
   (A) are always kind to strangers   (C) have a comfortable income
   (B) are careless of their children   (D) enjoy cooking outdoors

7. List the details that gave you the answer to question 6.

   (A) _____

   (B) _____

   (C) _____

8. What does "Distraught" say in her letter that implies that she considers herself a good mother? _____

_____

9. Why did the widow send her children over to "Distraught's" house? _____

_____

10. Presumably the expression *carrying on* means
    (A) repairing faucets   (C) continuing
    (B) lifting groceries   (D) having an affair

11. Apparently the word *distraught* means
    (A) disillusioned   (C) distressed
    (B) disparate   (D) dispersed

Dear Sandy,

I am worried sick about my husband. Ten years ago he was drinking so much that our marriage was foundering. Realizing he was ruining his own life and his children's and mine, he went to Alcoholics Anonymous. Within months, he was a new man: healthy, happy, a wonderful husband and father. He forswore drinking forever. Recently, however, he read someplace that alcoholics could drink a little if they did so cautiously. It's like a nightmare. His boss is ready to fire him, the children have moved out, and our marriage is once more on the brink of dissolving in alcohol. Is it possible for a reformed alcoholic to drink moderately?

Depressed in Milwaukee

Dear Depressed,

No, it is not possible for an alcoholic to drink moderately. Alcoholism is a disease for which the only cure is abstinence. Research with thousands of subjects has proven conclusively that an alcoholic should not drink at all; he has no more control over his drinking than he would over a ferocious bear. Unless your husband returns to AA for help, your woes will never cease.

B. DETAILED COMPREHENSION

Respond to each item as indicated.

1. The author is writing to
   (A) a doctor who specializes in nervous diseases
   (B) a newspaper columnist who gives advice to readers

    (C) Alcoholics Anonymous to enroll her husband
    (D) a lawyer to get a divorce

2. The reply to the letter is based upon
    (A) the writer's disdain for alcoholism
    (B) objective proof
    (C) personal experience
    (D) subjective data

3. According to this reading, an alcoholic at a cocktail party
    (A) could have no more than one drink
    (B) wouldn't be a good host
    (C) couldn't take his wife with him
    (D) had better drink water in a highball glass

4. Presumably the alcoholic can get help from
    (A) his wife   (C) his lawyer
    (C) his children   (D) none of the above

5. An alcoholic can control his drinking. True or false? _____

6. How did you get your answer to question 5?
    (A) It was stated in the reading.
    (B) It was implied in the reading.
    (C) The reading did not give the necessary information.

C. VOCABULARY WORK

Getting the Meaning from Context

Fill in the blank with the correct word according to the context of the sentence. How are the words used in the reading?

1. His ignorance of the best ways of investing in the stock market brought him to the _____ of ruin.
    (A) peak   (C) brink
    (B) bank   (D) break

2. His wife was _____ about his health.
    (A) sick   (C) wistful
    (B) worried sick   (D) ferocious

3. The ship _____ at sea, and all aboard were lost.
    (A) sailed   (C) foundered
    (B) flailed   (D) leaned

4. She went on a diet, _____ sweets and lost 20 pounds.
    (A) ate   (C) forswore
    (B) meted   (D) rebuilt

5. If you don't get to work on time, your boss will _____ you.
   - (A) hire
   - (B) fire
   - (C) praise
   - (D) rebel

6. An alcoholic's only hope for a cure lies in _____ from drinking.
   - (A) control
   - (B) ruin
   - (C) sickness
   - (D) abstinence

7. The district attorney proved _____ that the gang had murdered the federal agent.
   - (A) conclusively
   - (B) concretely
   - (C) cautiously
   - (D) carelessly

8. Little Red Ridinghood had a frightening escape from a _____ wolf.
   - (A) friendly
   - (B) grandmotherly
   - (C) likeable
   - (D) ferocious

9. Ophelia had so many _____ to recount that we all cried for her.
   - (A) stories
   - (B) news
   - (C) tales
   - (D) woes

10. For faster relief from pain, _____ the tablet in water.
    - (A) dissolve
    - (B) rotate
    - (C) elevate
    - (D) light

D. VOCABULARY BUILDING

Here are ten groups of words that are frequently confused and misused. Look at the definitions; then fill in the correct word in the sentences.

1. adapt, adopt
   Adapt means to adjust.
   Adopt means to take by choice.
   - (A) The committee decided to _____ the new regulations.
   - (B) It is difficult to _____ to a new environment.

2. adverse, averse
   Adverse means acting against.
   Averse means having a strong dislike.
   - (A) The jury made an _____ decision, so he was hanged.
   - (B) An anorexic is _____ to food.

3. allusion, delusion, illusion
   Allusion means an implied or indirect reference.
   Delusion means a false belief.
   Illusion means an unreal image.
   - (A) That poor man is under the _____ that he is Hitler.
   - (B) I am not familiar enough with mythology to understand all the _____ s to it in this poem.
   - (C) A good painter can give you the _____ of broad space in his works.

4. complement, compliment
Complement means to complete or make perfect.
Compliment means to praise.
   (A) I must _____ you on your choice of flowers for the party.
   (B) They are just the right flowers to _____ the table setting.

5. council, counsel
Council means an elected group to make decisions.
Counsel means advice.
   (A) The _____ advised the president to raise taxes.
   (B) The group was famous for its good _____.

6. elicit, illicit
Elicit means to draw out.
Illicit means against a law or rule.
   (A) The detective attempted to _____ information about the (B) _____ drug ring.

7. explicit, implicit
Explicit means clear and fully expressed.
Implicit means meant though not plainly expressed.
   (A) The manual gives _____ instructions on how to repair a bicycle.
   (B) There was definitely an _____ threat in the way he glared at her.

8. ingenious, ingenuous
Ingenious means clever at inventing things.
Ingenuous means simple, naive, and inexperienced.
   (A) An _____ high school student invented a video game.
   (B) Katy is so _____ she will believe anything you tell her.

9. infer, imply
Infer means to draw the meaning from.
Imply means to suggest.
   (A) I _____ from what you just said that the engagement is over.
   (B) Did you mean to _____ that you don't love me anymore?

10. immigrate, emigrate
Immigrate means to come into a country to make one's home there.
Emigrate means to leave one's country to go and live in another.
   (A) Many venturesome people _____ from England to Australia.
   (B) If you _____ to this country, you will have to learn the language.

Quiz 1

Write the word next to the definition. Your answers are words used in this section of the book.

1. A one-room apartment _____
2. Occupant of a building _____
3. Advanced in years _____
4. Repayment _____
5. Machine for heating a building _____
6. Hint _____
7. A clever trick to obtain an end _____
8. Charlatan, pretender to medical skill _____
9. Summit, highest point _____
10. Underwater vehicle _____
11. Distance around an object _____
12. Person with ideals _____
13. Tales of sorrow _____
14. Indirect reference _____
15. An elected group that gives advice _____

Reading 12

The following is a list of select restaurants in the metropolitan area. Critical comments are based upon the author's opinions. Prices are current.

The Banyan Tree, 2 East Monopoly Street **
A small sidewalk restaurant on a peaceful back street with a green and white striped awning, rattan chairs, and glass-topped tables. The menu is limited to exotic East Indian specialties, savory curries of all varieties being featured. Full luncheon comes to about $25. Open daily for lunch only.

The Boathouse, 433 River Road *
A delightful, convivial eating place decorated with sea urchin lamps, fishermen's nets, and seaweed wall coverings. Very informal atmosphere. A lighthouse bar. Specialties are, of course, seafood, my favorite being the *moules marinières* served in steaming black pots. A five-course dinner at $11. Open daily.

Cafe Henri, 17 Lorraine Street*
Soft lighting and muted decorator shades of beige and bronze give the dining room an intimate atmosphere. Basically French, the cuisine represents aromatic country fare, with rich, nutritious soups and assorted platters of sausages, patés, and cheeses. Wholesome fare at reasonable prices. Entrées $12.50 to $20.75.

Little Old San Juan, 62 Fortaleza Boulevard ***
A cozy Spanish decor, enhanced by mellow, red clay floor tiles, wrought-iron street lanterns, and walls lined with rows of painted pottery, gives this 100-

year-old landmark an aura of romantic old Spain. Gazpacho sprinkled with chopped onion, green pepper, rice and garlic croutons, and an irresistible array of Spanish dishes are exceptional. The paella laden with shellfish is more than worth the 30-minute wait. Wines both fine and *ordinario* from the vineyards of Spain. Entrées from $20. Closed Sundays.

No stars—Fair
   * Good
  ** Very good
 *** Excellent
**** Extraordinary

A. DETAILED COMPREHENSION

Answer the questions according to the nature of the item.

1. You may infer that this guide is
   (A) a paid-for advertisement
   (B) written by a gourmet restaurant critic
   (C) an introduction in a cookbook
   (D) none of the above

2. The author's intent is to
   (A) describe gourmet restaurants
   (B) give the reader a price list for dining out
   (C) recommend good places to eat
   (D) warn people about restaurants

3. Which restaurant serves the least expensive meals? _____
   _____

4. Which restaurant is recommended most highly? _____

5. Which restaurant is the most expensive? _____

6. Where could you get Indian food? _____

7. Where would you go for shrimp au gratin? _____

8. Which restaurant would most likely have a guitarist? _____
   _____

9. Which restaurant sounds like a good place for lovers? _____

10. You would infer that these restaurants are
    (A) in the United States   (C) for the wealthy only
    (B) in Europe   (D) informal

B. VOCABULARY WORK

Getting the Meaning from Context

Some words are used primarily to describe food and restaurants. Choose the correct synonym for each word from the choices given. Consider the word in the context in which it appears in the selection.

1. exotic
   - (A) delicious
   - (B) delightful
   - (C) unusual
   - (D) exciting

2. savory
   - (A) tasty
   - (B) East Indian
   - (C) hot
   - (D) spicy

3. convivial
   - (A) gathering
   - (B) festive
   - (C) communal
   - (D) gloomy

4. muted
   - (A) turned off
   - (B) silenced
   - (C) toned down
   - (D) drained

5. intimate
   - (A) intimidate
   - (B) private
   - (C) interior
   - (D) special

6. cuisine
   - (A) eating
   - (B) French
   - (C) cooking
   - (D) serving

7. aromatic
   - (A) fragrant
   - (B) fresh
   - (C) warm
   - (D) steaming

8. wholesome
   - (A) entire
   - (B) wholesale
   - (C) assorted
   - (D) healthy

9. reasonable
   - (A) moderate
   - (B) thoughtful
   - (C) cheap
   - (D) expensive

10. cozy
    - (A) smoky
    - (B) comfortable
    - (C) foreign
    - (D) courteous

11. enhanced
    - (A) added
    - (B) lighted
    - (C) intensified
    - (D) decorated

12. irresistible
    - (A) varied
    - (B) irregular
    - (C) overpowering
    - (D) irate

13. aura
    - (A) color
    - (B) atmosphere
    - (C) smell
    - (D) scenery

14. landmark
    - (A) restaurant
    - (B) change
    - (C) structure
    - (D) boundary

15. laden
    - (A) lifted
    - (B) lasted
    - (C) laced
    - (D) loaded

C. VOCABULARY BUILDING

When a word has more than one meaning, the dictionary will number each separate definition; the first meaning given is usually the most common use of the word. When looking up a word in the dictionary, you should know which definition provides the meaning of the word as it is used in the particular context.

Choose the appropriate definitions for the underlined words. Write the number in the space provided.

1. (1) on the surface; not deep
   (2) not serious; not complete
   _____ The article gave a superficial analysis of the country's economic woes.
   _____ The parachutist was treated for superficial cuts and bruises.

2. (1) working very well; sharp
   (2) severe; strong
   _____ She suffered from acute back pain after the accident.
   _____ Most animals have an acute sense of smell.

3. (1) thoroughly planned
   (2) intentional; on purpose
   _____ It was an accident; she didn't break the vase deliberately.
   _____ The President is taking deliberate steps to balance the federal budget.

4. (1) merciful in judgment
   (2) allowing less than the highest standards
   _____ Some people felt that the jury was too <u>lenient</u> with the man who shot the senator.
   _____ It is believed that <u>lenient</u> teachers produce mediocre students.

5. (1) concerning people who have a close relationship
   (2) personal; private
   _____ The two women are <u>intimate</u> friends.
   _____ They share even their most <u>intimate</u> thoughts.

6. (1) to become or make strong
   (2) to combine into fewer or one
   _____ The two major labor unions <u>consolidated</u> to form one large powerful union.
   _____ The United States is attempting to <u>consolidate</u> its position in the Caribbean.

7. (1) to eat or drink
   (2) to use up
   (3) to destroy
   _____ The entire apartment was <u>consumed</u> by fire.
   _____ The tennis player contracted hepatitis after <u>consuming</u> tainted fish.
   _____ Typing his boss's correspondence <u>consumed</u> most of the secretary's time.

8. (1) a particular government
   (2) a plan to improve one's health
   _____ After following a strict <u>regime</u>, the injured gymnast returned to competition.
   _____ The nation is sure to prosper under the new <u>regime</u>.

9. (1) causing a feeling of pity
   (2) worthless; unsuccessful
   _____ The supervisor is so <u>pathetic</u> that his entire staff is threatening to resign.
   _____ We were awakened by the kitten's <u>pathetic</u> cries.

10. (1) to cause to have no effect
    (2) to disprove; deny
    _____ Thermal insulation <u>negates</u> the effect of the cold.
    _____ The governor issued a statement in an attempt to <u>negate</u> the accusations against him.

Understanding Advertisements

1. List all the places you can think of where you see and hear advertisements for products and services.

   _____

   _____

   _____

   _____

   Did you name advertising billboards and posters? Where might you see them?

   _____

   _____

2. Do you have a favorite television commercial? Why do you like it?

   _____

   _____

   Is there a commercial that you particularly dislike? What is it that bothers you about the commercial? _____

   _____

   Make a list of at least three features that you consider necessary for a good television commercial.

   _____

   _____

   _____

   _____

Writers of advertising copy are amateur psychologists. They know just what will appeal to our instincts and emotions. In general, there are three major areas in our nature at which advertising aims—preservation, pride, and pleasure. Preservation, for example, relates to our innate desire to live longer, know more, and look better than our forefathers did. Pride encompasses all sorts of things—our desire to show off, to brag about our prosperity or our good taste, to be one of the élite. We all want to enjoy the fruits of our labors, and this is where the pleasure principle comes in. We want to be entertained, to eat and drink well, and to relax in comfortable surroundings.

Reading 13

As you read this advertisement, look for the means, both *overt* and *subtle*, employed to sell an extremely expensive car.

JAGUAR XJ-S: A CAR SO SWIFT, SILENT AND LUXURIOUS, THAT IT IS, IN EVERY SENSE…
BEYOND COMPARISON

The 1982 S-type Jaguar stands alone as a class of one. It is, to begin with, the only V-12 powered motorcar for sale in America. *Car and Driver* described the engine this way: "Its turbinelike smoothness and awesome torque simply set it apart from anything that might attempt to compete, even at half again the Jaguar's price."

The dramatically powerful engine is teamed with sports car engineering. Power rack and pinion steering is quick and precise. Four wheel independent suspension maintains balance and stability. And four wheel power disc brakes are both smooth and decisive.

The inner world of the S-type offers an experience of luxury on a level that few drivers will ever know. From the exotic burled elm veneers that enhance the dashboard and doors to the supple Connolly hides that cover virtually all of the passenger compartment, opulence is everywhere. Electronic conveniences pamper you: self adjusting heating and air conditioning; power window, doorlocks and antenna; cruise control and an AM/FM stereophonic radio with signal scanning tuner and Dolby® cassette player are all standard.

Standard too is the best warranty Jaguar has ever offered. For two years or 36,000 miles, whichever comes first, Jaguar will replace or repair any part which proves defective. The Pirelli tires are covered by the tire manufacturer's warranty. Your Jaguar dealer has full details on the 1982 limited warranty.

Courtesy of Jaguar Rover Triumph Inc.

DETAILED COMPREHENSION

Now look back at the advertisement and use note form to fill in the specific things offered to the purchaser of a Jaguar.

1. Show others your wealth.	
2. Show your good taste.	
3. Get a quality product.	
4. Save money.	
5. Look beautiful.	
6. Be comfortable.	
7. Enjoy entertainment.	

Advertisements for exotic places to go on your vacation are very different from ads for luxury cars. They must appeal to another side of your nature. After reading the following ad by the Jamaica Tourist Board, answer the questions.

Reading 14

JAMAICA

There's no place like home.

Here's you, at home in Jamaica in your very own villa, all pastels and privacy.
With Evangeline to pamper you: she's going shopping soon, to
surprise you with a lobster for dinner. Madly extravagant? Not at all.
There are hundreds of villas for rent, all over Jamaica.
Bring your family, or share one with your best friends, and the cost becomes
insidiously attractive. And what nicer way to experience the bountiful wonders of
Jamaica than to have your own special place to return to each evening,
where you can sit back with a rum punch, talk about tomorrow,
and say to yourself, "There's no place like home."

Make it Jamaica. Again.

Courtesy of the Jamaica Tourist Board

A. GENERAL COMPREHENSION

Respond to the following according to the nature of the item.

1. The ad implies that you
   (A) require entertainment by well-known singers
   (B) enjoy sightseeing in foreign places
   (C) don't want to spend a lot of money
   (D) need a lot of excitement on your vacation

2. The ad appeals to your need for
   - (A) quiet pleasure
   - (B) delicious food
   - (C) relaxation
   - (D) all of the above

3. To what major area in your nature does the ad appeal? _____
   _____

B. VOCABULARY WORK

Travel advertisements employ a special vocabulary, particular words that evoke images of pleasure and anticipation. The following words appear in this ad. Write a synonym or definition beside the word or expression.

1. pamper _____
2. madly extravagant _____
3. insidiously attractive _____
4. bountiful wonders _____
5. lobster _____
6. villa _____
7. rum punch _____

Now look at the ad on page 50 for the New York Health & Racquet Club. Can you describe the differences in its appeal from the other two ads? Write down the differences in the space below.

Reading 15

ONCE-A-YEAR SUMMER SALE!
SAVE $100 OR MORE!

This month only, every membership plan is substantially reduced. That's great! But the real excitement at HRC comes from what people do.

Nautilus
Ours is the most complete and advanced equipment available.

Free Classes
We offer over 120 free classes each week including aerobic and tap dance, calisthenics, yoga and more. You'll also enjoy free clinics in racquetball, squash and tennis. Don't forget about our whirlpools, saunas and swimming pools either.

Guarantee
Come to HRC for 3 days. If all that action leaves you less than satisfied you'll get a full refund.

5 Locations
By the way, your membership allows you to use all 5 locations in Manhattan 7 days a week.

Give us a call or drop by for more information.

Sale Ends Aug. 31st!

NEW YORK HEALTH & RACQUET CLUB

Courtesy of the New York Health & Racquet Club

A. GENERAL COMPREHENSION

Respond to the following according to the nature of each item.

1. The advertisement emphasizes
   (A) locations
   (B) a trial membership
   (C) reduced cost
   (D) opening hours

2. It can be inferred that if you join the club,
   (A) the sale ends on August 31
   (B) you will go to all five club locations
   (C) your figure will improve
   (D) you will get a refund

3. This ad appeals to people's
   (A) pleasure
   (B) pride
   (C) preservation
   (D) all of the above

4. From the context of the expression *free clinics,* it must mean
   (A) cost-free medical care
   (B) no charge for lessons
   (C) liberated movement
   (D) games

5. Membership in the club enables you to enjoy _____ in winter.
   (A) the cold
   (B) a full refund
   (C) dropping by
   (D) swimming

B. VOCABULARY WORK

Note the different words used in this ad to sell an exercise and recreation program in a big city. What words particularly appeal to people confined to metropolitan areas?

1. _____
2. _____
3. _____
4. _____
5. _____

What is the connotation of the words you just wrote?

_____

_____

The final advertisement appeals to people's desire to improve their minds. Of what major area is this an important aspect? After reading the ad, answer the questions.

Reading 16

An out-of-town college thrives in town.

At most big city universities the pace, the attitude and the life-style are geared to city life.

But there is a university in Manhattan that has its roots outside the city—Adelphi.

When we opened Adelphi University/ Manhattan, we brought with us all the values of a traditional non-urban university.

Such as classes small enough for you to get to know your professors. An educational environment designed to separate you from the daily rigors of life. And a staff of counselors and administrators schooled in the importance of the individual.

Yet, with all our emphasis on traditional values, it has always been our tradition to offer programs which reflect the needs of today. So you'll find we've pioneered in education for adults with programs for teachers, social workers, business majors, child care workers and others.

If you're looking for our kind of tradition, you can find it without leaving the city. Adelphi/Manhattan—thriving on 28th Street.

I am interested in the following:
<u>University College for Adults:</u> ☐ Degree ☐ Certificate
<u>Arts & Sciences</u> (Dept. of Educ.): ☐ Undergraduate ☐ Graduate
         <u>Social Work:</u> ☐ Undergraduate ☐ Graduate
         <u>Business:</u> ☐ Grad. Certificate Arts Mgmt.
         <u>Nursing:</u> ☐ Non Credit Continuing Education

Name_____
Address_____
City_____
State_____Zip_____
Tel. (day)_____
Tel. (evening)_____
Adelphi University/Manhattan, 22 East 28th St.
New York, N.Y. 10016 Tel. 212-347-9460
Adelphi University is committed to extending equal educational opportunity to all those who qualify academically.

ADELPHI
UNIVERSITY
MANHATTAN

Courtesy of Adelphi University
Agency: Herman Associates, New York City

A. DETAILED COMPREHENSION

Respond to the following according to the nature of the item.

1. According to the ad, why is Adelphi different from other city colleges?
   (A) It has been geared to the big city.
   (B) Its programs are needed today.
   (C) Its classes are small.
   (D) It caters to adults

2. List the values of a traditional non-urban university.

   (A) _____

   (B) _____

   (C) _____

3. The word *traditional* as used in this ad seems to mean
   (A) changing   (C) innovative
   (B) customary   (D) educational

4. This ad would appeal most to
   (A) counselors   (C) high school graduates
   (B) urban adults   (D) none of the above

5. This ad may be classified as
   (A) humorous   (C) low pressured
   (B) comparative   (D) separatist

6. The final line below the address means that Adelphi is
   (A) interested in admitting only qualified students
   (B) not following the law in its admission standards
   (C) committed to high standards of admission
   (D) an equal opportunity institution

B. VOCABULARY WORK

The vocabulary for this ad is obviously different from that used to sell a Jaguar. Here are words from the ad, some associated with education. What do they mean?

1. pace _____

2. geared _____

3. roots _____

4. non-urban _____

5. rigors of life _____

6. schooled _____

7. pioneered _____

8. social worker _____

9. extend _____

10. qualify _____

C. VOCABULARY BUILDING

Let's review some of the prefixes we studied earlier.

1. un		4. il	
2. in, im		5. non	
3. ir		6. dis	

What do they mean? _____

NOTE: A rule for the negative prefixes is *il* before *l; im* before *b, m,* or *p; ir* before *r;* and *in* or *un* before other letters.

Select the one word from the choices given that best completes each of these sentences. Write it in the space provided.

1. The dying man's speech was so _____ that no one was able to interpret his last request.
   (A) indiscreet   (C) incoherent
   (B) nonchalant   (D) impotent

2. Due to many years of _____, the Smiths had nothing to fall back on when it was time for them to retire.
   (A) illiteracy   (C) inflexibility
   (B) impunity   (D) imprudence

3. Certain pessimists feel that a nuclear war in our time is _____.
   (A) inevitable   (C) disconcerting
   (B) illicit   (D) impossible

4. The personnel manager could not even consider her for the position because of her _____ appearance.
   (A) inept   (C) unkempt
   (B) inflexible   (D) disheartened

5. We received the _____ news today that there would be no raises this year.
   (A) disreputable   (C) incongruous
   (B) uncanny   (D) disconcerting

6. It was truly miraculous that the child was _____ after falling six stories.
   (A) unscathed   (C) irreparable
   (B) uncanny   (D) illiterate

7. Modern architecture often seems _____ in a city rich in history.
   (A) unlikely   (C) incongruous
   (B) unwitting   (D) unkempt

8. Serpico is known for his ＿＿＿＿＿＿ efforts to expose fellow police officers who accepted bribes.
   (A) incalculable   (C) unwieldy
   (B) inexorable   (D) illicit

9. Barbara's parents received a report from her teacher that said, "Barbara is an excellent student, but she talks to her friends ＿＿＿＿＿＿ during class."
   (A) ineptly   (C) unerringly
   (B) incoherently   (D) incessantly

10. A civil war pits brother against brother and causes ＿＿＿＿＿＿ harm to a nation's morale.
    (A) uncompromising   (C) invariable
    (B) incalculable   (D) infallible

11. She divorced her husband after he had a(n) ＿＿＿＿＿＿ affair with his secretary.
    (A) nonchalant   (C) inequitable
    (B) incongruous   (D) illicit

12. Journalists often have to resort to ＿＿＿＿＿＿ questions to obtain information that will interest their readers.
    (A) indiscreet   (C) incalculable
    (B) inflexible   (D) unerring

13. There is still no ＿＿＿＿＿＿ cure for the common cold.
    (A) impotent   (C) infallible
    (B) impossible   (D) unwieldy

14. The boy's performance in school suffered greatly when he became a member of a(n) ＿＿＿＿＿＿ gang.
    (A) unlikely   (C) disreputable
    (B) inequitable   (D) unwieldy

15. Because her husband was ＿＿＿＿＿＿, Mary learned how to do home repairs herself.
    (A) uncompromising   (C) insubordinate
    (B) infallible   (D) inept

Write the number of the word in Column B that has the same meaning as the word in Column A. Put the number on the line provided.

	A		B
＿＿ a.	sure	1.	inexorable
＿＿ b.	unable to do things	2.	imprudent
＿＿ c.	unharmed	3.	incoherent
＿＿ d.	inflexible	4.	incongruous
＿＿ e.	unwise, not careful	5.	disreputable
＿＿ f.	forbidden	6.	infallible
＿＿ g.	disjointed, garbled	7.	incessant

_____ h. not neat   8. illiterate
_____ i. very great   9. incalculable
_____ j. of bad character   10. disconcerted
_____ k. unable to read and write 11. illicit
_____ l. inappropriate   12. inept
_____ m. constant   13. unscathed
_____ n. upset   14. inevitable
_____ o. unavoidable   15. unkempt

Quiz 2

Choose the word among the four alternatives that is the *opposite* (antonym) of the underlined word.

1. I ate lunch with a most <u>convivial</u> group of my friends.
   (A) lively   (C) unsociable
   (B) large   (D) old

2. I prefer <u>muted</u> colors in my living room.
   (A) changeable   (C) dull
   (B) bright   (D) mauve

3. She came for Christmas <u>laden</u> with gifts for everyone.
   (A) later   (C) unloaded
   (B) provided   (D) lifted

4. She had a <u>cozy</u> little apartment in Boston.
   (A) uncomfortable   (C) lazy
   (B) dirty   (D) warm

5. She was a very <u>superficial</u> person with a large group of frivolous friends.
   (A) superior   (C) attractive
   (B) deep   (D) horrible

6. The convicted robber hoped the judge would give him a <u>lenient</u> sentence.
   (A) easy   (C) acute
   (B) unmerciful   (D) frightening

7. Hector takes his dates to <u>intimate</u> restaurants where there is candlelight.
   (A) public   (C) noisy
   (B) quiet   (D) dark

8. As he lay dying, his speech was <u>incoherent</u>.
   (A) inaudible   (C) interesting
   (B) organized   (D) indecent

9. If you want to make a good impression on my father, you will have to be less <u>unkempt</u> than you are now.
   (A) discreet   (C) literate
   (B) uncanny   (D) neat

10. His career in the <u>illicit</u> drug trade ended with the police raid this morning.
   (A) irregular   (C) elicited
   (B) legal   (D) secret

11. Having planned our weekends to watch football, we found the news of the players' strike most <u>disconcerting</u>.
   (A) pleasing   (C) refreshing
   (B) activating   (D) debilitating

12. A frightening number of <u>illiterate</u> students are graduating from college.
   (A) able to read and write
   (B) able to enjoy intramural sports
   (C) unable to pass an examination in reading and writing
   (D) inflexible

13. John was so <u>insubordinate</u> that he lost his job within a week.
   (A) fresh   (C) indiscreet
   (B) understanding   (D) obedient

14. I cannot stand professors who think they are <u>infallible</u>.
   (A) imperfect   (C) inept
   (B) inexorable   (D) inflexible

15. My brother-in-law talks <u>incessantly</u>.
   (A) indiscreetly   (C) seldom
   (B) inevitably   (D) sensibly

Reading 17

The business of tennis clothes has grown astoundingly in the past few years. Over $250 million is spent annually on the trappings of tennis. Apparently everyone wants to look like a pro, even though 20% of the clientele has never even played the game.

Manufacturers pay the stars lucrative fees for wearing their brands of clothes and wielding their racquets on center court. Chris Evert-Lloyd, for example, is rumored to have signed a five-year contract for $5 million with Ellesse, a producer of fancy, expensive tennis wear. John McEnroe gets a reported $600,000 for playing with a Dunlop racquet, $330,000 for sporting Tacchini clothes, and $100,000 for tying his Nike tennis shoes. Obviously, in a bad year, these stars make more as fashion models than as athletes.

Not only tennis players get free clothing, but also all the people involved in the game—the referees, linespeople, ball boys and girls—are living advertisments for tennis wear producers. Where, traditionally, conservative white clothing was required for the entire tennis coterie, changing times have seen a new vogue in tennis outfits. Flamboyant colors, designers' nameplates, geometric figures, and bold lines distinguish the new tennis togs from their predecessors.

A. GENERAL COMPREHENSION

Respond to each item according to its nature.

1. It can be inferred from the passage that
   (A) tennis clothing appeals to the wealthy
   (B) tennis stars get huge sums for endorsements
   (C) the price of tennis racquets has remained stable
   (D) bright colors entice people to buy tennis wear

2. The author's intention is to
   (A) explain why the cost of tennis clothes has risen
   (B) defend tennis wear manufacturers from complaints about their high prices
   (C) describe the means of advertising expensive tennis clothes
   (D) describe the new tennis clothing

3. A good title for this passage would be
   (A) The Stars at Play
   (B) Big Business in Tennis Wear
   (C) The High Cost of Playing Tennis
   (D) Tennis Stars' Flamboyant Clothes

4. It is stated that John McEnroe
   (A) wears flamboyant clothing on the court
   (B) may be earning over $1 million for endorsing tennis products
   (C) is a fashion model more than he is a tennis player
   (D) has had a bad year in tennis competition

5. It is implied that
   (A) tennis clothing is bought by the well-to-do
   (B) everyone who wears expensive tennis wear plays tennis
   (C) tennis officials would prefer to wear traditional white clothing
   (D) fashion models wear tennis clothing

B. VOCABULARY WORK

Find the word that correctly completes these sentences.

1. Manufacturing tennis clothing has become a(n) _____ business.
   (A) astounding   (C) lucrative
   (B) traditional   (D) reported

2. More _____ tennis players still wear white on the court.
   (A) flamboyant   (C) conservative
   (B) athletic   (D) distinguished

3. The cost of the _____ of tennis is prohibitive to the average American.
   (A) court   (C) pro
   (B) net   (D) trappings

4. McEnroe _____ a Dunlop racquet.
   (A) plays   (C) changes
   (B) wields   (D) makes

5. Salvador Dali is one of a _____ of living modern artists.
   (A) coterie   (C) vogue
   (B) painter   (D) gallery

6. Apparently short skirts are in _____ this year.
   (A) acclaim   (C) vogue
   (B) tennis   (D) tradition

7. Since he usually wears red on the court, he has a reputation for preferring
   _____ tennis wear.
   (A) white   (C) flat
   (B) conservative   (D) flamboyant

8. Maria's boutique appealed to a very wealthy _____.
   (A) city   (C) clientele
   (B) manufacturer   (D) clothing

C. VOCABULARY BUILDING

The following is a list of common word elements that give the meaning of a number. Study them and look up the meaning of any words you do not know in the Example column.

Element	Meaning	Examples
mono, uni	one	monotheist, monosyllable, unilateral
du, bi, di	two	duet, binoculars, bipartisan, bicentennial, dichotomy, bisect
tri	three	tricycle, trilingual, triplet
quadr, quat	four	quadrangle, quatrain
quint, penta	five	quintuplet, pentagon
sext, hexa	six	sextet, hexagon
sept	seven	septennial
oct	eight	octagon
non, nov	nine	nonagenarian
deca	ten	decade
cent	hundred	centennial
poly, multi	many	polytheist, multilingual

Refer to the words in the Examples column to complete these sentences.

1. I speak French, Spanish, and English; I am _____.
   able to speak three languages

2. Joe's vocabulary seems limited to _____; all he ever says
   one-syllable words
   is yes or no.

3. Pavarotti and Sutherland sang an operatic _____ at the benefit performance last night.
   music for two singers

4. A six-sided figure is a(n) _____.

5. The five branches of the United States armed forces are directed from a five-sided building known as the _____.

6. We bought our two-year-old daughter a(n) _____.
   bicycle with three wheels

7. A(n) _____ believes that there is more than one God, whereas a(n) _____ believes in the existence of only one.

8. A poem or part of a poem made up of a group of four lines is referred to as a(n) _____.

9. Since we had seats in the upper balcony, we watched the play through _____.
   two lenses

10. The president appointed a(n) _____ committee in the hopes of pleasing both political parties.
    two-party

11. The 1970s was a(n) _____ remembered for worldwide political instability and economic woes.
    10 years

12. Although modern science has improved our chances of living longer, there are still relatively few _____s.
    people between 90 and 100

13. A woman who gives birth to three children at the same time is the mother of _____s.

14. While we live under the threat of nuclear war, _____ disarmament seems futile.
    one-sided

15. On July 4, 1976, the United States celebrated its _____.
    200 years

Reading 18

The oil embargoes of 1973–1975 caused vast chagrin among the manufacturers of automobiles around the world. In particular, American companies were obliged to create innovations in producing small cars that would compete in the market with those flowing into the American market from Japan and Europe. No longer could Americans afford ostentatious, gas-guzzling vehicles.

Of paramount importance to today's car owner is the cost of gasoline. American manufacturers have collaborated to supply their clientele with small cars that provide the amenities of the stereotyped large American car, yet get better mileage than any other car in the history of American car production. It has become a question of ardently competing with foreign car manufacturers or succumbing to the intense competition and losing a lucrative business through apathy.

The American car industry has been rejuvenated. The fuel consumption of the new cars has decreased by 49% since 1977; mileage has risen from an average 17.2 miles per gallon to 25.6 miles per gallon. These figures are indicative of a major turnaround in engineering, manufacturing, and design. The industry has made pertinent use of the computer by installing a microprocessor, a thin piece of silicon about the size of an aspirin, in new cars. This miniature computer measures engine speed, engine load, and other functions, and sends messages to the fuel system and other parts of the car's mechanism, thus producing lower gas consumption and cleaner exhaust.

By designing sleek, roomy, beautiful, sporty models, the automobile industry has enticed both the average-income and the affluent car buyer into purchasing small cars. In addition to saving on gas, today's car is built to save on maintenance and repair expenses. Fewer oil changes, lubrications, and maintenance checks are required. Furthermore, the manufacturer is including the costs of maintenance in the buyer's purchase price. New car advertisers now claim that all the buyer has to pay for is gas. To fight corrosion, new coatings have been developed that protect against the havoc caused by road salts, gravel, and other materials. Hence, when car owners are ready to turn in last year's car for a new one, they will find that their well-preserved used cars will have an unusually high trade-in value.

Fuel efficient, safe, emission free, economical, and beautiful, today's cars are better bargains than any ever produced before.

A. DETAILED COMPREHENSION

Respond to the following according to the nature of each item.

1. What significance did oil embargoes have in the automobile industry?
   (A) Car manufacturers worldwide had to produce fuel-efficient automobiles.
   (B) Automobile manufacturers had to make smaller cars.
   (C) The Japanese exported cars to America.
   (D) Americans continued to drive American cars.

2. In the second paragraph there is a statement that implies that
   (A) Americans love large cars
   (B) American auto manufacturers had been indifferent to the need for smaller cars
   (C) Americans will not buy uncomfortable small cars
   (D) all of the above

3. The microprocessor is
   (A) responsible for the American car industry's rejuvenation
   (B) a major turnaround in American car manufacturing
   (C) a computer that saves gas and helps create cleaner emission
   (D) a pertinent use of fuel consumption

4. The new, small American cars are being bought
   (A) by middle-class and rich clientele
   (B) because they save fuel
   (C) because of inflation
   (D) by Americans who want to help American business

5. New cars are a better bargain than those manufactured in years past because they
   (A) cost less to run and are built to last longer
   (B) have a built-in computer
   (C) save fuel, have more safety features, cost less to maintain, and have a higher trade-in value
   (D) are a lot smaller and don't rust because of better coatings

6. From the information given in the reading, you can infer that anticorrosive coatings will not only protect a new car's body, but also
   (A) make the car run better
   (B) increase the trade-in value of the car
   (C) increase the car's mileage
   (D) make the car safer to drive

7. From the passage you can infer that
   (A) new cars are fuel efficient, sleek, and beautiful
   (B) Americans want their cars to be both beautiful and practical in terms of comfort and cost
   (C) Americans will continue to buy European and Japanese cars because they are cheaper
   (D) if oil becomes plentiful and cheap again, Americans will not return to buying large cars

8. Another inference from the article is that
   (A) the most important consideration in buying a car is the cost of gas
   (B) gas shortages caused American manufacturers to change their production methods
   (C) today's cars are more sensible buys than those in the past
   (D) large cars are more comfortable than small cars

B. VOCABULARY WORK

Getting the Meaning from Context

Select a word from the list below that best completes the following sentences.

compete	vast
chagrin	affluent
innovation	lucrative
amenities	rejuvenated
apathy	stereotype

1. The use of audiovisual materials in foreign language teaching was one of the most important _____s in recent years.

2. _____ Middle Easterners have been buying some of England's ancient estates.

3. Wearing his ten-gallon hat, the Texan has become the _____ of the American Westerner.

4. Doing volunteer work at the hospital is not a very _____ pastime.

5. You have made a(n) _____ improvement in your handwriting since you took that calligraphy course.

6. In order to _____ in today's market, we are going to lower our prices.

7. Mrs. Golightly had cosmetic surgery and appears much _____.

8. Imagine his _____ when he discovered he had forgotten to pay his electric bill and the company turned off his power.

9. The automatic washing machine is one of the _____ without which I cannot live.

10. Many a crime has gone unpunished because of the _____ of bystanders.

Synonyms

Choose the best synonym for the underlined word.

1. She was overcome by <u>chagrin</u> at the check-out counter when she discovered she had left her wallet at home.
   - (A) anger
   - (B) poverty
   - (C) embarrassment
   - (D) challenge

2. The space shuttle covered <u>vast</u> distances.
   - (A) very
   - (B) huge
   - (C) varying
   - (D) hard

3. Dr. Jones suggested that final examinations be discontinued, an <u>innovation</u> I heartily support.
   - (A) entrance
   - (B) change
   - (C) inner part
   - (D) test

4. She plans to <u>compete</u> in the marathon.
   - (A) contend
   - (B) compare
   - (C) delay
   - (D) register

5. His new yacht is certainly an <u>ostentacious</u> display of his wealth.
   - (A) ossified
   - (B) showy
   - (C) large
   - (D) expensive

6. The doctor warned her that adequate diet was of <u>paramount</u> importance in effecting a cure.
   - (A) moving
   - (B) chief
   - (C) healing
   - (D) saving

7. Occasionally the most unlikely people manage to <u>collaborate</u> successfully.
   - (A) put together
   - (B) stand together
   - (C) work together
   - (D) get together

8. Peter advised his <u>clientele</u> that he would be on vacation for the month of January.
   - (A) clinic
   - (B) customers
   - (C) salespeople
   - (D) contact

9. I'd rather stay in a hotel with all the <u>amenities</u> than camp in the woods.
   - (A) conveniences
   - (B) friends
   - (C) expenses
   - (D) sports

10. The night before this exam I tried not to <u>succumb</u> to sleep.
    - (A) scoff
    - (B) save
    - (C) yield
    - (D) try

11. He inherited a <u>lucrative</u> business from his father.
    - (A) lucid
    - (B) wealthy
    - (C) losing
    - (D) profitable

12. <u>Apathy</u> toward his studies prevented his graduation.
    - (A) indirection
    - (B) indifference
    - (C) indecision
    - (D) indication

13. Her large weight loss has <u>rejuvenated</u> her.
    - (A) slimmed again
    - (B) subjugated again
    - (C) made young again
    - (D) made comfortable again

14. Her early skill with numbers was <u>indicative</u> of a genius in mathematics.
    - (A) giving direction
    - (B) giving indication
    - (C) giving assistance
    - (D) giving approval

15. Do you think your question is <u>pertinent</u> to the matter we are discussing?
    - (A) perceptive
    - (B) appropriate
    - (C) discriminating
    - (D) apparent

16. Although he knew she had work to do, he tried to <u>entice</u> her to go to the beach.
    - (A) trace
    - (B) enervate
    - (C) tempt
    - (D) thrice

17. Having spent all my money on tuition, I am not <u>affluent</u> enough even to go to the movies.
    - (A) destitute
    - (B) arrogant
    - (C) wealthy
    - (D) afraid

18. A domineering husband, he is the <u>stereotype</u> of a male chauvinist.
    (A) musician (C) disagreeable type
    (B) fixed conception (D) opposite

19. The senator formerly supported the President's budget plans <u>ardently</u>.
    (A) expertly (C) arduously
    (B) zealously (D) entirely

20. The hurricane caused great <u>havoc</u> in the islands.
    (A) winds (C) destruction
    (B) treatment (D) immersion

Quiz 3

Choose the word from the alternatives that has the *same meaning* as the underlined word in the sentence.

1. Don't you love the new <u>flamboyant</u> tennis clothes?
    (A) athletic (C) expensive
    (B) flaming (D) showy

2. Grandma has just bought herself a new <u>tricycle</u>.
    (A) three-wheeled bike (C) trash can
    (B) triple-sided bird cage (D) trident

3. The football player gave only <u>monosyllabic</u> replies to his professor's questions.
    (A) monotonous (C) one-syllable
    (B) monstrous (D) monopolistic

4. The <u>bicentennial</u> celebration lasted for six months.
    (A) divided by 100 (C) 100 years'
    (B) 200 years' (D) 50 years'

5. The police attribute the increase in the crime rate to the <u>apathy</u> of bystanders who do not help victims.
    (A) lack of weapons (C) lack of time
    (B) lack of concern (D) lack of attention

6. Fashion modeling can be a <u>lucrative</u> business.
    (A) ludicrous (C) profitable
    (B) laughable (D) competitive

7. Imagine my <u>chagrin</u> when I discovered I had on unmatched socks.
    (A) disappointment (C) embarrassment
    (B) terror (D) change

8. Only an <u>affluent</u> person could maintain a 60-foot yacht.
    (A) very brave (C) very mechanical
    (B) very capable (D) very rich

9. In recent years there have been many <u>innovations</u> in teaching that have made learning easier.
   (A) new machines   (C) new teachers
   (B) new prohibitions   (D) new methods

10. The fireman <u>enticed</u> the cat from the treetop with a can of tuna fish.
    (A) entranced   (C) enlisted
    (B) tempted   (D) assisted

11. A good night's sleep is of <u>paramount</u> importance to a student who plans to take an examination.
    (A) chief   (C) minimum
    (B) restful   (D) instructive

12. Only a <u>bipartisan</u> senate committee can make a decision in this case.
    (A) deliberating   (C) two-party
    (B) sage   (D) decisive

13. Have you seen the new <u>octagonal</u> dishes?
    (A) round   (C) six-sided
    (B) seven-sided   (D) eight-sided

14. The American car industry has been <u>rejuvenated</u> by its switch from large to small car production.
    (A) depressed   (C) reinvigorated
    (B) rewarded   (D) rejected

15. The writer, the artist, and the editor <u>collaborate</u> to perfect the book.
    (A) keep in touch   (C) study methods
    (B) work in their offices   (D) work closely together

Now see if you can do this crossword puzzle, which is a review of the vocabulary used in Part I.

Across

1. Powerful
5. Adjust
10. Eager
14. Prefix meaning *out*
15. Praise
17. Either/____
18. Synonym for *kind, type*
20. Prefix meaning *nine*
21. Suffix meaning *person who does something*
22. Triplets
23. Neuter pronoun
24. Abbrev. for *Rhode Island*
26. Camper's "house"
27. Abbreviation for *place*
28. Prefix meaning *not*
29. Cause to have no effect
32. Prefix meaning *three*
33. Abbreviation for *small bedroom*
35. Prefix meaning *not*
36. Negatives
38. Fierce animal
39. Preposition: ____ Monday
40. Abbreviation for *advertisement*
41. Very poor
45. Exist
46. Prefix meaning *from*
47. Neuter pronoun
48. Work together
52. Advanced degree
53. Delicious
54. Huge
55. Article
56. Abbreviation for *elevation*
57. Possessive adjective
58. Slang for *doctors*
59. Prefix meaning *two*
60. Preposition: ____ home
61. ____ soon ____ possible
62. Foot covering
63. Decade
64. Abbreviation for *near*
65. Troubles
67. Tempt
69. Pay back
72. Adverb suffix
73. Where a bird lives
74. Someone who is penniless has ____ money
75. Abbreviation for *street*

Down

1. Suffix meaning *after*
2. Very bad
3. Make longer, increase
4. Prefix meaning *three*
5. Severe
6. Auxiliary verb
7. Neither moral nor immoral
8. Afternoon
9. Deca
10. Acting against
11. Musical piece for two
12. Antonym of *yes*
13. Speaking three languages
16. Someone illiterate is ____ literate.
19. Exclamation
23. Negative prefix used with *coherent*
25. ____ rained last night.
27. Prefix meaning *for*
30. Alcoholic drink
31. ____tire, whole
32. Rise and fall of the sea
33. Condition of being sane
34. Abbreviation for *mister*
37. Opposite of *subtle*
38. Loaded
39. Full of oil
42. Latin for *and*
43. First word in letter salutation
44. Ruin, destruction
45. Employer
48. Eat or drink
49. See 17 across
50. Antonym of *front*
51. Spoil
52. British spelling of *meters*
53. Prefix meaning *above*
58. Someone who does things
59. Another definition for 29 across
60. Suffix meaning *relating to*
62. Hurt your toe
63. ____ the truth
65. Antonym of *lose*
66. Use the eyes
68. Preposition: ____ January
70. Abbreviation for *Social Security*
71. Abbreviation for *extra-terrestrial*

PART II.
HOW THOUGHTS
ARE RELATED

In the preceding section, we talked about various aspects of reading comprehension: finding the main idea and suporting details, getting meaning from context, determining the author's intent or purpose, scanning for specific information, and vocabulary building through knowledge of common word elements and recognition of synonyms. Besides providing you with a thorough review, this section of readings will concentrate on thought relations within sentences, paragraphs, and longer passages. It is important to be able to recognize and understand signal words or *connectives*, which introduce, connect, order, and relate individual ideas to larger and often more general concepts.

Study these connectives, paying close attention to their function.

Connectives	Function
and, also, as well as, besides, finally, furthermore, in addition to, in conclusion, moreover	more information will follow
examples, for example, kinds, types, sorts, ordinal numbers (1,2,3, etc.), others, several, some, such as, the following, ways	examples will follow
even if, however, in spite of, instead of, nevertheless, on the other hand, rather, still, yet, despite	an opposite idea will follow
all but, except	exceptions will follow
as a result of, because, due to, in order to, on account of, since	cause
as a consequence, as a result, consequently, so, so as to, so that, therefore	effect
after, as soon as, before, if, provided that, should, while, without, unless, until, following	conditions to be met
as, before. . .after, like some. . .other, than, once. . .now	comparison

Look at the following example. Note that the connectives are underlined and the ideas connected are circled. Can you determine the function of each connective? If necessary, refer back to the table.

69

Mr. Green had sent his secretary to pick up his car, which he had taken to the garage in order to have the brakes repaired. While returning with Mr. Green's car, the secretary, driving on Main Street, entered the intersection at Elm after the light changed from green to red. She sounded her horn but nevertheless collided with a car that had entered the intersection from Elm Street after the light had turned green.

As you read this passage, underline the signal words and circle the related ideas. Then give the function of each.

Reading 1

1) When a death occurs, the family has religious, social, and legal responsibilities. If the deceased has left an explicit set of papers in an accessible file, arrangements will be much easier for the family to make. For example, such papers should include the deed for a burial plot (if there is one), a statement as to whether cremation or burial is desired, a copy of the birth certificate, and the names and addresses of all family members and friends who should be notified. Furthermore, the papers should include information on bank accounts, safe deposit boxes, and insurance policies, as well as the will. The person in charge of the funeral will need to know how much money is available in order to determine the expenses he or she may reasonably incur for the family.

2) If feasible, the person who makes the funeral arrangements should not be one of the bereaved. A melancholy widow may not be able to make objective decisions regarding expenses, such as for a coffin. Whoever makes the funeral arrangements realizes that he or she is deputized to make legally binding contracts with a funeral director and others, which will probably be honored some months later when funds from the estate are released.

3) One of the duties of the person in charge of the funeral is to prepare a death notice for the newspapers. Often the mortician arranges for the insertion of the notice. Included in the information should be the date of death, the names of the family members, and the time and place of the forthcoming interment.

A. GENERAL COMPREHENSION

Answer the following questions about main ideas and supporting details.

1. The main idea of paragraph 1 is that
   (A) funerals are melancholy occasions
   (B) everybody should leave a will so that survivors will know how much property they inherit
   (C) everybody should put important papers together for his or her survivors
   (D) all friends and relatives of the deceased should be advised of the funeral arrangements

2. The supporting details of paragraph 1
   (A) give instructions about making funeral arrangements
   (B) specify the types of papers required to make funeral arrangements simpler
   (C) explain why a birth certificate is an important requisite for a death certificate
   (D) none of the above

3. The main idea of paragraph 2 is
   (A) in the first sentence
   (B) implied
   (C) in the last sentence
   (D) not clearly stated

4. The supporting details in paragraph 2
   (A) tell why widows spend too much on funeral arrangements
   (B) explain the duties of a funeral director
   (C) emphasize the unpleasant nature of funeral arrangements
   (D) explain why a disinterested person should make funeral arrangements

5. What is the main idea of paragraph 3? Is it stated or implied?

   _____

   _____

6. List the supporting details of paragraph 3.

   (a) _____

   (b) _____

   (c) _____

B. VOCABULARY WORK

Choose the correct synonym of the following underlined words.

1. The deceased left you all her diamonds.
   (A) missing person   (C) wealthy person
   (B) dead person   (D) relative

2. She left explicit instructions regarding her burial.
   (A) vague   (C) irregular
   (B) exciting   (D) clear

3. Because the information was easily accessible, we found it immediately.
   (A) acceptable   (C) reachable
   (B) accessory   (D) probable

4. Property deeds belong in a safe deposit box.
   (A) actions   (C) wills
   (B) legal papers   (D) addresses

5. He was careful not to incur too many bills for the widow to pay.
   (A) inquire   (C) acquire
   (B) pay   (D) change

6. A funeral is a melancholy event.
   (A) meaningful   (C) expensive
   (B) medical   (D) sorrowful

7. The family <u>deputized</u> a close friend to make the funeral arrangements.
   - (A) disputed
   - (B) deprived
   - (C) delegated
   - (D) dispatched

8. The funeral director gave the <u>death notice</u> to the local newspaper.
   - (A) obituary
   - (B) funeral
   - (C) burial
   - (D) biography

9. The <u>undertaker</u> waited three months after the funeral for his bill to be paid.
   - (A) tax collector
   - (B) beginner
   - (C) mortician
   - (D) priest

10. In tropical countries the <u>interment</u> takes place within twenty-four hours of a death.
    - (A) intermittent
    - (B) burial
    - (C) mourning period
    - (D) interruption

Now try to find the signal words and their functions in this paragraph.

Reading 2

The Central Park Conservancy raised $39,000 in private donations to employ twenty-five high school students from the New York area. With commendable zeal, the participants are embellishing the park, as well as weeding and cleaning unkempt areas. Although their employment is merely interim work over the summer, the youths share an affinity for horticulture. Collaboration with the Conservancy only whets their appetites for further endeavors with nature and ecology.

VOCABULARY WORK

Getting the Meaning from Context

Choose the alternative that best completes the sentence.

1. John and Mary _____ on all their books; she writes the text and he does the artwork.
   - (A) study
   - (B) collaborate
   - (C) discuss
   - (D) divide

2. His efforts to keep the peace were so _____ that he was awarded the Nobel Peace Prize.
   - (A) lucrative
   - (B) mercenary
   - (C) commendable
   - (D) heavy

3. They worked from dawn to dusk with such _____ that they were exhausted.
   - (A) boredom
   - (B) detraction
   - (C) debility
   - (D) zeal

4. Before they sold their house, they spent two months _____ it.
   - (A) trying
   - (B) embellishing
   - (C) sifting
   - (D) planting

5. The _____ in the program were high school students.
   (A) donations
   (B) endeavors
   (C) gardens
   (D) participants

6. In the _____ between shows, the actress went to Paris.
   (A) rush
   (B) closing
   (C) interim
   (D) practice

7. He felt such a close _____ for animals that he became a veterinarian.
   (A) distaste
   (B) affinity
   (C) approach
   (D) likeness

8. A bite of chocolate cake only _____ my desire for more.
   (A) spares
   (B) lets
   (C) changes
   (D) whets

9. Working in the park stimulates his interest in _____.
   (A) archaeology
   (B) horticulture
   (D) zoology
   (D) biology

10. We'll have to clean up this _____ yard before the guests arrive.
    (A) tired
    (B) unlikely
    (C) undone
    (D) unkempt

Here is a longer passage. Look at the first sentence. Can you guess what the article is about?

Before you do the exercises that follow the reading, locate all the signal words and determine their functions. You will probably find that this will help you achieve a better understanding of the information included here.

Reading 3

Divorce settlements attempt to make an equitable distribution of a couple's assets. Wrangles are common over who gets the car, the furniture, or the dog, but people overlook future needs and income. Two important issues will have to be decided by the courts. Can the divorced wife continue to have health coverage under her former husband's policy? Is the divorced wife entitled to a share of her ex-husband's pension?

So far the subject of health insurance has created much dissension. Most insurance companies exclude former wives from their definition of a worker's dependents. In order to circumvent his ex-wife's exclusion from his health plan, many a husband has concealed his divorce from his employer. Divorced spouses of military men anticipate that a newly approved bill will allow them 180 days' medical coverage and continued coverage for serious ailments if they were married for at least 20 years during their husbands' service career.

Ex-wives are faring better in the pension-sharing dilemma than they are in obtaining health coverage. The courts have set a precedent in awarding pension funds to divorced women, particularly if there are defaults in alimony and child-support payments. Nevertheless, the Employee Retirement Income Security Act prohibits the payment of a pension to anyone other than the worker. Litigation of ex-wives seeking a share in their former husbands' pensions contends that the

ERISA was passed for the purpose of protecting workers from creditors' attempts to attach pensions, not from their ex-wives. In a recent decision, the Supreme Court gave exclusive pension rights to the military retiree whose retirement plan is not under the jurisdiction of state property laws. On the other hand, the former wives of retired foreign service personnel are legally entitled to a share of these retirees' pensions in proportion to the length of their marriage.

Obviously, there is no panacea for the ills besetting the legal system. Divorced women can only pray for significant benefits from future legislation.

A. DETAILED COMPREHENSION

Mark the following statements *true* or *false*. Then indicate how you got your answer by adding on the blank line *stated, implied,* or *no info.* if there is no information given.

1. _____ Divorce settlements make fair distributions of couples' property. _____

2. _____ In the emotional atmosphere of getting a divorce, wives seldom plan for the distant future. _____

3. _____ Health insurance companies cover ex-wives in the workers' policies. _____

4. _____ A divorced man can continue his wife's health insurance coverage by observing the "silence is golden" rule. _____

5. _____ The author of this selection has no sympathy for divorced women and their demands. _____

6. _____ Sailors' former wives will get some health insurance benefits under any conditions. _____

7. _____ Ex-wives have gone to court and have failed to get a share of their ex-husbands' pensions. _____

8. _____ There is a specific law that prohibits ex-wives from legally attaching their former husbands' pensions. _____

9. _____ A pension must be paid to the retired person and to no other person. _____

10. _____ Some laws regarding pensions favor ex-wives while other laws discriminate against them. _____

B. RESTATING

Choose the alternative that has the same meaning as the initial sentence.

1. Insurance companies exclude former wives from their definition of a worker's dependents.
   (A) Insurance companies do not consider ex-wives as dependents.
   (B) An ex-wife is defined as an exclusion by insurance companies.

    (C) Insurance companies' definition of a worker's dependents includes ex-wives.

    (D) By definition, ex-wives are excluded from insurance companies.

2. Ex-wives are faring better in sharing pensions than in obtaining health coverage.

    (A) Ex-wives get more health coverage than pension shares.

    (B) The fare in the dilemma costs more for health coverage.

    (C) Pension sharing is faring better than health coverage.

    (D) Ex-wives get less health coverage than pension shares.

3. The law was passed to protect workers from creditors' attempts to attach pensions, not from their former wives.

    (A) The law did not intend to keep ex-wives from sharing workers' pensions.

    (B) Creditors' attempts to attach pensions are the same as the ex-wives' attempts.

    (C) The law was passed to keep ex-wives from attaching workers' pensions.

    (D) Former wives, nevertheless, can legally attach workers' pensions.

4. The former wives of retired foreign service personnel are legally entitled to a share of these retirees' pensions in proportion to the length of their marriage.

    (A) Former wives of foreign service men get an equal share of their ex-husbands' pensions.

    (B) Legally a share of retired foreign service personnel pensions depends on a lengthy marriage.

    (C) An ex-wife of a foreign service employee who was married for twenty years gets a larger share of her ex-husband's pension than an ex-wife who was married for ten years.

    (D) Foreign service employees who retire do not have to give a proportion of their pension to their former wives.

5. The Supreme Court decision gave exclusive pension rights to military men whose retirement plan is not under the jurisdiction of state property laws.

    (A) State property laws exclude military men, so their ex-wives get a share of their pensions.

    (B) Although state laws require former husbands to share their pensions with their ex-wives, military men are outside state jurisdiction, and federal law has ruled that their pensions are their own.

    (C) Under the jurisdiction of state property laws, the Supreme Court has ruled that pensions of retired military men belong exclusively to them.

    (D) Former wives of military men petitioned the Supreme Court to pass a law giving them exclusive rights to their ex-husbands' pensions.

C. VOCABULARY WORK

Synonyms

    In the exercise at the top of page 76, put the number of the synonym in Column B beside the word in Column A.

	A		B
_____	a. equitable	1.	illness
_____	b. assets	2.	example
_____	c. wrangle	3.	cure
_____	d. ailment	4.	quarrel
_____	e. fare	5.	succeed
_____	f. dilemma	6.	impartial
_____	g. precedent	7.	property
_____	h. default	8.	fail
_____	i. panacea	9.	predicament

D. VOCABULARY BUILDING

In this group of words, the noun is formed by adding *ion* to the verb. Note the spelling change in some of them.

Verb	Noun
anticipate	anticipation
celebrate	celebration
circumvent	circumvention
direct	direction
donate	donation
exhilarate	exhilaration
insert	insertion
intimidate	intimidation
legislate	legislation
litigate	litigation
object	objection
participate	participation
select	selection

If there are any words that you do not understand from the list above, look them up in your dictionary. Then select the word from the four choices that best completes the sentence. Write the correct form in the space provided.

1. Recent _____ has raised taxes on luxury items.
   object   celebrate   legislate   donate

2. Half the enjoyment of a vacation is the _____ of it.
   insert   direct   object   anticipate

3. Unless a will is written clearly, _____ among family members may be inevitable.
   legislate   litigate   celebrate   select

4. I hope you don't _____ to my smoking.
   intimidate   participate   circumvent   object

5. Americans _____ the Fourth of July with a bang.
   donate   celebrate   direct   legislate

6. We were surprised by the _____ of candidates for the legislature.
   insert   anticipate   direct   select

7. The police department _____ trouble at the antinuclear demonstration this afternoon.
   object   anticipate   participate   circumvent

8. It is difficult to _____ additional material in a manuscript once it has been prepared for the printer.
   insert   direct   donate   celebrate

9. He gave a generous _____ to the public television station.
   donate   celebrate   participate   direct

10. Thousands of runners _____ in the annual Boston Marathon.
    celebrate   exhilarate   intimidate   participate

Now read these short passages for general comprehension and vocabulary practice.

Reading 4

The baptism of His Royal Highness Prince William Arthur Phillip Louis of Wales was a brief, quiet ceremony at Buckingham Palace in London. The little prince shared the honors of the day with his great-grandmother, who was celebrating her 82nd birthday. Thousands of her ardent admirers outside the palace sang "Happy Birthday" to the accompaniment of the Coldstream Guards band.

Clad in a lace and silk christening dress first worn by the future Edward VII in 1841, Prince William affably responded to the baptismal water poured over his head by the Archbishop of Canterbury. Instead of the fierce cry that the superstitious believe expels the Devil from the infant, the prince managed only a squeak or two. His parents and godparents promised to bring him up "to fight against evil and follow Christ."

Following a session with photographers, the baby was removed from the scene by his nanny. The parents and guests celebrated with a palatial luncheon of champagne and christening cake, the top layer of Prince Charles and Princess Diana's wedding cake. Godparents include ex-King Constantine of Greece, Princess Alexandra, Lord Romsey, the Duchess of Westminster, Sir Laurens de Post, and Lady Susan Hussey.

A. GENERAL COMPREHENSION

Mark the following *true* or *false* according to the article. If the statement is false, go back to the reading and find the word or words that make it false.

1. _____ The baptism was a lengthy ceremony.

   _____

2. _____ The baby cried when the baptismal water was poured on him.

   _____

3. _____ Crowds outside the palace sang to celebrate the baby's baptism.

_____

4. _____ The Coldstream Guards band played "Happy Birthday."

_____

5. _____ The prince wore a new christening robe.

_____

6. _____ The ceremony was very private.

_____

7. _____ The christening cake was made especially for the baptismal ceremony.

_____

8. _____ A nanny is a person who takes care of children.

_____

9. _____ The prince's godparents are titled people.

_____

10. _____ It is a superstition that godparents bring a child up to fight against evil and follow Christ.

_____

B. VOCABULARY WORK

Synonyms

Choose the correct synonym for the underlined word in the following sentences. Use your dictionary if you need to.

1. Tom insisted upon a fair <u>share</u> of the partnership's profits.
   (A) spare   (C) merit
   (B) division   (D) help

2. The president held a <u>brief</u> press conference.
   (A) documented   (C) pleasant
   (B) long   (D) short

3. In spite of his rude behavior on the tennis court, John has many <u>ardent</u> admirers.
   (A) arduous   (C) wild
   (B) eager   (D) fabulous

4. An <u>affable</u> response frequently turns away wrath.
   - (A) pleasant
   - (B) loud
   - (C) polite
   - (D) angry

5. It is extremely hazardous to try to break up a <u>fierce</u> dog fight.
   - (A) cross
   - (B) ravenous
   - (C) noisy
   - (D) violent

6. <u>Superstition</u> may easily lead you astray.
   - (A) irrational belief
   - (B) succession
   - (C) logic
   - (D) misdirection

7. Queen Victoria's <u>palatial</u> country home draws many visitors to the Isle of Wight.
   - (A) palatine
   - (B) paltry
   - (C) palace-like
   - (D) partial

8. The little boy certainly has distinguished <u>godparents</u>.
   - (A) mother and father
   - (B) sponsors at the baptism
   - (C) religious supporters
   - (D) loving relatives

9. The principal threatened to <u>expel</u> him from school if he didn't behave better.
   - (A) excise
   - (B) exert
   - (C) send out
   - (D) try out

10. He sang the hymn to the <u>accompaniment</u> of the church choir.
    - (A) voices
    - (B) support
    - (C) meter
    - (D) music

The following article describes another type of event. Read it quickly and answer the questions to check your comprehension.

Reading 5

Flora Jones Wed in Forest Hilltop to Francis Smith

Two well-known residents of Forest Hilltop, Flora Jones and Francis Smith, were married in a meadow near Smith's cabin on Sunday, August 4.

The double-ring nuptials were performed by Horace Dooley, minister of his own Church of the True Faith.

The bride was attended by Colleen Jones, the bride's daughter by a previous marriage, and Kristina Svenson, a longtime resident of Forest Hilltop. Verity Smith, the groom's daughter by a previous marriage, acted as flower girl.

The duties of best man were shared by Daniel Lion and Rory Whitney. Mr. Lion read a selection of poetry by Shakespeare, and Mr. Whitney read a selection from Wordsworth's *Prelude*. Music for the ceremony was provided by the bride's brother, James, from London, who accompanied vocalist Marilyn Horn, a Forest Hilltop neighbor.

Also performing at the ceremony was Samuel Cantor, a friend of the groom from Los Angeles, who sang several of his own compositions, accompanied by James Guidry, of Washington, D.C., and William Morris, of New York City.

Playing the flute, James Guidry led a procession of wedding guests and the groom's party from the groom's cabin to the meadow site of the wedding. Following the ceremony, the wedding party and guests strolled back to the cabin, where a reception was held for over 100 guests.

A. DETAILED COMPREHENSION

Answer the following according to the nature of the item.

1. What type of place is Forest Hilltop?
   (A) urban
   (B) suburban
   (C) rural
   (D) metropolitan

2. This wedding would be considered
   (A) traditional
   (B) original
   (C) lovable
   (D) familial

3. The wedding was performed by
   (A) a man who has formed his own sect
   (B) a friend of the family
   (C) the bride's brother
   (D) the bride and groom

4. Apparently a vocalist is a
   (A) female
   (B) wedding guest
   (C) singer
   (D) neighbor

5. Apparently Mr. Cantor is noted for
   (A) his friendship with the groom
   (B) his attendance at the wedding
   (C) writing music
   (D) his residence in Los Angeles

6. Included in the wedding ceremony was
   (A) a dance
   (B) a cabin
   (C) a welcome speech
   (D) a poetry recital

7. The wedding took place
   (A) in a cabin
   (B) in a church
   (C) outdoors
   (D) in a city

8. The reader knows that this is not the first marriage for both bride and groom because
   (A) it included two daughters
   (B) the guests came from many different places
   (C) it took place in a meadow
   (D) the minister was of the Church of the True Faith

9. Because a cabin is usually a small building, the reader infers that
   (A) it is constructed of wood
   (B) the reception was held outside the cabin
   (C) it was a temporary residence
   (D) the bride and groom will not live in it

10. Presumably this wedding announcement appeared in
    (A) a metropolitan newspaper   (C) a musical review
    (B) an alumni bulletin   (D) a small-town newspaper

B. VOCABULARY WORK

Can you think of words that mean the opposite of these words from the reading?

		Antonyms
1.	well-known	_____
2.	married	_____
3.	near	_____
4.	longtime	_____
5.	best	_____
6.	friend	_____
7.	to	_____
8.	resident	_____
9.	provide	_____
10.	led	_____

C. VOCABULARY BUILDING

Knowing the meaning of the prefixes *con, com, co, col,* and *cor* can help you understand a great number of words in English. All of these prefixes add the sense of "with" or "together." Study this list of words and fill in the blanks with a synonym or definition for each. Use your dictionary if you need to.

1. collaborate _____

2. combat _____

3. compatible _____

4. compete _____

5. complement _____

6. component _____

7. concoction _____

8. concur _____

9. concise _____

10. concentrate _____

11. congenital _____

12. conclave _____

13. confide _____

14. congestion _____

15. confer _____

Now use the vocabulary words to complete these sentences. Be sure to use the correct form.

1. The spy was hanged for _____ with the enemy.
   working together

2. I spend my weekends at my beach house, far from the noise and

   _____ of the big city.
   overcrowding

3. The defense attorney could not find a witness whose version of the incident

   _____ with that of the accused.
   agreed

4. Certain drugs have been blamed for _____ defects and should not
   since birth

   be prescribed for pregnant women.

5. The children are making so much noise that I can't _____
   on my work.   give complete attention

6. Reading is an essential _____ of any language course.
   part

7. How did you ever come up with that unappetizing _____?
   mixture

8. The priest promised to _____ evil and help those in need.
   fight

9. If only we had made sure that we were truly _____ before
   able to live together

   we made our nuptial vows!

10. The decision concerning the withdrawal of troops was made at a

    _____ between the Attorney General and the President.
    meeting

11. Every morning at nine the boss and her secretary _____ on the
    talk together

    work plan for the day.

12. If he is serious about a career in journalism, he ought to develop a more

    _____ style of writing.
    short and clear

13. White wine is a _____ to a good seafood dinner.
    something that completes

14. Thousands of athletes from around the world _____ in the Olympic
    try to win

    Games.

15. Only my older sister knows my secrets; she and I have _____ in
    talked freely

    each other since we were children.

Quiz 4

Choose the alternative that has the *same meaning* as the underlined word.

1. He reads periodicals that are <u>pertinent</u> to his profession.
   (A) appropriate
   (B) apparent
   (C) perceptive
   (D) discriminating

2. I like chocolate <u>as well as</u> licorice.
   (A) but the opposite
   (B) in spite of
   (C) and
   (D) rather than

3. Before Smith went on vacation, he left <u>explicit</u> instructions for the painting of his apartment.
   (A) colorful
   (B) clear
   (C) verbal
   (D) written

4. I'm looking for a little cabin in the woods where I won't be <u>accessible</u> to my relatives.
   (A) acceptable
   (B) probable
   (C) reachable
   (D) accessory

5. John and Mary worked on their garden with such <u>zeal</u> this summer that they grew more tomatoes than they could eat.
   (A) fertilizers
   (B) garden tools
   (C) unwillingness
   (D) enthusiasm

6. No one could decide whether she married him for <u>mercenary</u> motives or she loved him in spite of his millions.
   (A) money-loving
   (B) mercurial
   (C) unknown
   (D) lucrative

7. Because he had <u>defaulted</u> in his car payments, the bank repossessed the car.
   (A) erred
   (B) deprived
   (C) failed
   (D) delayed

8. Because he had invited two girls to the dance, he found himself in a terrible <u>dilemma</u>.
   (A) predicament
   (B) romance
   (C) argument
   (D) discussion

9. No matter how hard we try, there is no way to <u>circumvent</u> taxes.
   (A) pay in installments
   (B) get around
   (C) travel around
   (D) round up

10. Because their birthdays occurred in the same month, they <u>shared</u> a birthday party.
    (A) celebrated
    (B) spared
    (C) merited
    (D) experienced together

11. He's such an <u>affable</u> fellow that people sometimes take advantage of him.
    (A) accessible
    (B) good-natured
    (C) wealthy
    (D) weak

12. A recent bride enjoys <u>concocting</u> special dinners for her husband.
    (A) putting together
    (B) inventing
    (C) coordinating
    (D) cooperating

13. Married couples can get a divorce if they find they are not <u>compatible</u>.
    (A) able to budget their money
    (B) capable of having children
    (C) capable of living harmoniously
    (D) able to share an apartment or house

14. The <u>consensus</u> among his sisters was that he ought to get married.
    (A) agreement
    (B) survey
    (C) statistics
    (D) concentration

15. The newscaster gave a <u>concise</u> account of the tragedy.
    (A) long and detailed
    (B) sad and depressing
    (C) complicated and intricate
    (D) short and clear

The last reading described a rather elaborate and somewhat unusual wedding. Now read this selection about a summer camp for adults. Then do the comprehension and vocabulary exercises that follow.

Reading 6

The Audubon Society operates a summer camp for adults on Hog Island, Maine, a 333-acre wildlife sanctuary. Singing paeans to nature and the wilds of Maine, campers delight in meandering down nature trails overhung with spruce and moss. The average age of the campers is 45–50, but the amenities provided are reminiscent of those at summer camps for children—dormitories divided for men and women, wake-up bells at 6:30, sharing chores, and communal meals in a dining room overlooking the rugged Maine coast.

A routine day of exploration begins at 8:30, when instructors, all qualified naturalists, lead small groups of campers around Muscongus Bay, the habitat of prolific lobsters and the site of island homes for terns, gulls, and cormorants. Deer, seals, and occasional whales and porpoises enliven the scene. Each daytrip encompasses a specific theme in nature, such as the weather, birds, or animal and plant ecology. Most of the campers are not stereotyped ecology fanatics but, rather, city dwellers exhilarated by this opportunity to gain a rudimentary insight into the wonders of the natural world.

An all-day boat trip to Eastern Egg Rock, a remote island, elicits the campers' greatest enthusiasm. Once the habitat of innumerable puffins whose eggs were pilferred by poachers, the island currently has very few birds. Since 1974, the Audubon Society has been bringing puffins from Newfoundland to augment the population, but it wasn't until 1981 that any produced young.

The campers' program continues without cessation into the evening hours. Lectures, slide shows, films, and "how-to" courses complement the day's adventures. Compatible campers end their day seated placidly before a blazing fire, discussing their life together in the great outdoors.

A. DETAILED COMPREHENSION

Answer the following questions according to the nature of the item.

1. Would the Audubon camp be a good place for a devoted bird watcher to go? Say why or why not. _____

    _____

2. The instructors at the camp are
    (A) young people
    (B) middle-aged
    (C) trained in nature subjects
    (D) inclined to spend too much time instructing

3. Presumably the camp's facilities are
    (A) rugged but comfortable   (C) built for children
    (B) damp and dirty   (D) modern

4. A common practice at a summer camp is to
    (A) separate the instructors and campers
    (B) take turns doing household work
    (C) take boat trips to islands
    (D) provide for adults

5. Where is there a multitude of lobsters? _____

    _____

6. Why are there so few puffins on Eastern Egg Rock? _____

    _____

    _____

7. How successful has the Audubon Society been in increasing the puffin population? _____

    _____

8. True or false? The campers eat dinner and then relax after the day's exploration. _____

9. True or false? There are numerous whales and porpoises along the coast of Maine. _____

10. At the end of a busy day in the outdoors, most campers are
    (A) ready for bed   (C) cold and hungry
    (B) eager for more information   (D) stereotyped ecology fanatics

11. We may infer that Newfoundland is
    (A) distant from Maine
    (B) only an all-day boat trip from the camp

    (C) increasing its population
    (D) a habitat for puffins

12. We may infer that puffins
    (A) augment their numbers regularly
    (B) take a long time to get used to a place
    (C) are native to Maine
    (D) emigrate from Newfoundland every spring

B. VOCABULARY WORK

Synonyms

Put the number of the definition or synonym in Column B beside the appropriate word in Column A.

A	B
_____ a. stereotype	1. move slowly and aimlessly
_____ b. meander	2. increase
_____ c. pilfer	3. elementary, initial
_____ d. complement	4. jubilant song
_____ e. amenity	5. draw out
_____ f. augment	6. steal
_____ g. paean	7. pleasantness
_____ h. rudimentary	8. fixed pattern representing a type of person
_____ i. habitat	9. natural locality of plant or animal
_____ j. elicit	10. make complete

Sentence Completion

Now use the words above to complete these sentences.

1. On Sundays I love to _____ through the woods and bird watch.

2. Comprehending calculus is impossible if you have only a _____ knowledge of mathematics.

3. Wildlife sanctuaries protect the _____ of birds and the plants on which they feed.

4. Absent-minded and thoughtful, Dr. James is the _____ of a college professor.

5. He will have to find a second job to _____ his income.

6. Vocabulary exercises _____ the work required for reading comprehension.

7. The detective tried to _____ the truth from the captured felon.

8. The superintendent was trying to catch the person who had _____ from the children's desks.

9. The hotel we stayed in last weekend didn't have a single _____, so we left after one night.

10. At the Thanksgiving service, the congregation sang a _____ to the Lord.

Prefixes and Suffixes

There are words in the passage with the following prefixes and suffixes. Write them in the space provided. Then use the line at the right to define each of them.

1. _____ic   _____

2. in_____   _____

3. _____ty   _____

4. _____able   _____

5. _____ers   _____

6. _____ary   _____

7. _____ible   _____

8. out_____   _____

9. over_____   _____

10 en_____   _____

11. _____ation   _____

The Women's Rights Movement came into existence in the early nineteenth century. This international movement originally concentrated on obtaining suffrage (voting rights) and has worked to achieve dignity and equality for women: equality of employment opportunity and freedom from social and political limitations. As a result, women around the world now hold positions and perform tasks that were once restricted to men. List some of the jobs that women perform today that would not have been available to them years ago.

Reading 7

The adage that "a woman's place is in the home" no longer applies to the dauntless ladies in space. The first woman in space was a Soviet who orbited the earth with a male companion in 1963 and landed unscathed after a three-day sojourn aboard a spacecraft. Seemingly, it was inevitable that another Soviet woman would repeat her feat. The second woman in space was Svetlana Savitskaya, a parachutist and test pilot, who served as researcher aboard Soviet Soyuz T-7, which had a rendezvous with Salyut 7, the space station in which the longest manned orbital flight was completed.

Ms. Savitskaya's aptitude for space travel was patent in her past experience in aviation. Holder of several women's records in aviation, she had flown sundry types of aircraft and made over 500 parachute jumps. Her father was a Soviet Air Force marshal, and her husband a pilot. Without a qualm she boarded the spacecraft with her commander, Lieutenant Colonel Leonid Popov, and another rookie astronaut who was the flight engineer.

Soviet authorities announced that they were looking forward to gaining further information about the "weaker sex," so-called in the Soviet newspaper *Tass*, under the stressful conditions of space travel. Sex, however, is not considered an impediment but, rather, a benefit in space, for the Soviets have lauded women for their precision and accuracy in carrying out experiments.

As planned, the Americans put their first woman in space in mid-1983. Sally Ride was their choice. Ms. Ride joined the NASA program with five other women and thirty-four men to train as astronauts in the space shuttle program. She faces an epoch when space travel will no longer be a glamorous adventure but, rather, a commonplace day's work.

A. DETAILED COMPREHENSION

Choose the correct alternative.

1. True or false? A woman's place is in the home. _____ How did you get your answer?
   (A) It was stated.   (C) No information was given.
   (B) It was implied.

2. You can infer that women have been included in the space program as a result of
   (A) public outcry   (C) their qualifications
   (B) their husbands   (D) their connections

3. Soviet authorities apparently think that men and women are
   (A) equal   (C) weaker
   (B) different   (D) inevitable

4. The Soviet Salyut 7 was
   (A) joined by Soyuz T-7   (C) an experiment
   (B) manned by a woman   (D) a training craft

5. Ms. Savitskaya was chosen to travel into space because
   (A) her father was in the Soviet Air Force
   (B) she was dauntless
   (C) her husband was an astronaut
   (D) she was experienced in aviation

6. True or false? Ms. Savitskaya showed no fear of space travel.
   _____ How did you get your answer?
   (A) It was stated.   (C) No information was given.
   (B) It was implied.

7. From the use of the term *weaker sex,* you can infer that the Soviets
   (A) think that Soviet women are not strong
   (B) entertain a bias against women
   (C) think that Soviet men are better than women
   (D) question the women's movement

8. True or false? No American woman has traveled in space. _____
   How did you get your answer?
   (A) It was stated.   (C) No information was given.
   (B) It was implied.

9. An American woman has traveled
   (A) to the moon   (C) in the space shuttle
   (B) to NASA   (D) with the Soviets

10. Space travel will soon be
   (A) glamorous   (C) an everyday experience
   (B) adventuresome   (D) a lot of work

B. VOCABULARY WORK

Synonyms

Choose the synonym for the underlined word.

1. The spacecraft orbited the earth three times.
   (A) circled   (C) flew
   (B) ordered   (D) spaced

2. You can't fight the inevitable.
   (A) inaccurate   (C) unavoidable
   (B) improper   (D) inestimable

3. As a rookie baseball player, he doesn't get paid much.
   (A) rotten   (C) experienced
   (B) novice   (D) practicing

4. Her employer lauded her for her flawless typing.
   (A) lowered   (C) fired
   (B) promoted   (D) praised

5. The epoch of space travel has just begun.
   (A) fear   (C) period
   (B) moment   (D) event

Now complete the following sentences with one of these words. If you have trouble, go back to the reading and look at the context in which the words appear.

adage	impediment	sojourn
aptitude	qualm	sundry
dauntless	rendezvous	unscathed
feat		

1. By a miracle, he fell from the second floor and was _____.

2. I have absolutely no _____ for sports, so don't ask me to play tennis.

3. After a long _____ in the country, he returned to New York City.

4. Only a(n) _____ person would attempt to climb Mount Everest.

5. Because of a speech _____, Mary goes for therapy every week.

6. Swimming the English Channel is a daring _____.

7. "The early bird catches the worm" is a funny _____.

8. The experienced parachutist leaped from the plane without a(n) _____.

9. John had a(n) _____ with his girlfriend at an Italian restaurant last night.

10. Women have joined the space program for _____ reasons.

C. VOCABULARY BUILDING

When reading in English, you will come across foreign words that have been incorporated into the language. Below is a list of some of the most commonly used foreign words. Find out what they mean; then do the exercises that follow.

1. ad infinitum	11. élite	21. non sequitor
2. alumnus, alumna	12. ennui	22. nouveau riche
3. bête noire	13. rapport	23. par excellence
4. carte blanche	14. faux pas	24. parvenu
5. cliché	15. forte	25. pecadillo
6. connoisseur	16. gourmet	26. potpourri
7. coquette	17. macabre	25. savoir faire
8. coup de grace	18. magnum opus	28. suave
9. dilettante	19. misanthrope	29. tyro
10. double entendre	20. misogynist	30. virtuoso

Now study these sentences that give you examples of how these words are generally used in English sentences.

1. She talked about her troubles *ad infinitum*, so we all went home early.
2. He is an *alumnus* of Boston University, and she is an *alumna* of Princeton.
3. My *bête noire* has always been spelling.
4. The Queen was given *carte blanche* wherever she went.
5. The speaker's lecture was full of *clichés*, which annoyed his audience greatly.
6. As a *connoisseur* of modern art, he was invited to all of the gallery openings.
7. Carmen was a *coquette* whom no man could resist.

8. As far as he was concerned, the *coup de grace* in the divorce settlement was his wife's getting the dog.
9. He will never be anything more than a *dilettante* in art.
10. At the bachelors' party, everything that was said seemed to have a *double entendre*.
11. Only the *élite* were invited to the royal wedding.
12. That movie was so bad that I nearly passed out from *ennui*.
13. It is important for teachers to establish a good *rapport* with their students.
14. Not thanking the hostess for dinner was a *faux pas* on my part.
15. Mathematics is definitely John's *forte*.
16. Charlie's Chophouse is not for *gourmets*.
17. The children were frightened by the *macabre* Halloween decorations.
18. After thirty years of intense work on his *magnum opus*, he found a publisher.
19. His denunciation of just about everyone and everything earned him the reputation of a *misanthrope*.
20. He was so old when he got married that his friends had begun to think that he was a *misogynist*.
21. Helen's conversation is so full of *non sequitors* that we cannot understand her.
22. The neighbors are obviously *nouveau riche* and don't have the vaguest notion of good taste.
23. Perlman is a violinist *par excellence*.
24. A *parvenue*, he was not accepted by the old families of Bar Harbor.
25. His wife was used to his *pecadillos* and forgave them.
26. Stew is a *potpourri* of meat and vegetables.
27. She showed a great deal of *savoir faire* for such a young girl.
28. A *suave* gentleman never lacks invitations to dinner.
29. A *tyro* in the business world usually earns very little money.
30. Leonard Bernstein is a *virtuoso* in the music world.

Now fill in the blanks in the following sentences with one of the words from the list.

1. A(n) _____ is a person who knows good food and drink.

2. A(n) _____ is a person who is newly rich.

3. A(n) _____ is a flirt.

4. A(n) _____ is a person who dabbles in arts or sciences.

5. A(n) _____ hates women.

6. A(n) _____ hates mankind.

7. A(n) _____ is an expert in a field.

8. A(n) _____ is a beginner in a field.

9. A(n) _____ is a male graduate of a school.

10. A(n) _____ is a female graduate.

11. A(n) ⎯⎯⎯⎯⎯⎯ is a critical judge of an art.

12. A(n) ⎯⎯⎯⎯⎯⎯ is a great work by an artist or writer.

13. A(n) ⎯⎯⎯⎯⎯⎯ is something you hate and avoid.

14. ⎯⎯⎯⎯⎯⎯ is a feeling of community with a group.

15. A(n) ⎯⎯⎯⎯⎯⎯ is a slight offense.

16. ⎯⎯⎯⎯⎯⎯ is without end or limit.

17. Your ⎯⎯⎯⎯⎯⎯ is your strong point.

18. A(n) ⎯⎯⎯⎯⎯⎯ is a social blunder.

19. A(n) ⎯⎯⎯⎯⎯⎯ is a mixture of things.

20. A(n) ⎯⎯⎯⎯⎯⎯ is a trite phrase.

Computers have made tremendous changes in our lives. List some places where computers can be found and tell what you know about their function.

⎯⎯⎯⎯⎯⎯⎯⎯⎯⎯⎯⎯⎯⎯⎯⎯⎯⎯⎯⎯⎯⎯⎯⎯⎯⎯⎯⎯⎯⎯⎯

⎯⎯⎯⎯⎯⎯⎯⎯⎯⎯⎯⎯⎯⎯⎯⎯⎯⎯⎯⎯⎯⎯⎯⎯⎯⎯⎯⎯⎯⎯⎯

⎯⎯⎯⎯⎯⎯⎯⎯⎯⎯⎯⎯⎯⎯⎯⎯⎯⎯⎯⎯⎯⎯⎯⎯⎯⎯⎯⎯⎯⎯⎯

⎯⎯⎯⎯⎯⎯⎯⎯⎯⎯⎯⎯⎯⎯⎯⎯⎯⎯⎯⎯⎯⎯⎯⎯⎯⎯⎯⎯⎯⎯⎯

Now read this article about the use of computers in contemporary classrooms.

Reading 8

Traditional methods of teaching no longer suffice in this technological world. Currently there are more than 100,000 computers in schoolrooms in the United States. Students, mediocre and bright alike, from the first grade through high school, not only are not intimidated by computers, but have become avid participants in the computer epoch.

Kids operating computers implement their curriculum with great versatility. A music student can program musical notes so that the computer will play Beethoven or the Beatles. For a biology class, the computer can produce a picture of the intricate actions of the body's organs, thus enabling today's students to envisage human biology in a profound way. A nuclear reactor is no longer an enigma to students who can see its workings in minute detail on a computer. In Wisconsin, the Chippewa Indians are studying their ancient and almost forgotten language with the aid of a computer. More commonly, the computer is used for drilling math and language concepts so that youngsters may learn at their own speed without trying the patience of their human teachers. The simplest computers aid the handicapped, who learn more rapidly from the computer than from humans. Once irksome, remedial drills and exercises now on computer are conducive to learning because the machine responds to correct answers with praise and to incorrect answers with frowns and even an occasional tear.

Adolescents have become so exhilarated by computers that they have developed their own jargon, easily understood by their peers but leaving their disconcerted parents in the dark. They have shown so much fervor for computers that they have formed computer clubs, beguile their leisure hours in computer stores, and even attend computer camps. A Boy Scout can get a computer merit badge. One ingenious young student devised a computer game for Atari that will earn him $100,000 in royalties.

This is definitely the computer age. It is expected that by 1985 there will be between 300,000 and 650,000 computers in American schools. Manufacturers of computers are presently getting tax write-offs for donating equipment to colleges and universities and are pushing for legislation to obtain further deductions for contributions to elementary and high schools. Furthermore, the price of computers has steadily fallen to the point where a small computer for home or office is being sold for less than $100. At that price every class in the country will soon have computer kids.

A. DETAILED COMPREHENSION

Choose the best answer.

1. The expression *traditional methods of teaching* in the first sentence refers to
   (A) teachers who punish students for not learning
   (B) technological methods of teaching
   (C) teachers, textbooks, and class drills
   (D) teaching the so-called "three R's"

2. In order to operate a computer, a student does not have to be
   (A) especially bright   (C) versatile
   (B) in grade school   (D) musical

3. Today's students with the aid of computers
   (A) have more trouble learning
   (B) can understand more complex concepts
   (C) try to confuse their parents
   (D) build nuclear reactors

4. A computer is a robot teacher because it
   (A) is human
   (B) enables students to learn through mechanical means
   (C) teaches machines
   (D) shows human emotions

5. When the author says parents are "left in the dark," he means that they
   (A) didn't pay the electrical bill   (C) don't understand
   (B) have deficient eyesight   (D) go out at night

6. Teachers ought to like to have their students use computers because computers
   (A) are fun to work with
   (B) take over some of the teachers' tedious jobs

    (C) cost less than teachers' salaries
    (D) are being used all over the United States

7. Students' reactions to computers are
    (A) negative   (C) fervent
    (B) jargonistic   (D) original

8. Computers are used most for
    (A) scientific subjects   (B) drills and exercises
    (B) language instruction   (D) Boy Scout merit badges

9. According to the passage, one exceedingly clever student has
    (A) learned an Indian language   (B) invented a video game
    (B) overcome a handicap   (C) played music on a computer

10. Computer manufacturers donate equipment to schools
    (A). in 1985
    (B) to increase their sales
    (C) to get tax deductions
    (D) to teach students how to operate computers

11. The author of this article implies that
    (A) computers make learning today easier than it was in the past
    (B) students today have to be smarter than their parents
    (C) computers are difficult to operate
    (D) anyone who can't operate a computer is a dunce

12. By 1985 it is estimated that the number of computers in schools will
    (A) be at least twice that of today
    (B) be considerably lower than the number today
    (C) triple at least
    (D) continue as it is today

13. The price of a computer is now
    (A) too high for most schools
    (B) within the range of most schools' budgets
    (C) rising
    (D) preventing schools from buying computers

B. VOCABULARY WORK

Getting the Meaning from Context

Determine the meaning of the underlined word from the context.

1. Students beguile their leisure hours in computer stores.
    (A) cause time to pass unnoticed   (C) waste regrettably
    (B) begin   (D) fool around

2. He devised a computer game and sold it to Atari.
    (A) played   (C) invented
    (B) bought   (D) divided

3. Manufacturers are <u>donating</u> computers to schools.
   (A) giving
   (B) going
   (C) dedicating
   (D) deducting

4. I am not <u>ingenious</u> enough to invent a video game.
   (A) studious
   (B) clever
   (C) glorious
   (D) indigenous

5. <u>Currently</u> students appear to be learning and having fun simultaneously.
   (A) electrically
   (B) concurrently
   (C) sometimes
   (D) at the present time

6. Even a <u>mediocre</u> student can learn to operate a computer.
   (A) brilliant
   (B) thoughtful
   (C) average
   (D) attentive

7. It is said that you can <u>intimidate</u> your enemies by speaking in a low voice and carrying a big stick.
   (A) frighten
   (B) attack
   (C) harass
   (D) make peace with

8. <u>Avid</u> opera lovers are willing to stand in line for hours.
   (A) musical
   (B) averse
   (C) eager
   (D) tedious

9. Einstein was a <u>brilliant</u> mathematician.
   (A) shining
   (B) very intelligent
   (C) famous
   (D) foreign

10. The teacher was amazed by the students' <u>versatility</u> in handling the computer.
    (A) verse
    (B) enthusiasm
    (C) variety of skills
    (D) version

11. A computer described the <u>intricate</u> details of managing a bakery.
    (A) containing many detailed parts
    (B) closely guarded
    (C) interior
    (D) inversely related

12. A computer may be used in the math classroom to <u>implement</u> the lesson.
    (A) implant
    (B) learn
    (C) entreat
    (D) carry out

13. Physics is an <u>enigma</u> to me.
    (A) energy
    (B) problem
    (C) mystery
    (D) trial

14. A hundred dollars will <u>suffice</u> to buy a home computer.
    (A) be saved
    (B) be charged
    (C) be suffered
    (D) be enough

15. The kids spoke a <u>jargon</u> of their own that no one else understood.
    (A) accent
    (B) unintelligible talk
    (C) vocabulary
    (D) foreign language

16. It was a <u>minute</u> crack in the motor block that ruined the car.
    (A) hidden
    (B) multiple
    (C) many-sided
    (D) very small

17. Studying vocabulary can be an <u>irksome</u> task.
    (A) easy
    (B) pleasant
    (C) tedious
    (D) irate

18. The tennis player protested the call with great <u>fervor</u>.
    (A) passion
    (B) favor
    (C) fever
    (D) dislike

Earlier on we talked about signal words or connectives. The author of the next selection makes frequent use of pronouns and other words that refer to something mentioned in another part of the text. Read the text, using the questions at the bottom of the page to help you determine what the underlined words refer to. Note that the style of this selection is very different from the others presented in this book, so don't worry if you don't understand everything in it. After all, the paragraph was taken from a novel by Anthony Trollope entitled *The American Senator*. Trollope was a prolific British writer known for his satirical novels, in which he criticized the upper middle class in England. *The American Senator* was first published in 1877.

Reading 9

On the Monday afternoon the Trefoils arrived. Mr. Morton, with his mother and both the carriages, went down to receive <u>them</u>[1]—with a cart also for the luggage, <u>which was fortunate</u>,[2] as Arabella Trefoil's big box was very big indeed, and Lady Augustus, though she was economical in most things, had brought a comfortable amount of clothes. Each of <u>them</u>[3] had her own lady's maid, so that the two carriages were necessary. How it was that <u>these ladies</u>[4] lived so luxuriously was a mystery to their friends, as for some time past they had enjoyed no particular income of their own. Lord Augustus had spent everything that came to his hand, and the family owned no house at all. Nevertheless Arabella Trefoil was to be seen at all parties magnificently dressed, and never stirred anywhere without her own maid. It would have been as grievous to her to be called on to live without food as to go without <u>this necessary appendage</u>.[5] She was a big, fair girl whose copious hair was managed after such a fashion that no one could guess what was her own and <u>what</u>[6] was purchased. She certainly had fine eyes, though I could never imagine how any one could look at them and think it possible that she should be in love. They were very large, beautifully blue, but never bright; and the eyebrows over them were perfect. Her cheeks were somewhat too long and the distance from her well-formed nose to her upper lip too great. Her mouth was small and her teeth excellent. But the charm of which men spoke the most was the brilliance of her complexion. If, as the ladies said, <u>it</u>[7] was all paint, she, or her maid, must have been a great artist. <u>It</u>[8] never betrayed itself to be paint. But the beauty on which she prided herself was the grace of her motion. Though she was tall and big she never allowed an awkward movement to escape from her. She certainly did <u>it</u>[9] very well. No young woman could walk across an archery ground with a finer step, or manage a train with more perfect ease, or sit upon her horse with a more complete look of being at home <u>there</u>.[10] No doubt she was slow, but though slow she never seemed to drag. Now she was, after a certain fashion, engaged to marry John Morton and perhaps she was one of the most unhappy young persons in England.

The questions that follow refer to the numbered words in the passage above.

1. Who? _____

2. What was fortunate? _____

3. To whom does *them* refer? _____

4. What are their names? _____

5. What is *this necessary appendage?* _____

6. To what does *what* refer? _____

7. What is *it?* _____

8. What is *it?* _____

9. And to what does this *it* refer? _____

10. Where is *there?* _____

A. DETAILED COMPREHENSION

Respond to the following according to the nature of the item.

1. After reading this passage, we can infer that
   (A) Arabella Trefoil is the heroine of Trollope's novel
   (B) the author does not especially like Miss Trefoil
   (C) Miss Trefoil is very rich
   (D) Miss Trefoil has a maid

2. After describing each of Miss Trefoil's features, the author
   (A) tells us how beautiful they are
   (B) makes us admire her
   (C) adds something to negate their beauty
   (D) discusses her attitude toward her maid

3. Miss Trefoil's full hair, it is implied, is
   (A) exceedingly pretty   (C) dyed
   (B) not entirely natural   (D) very fashionable

4. True or false? The author thinks Miss Trefoil's eyes are beautiful.
   _____

5. Women sometimes criticize each other. What nasty remark do they make
   about Arabella Trefoil? _____

   _____

6. Miss Trefoil's complexion appears brilliant because
   - (A) she gets plenty of fresh air
   - (B) she is a horseback rider
   - (C) she is a great artist
   - (D) she uses makeup skillfully

7. Apparently Miss Trefoil and Lady Augustus
   - (A) have plenty of money
   - (B) live beyond their means
   - (C) like to visit friends
   - (D) have limited wardrobes

8. Lord Augustus, it is implied, has
   - (A) provided his wife and daughter with luxury
   - (B) moved from the family home
   - (C) wasted his inheritance
   - (D) become a mystery to his friends

9. Presumably the ladies' maids show that
   - (A) the ladies are helpless without service
   - (B) the ladies are wealthy
   - (C) a large group visited the Mortons
   - (D) two carriages were needed to transport the group

10. The reader can infer that Miss Trefoil is planning to marry for
    - (A) new clothes
    - (B) love
    - (C) money
    - (D) position

11. Miss Trefoil considers her maid more essential than her
    - (A) mother
    - (B) fiancé
    - (C) dinner
    - (D) clothes

12. The reason Miss Trefoil is unhappy is that
    - (A) her clothes are expensive
    - (B) she did not want to visit the Mortons
    - (C) she and her mother do not get along well
    - (D) she does not love her fiancé

B. VOCABULARY WORK

Getting the Meaning from Context

Determine the meaning of the underlined word from the context; then select the best synonym.

1. Mr. Morton went down to receive them.
   - (A) get
   - (B) welcome
   - (C) say goodbye to
   - (D) sign for

2. Lady Augustus, though economical in most things, spent a lot of money on clothes.
   - (A) awkward
   - (B) extravagant
   - (C) thrifty
   - (D) careless

3. They lived luxuriously even though they had no income.
   - (A) expensively
   - (B) cheaply
   - (C) usury
   - (D) beautifully

4. Arabella never <u>stirred</u> anywhere without her maid.
(A) mixed   (C) stayed
(B) moved   (D) resided

5. It would be <u>grievous</u> to her to live without her maid.
(A) pleasant   (C) painful
(B) grateful   (D) tearful

6. The maid was a necessary <u>appendage</u> to Arabella.
(A) something added   (C) dependent
(B) application   (D) servant

7. It never <u>betrayed</u> itself to be paint.
(A) made known   (C) bewildered
(B) fooled   (D) bestowed

8. She was graceful and never moved <u>awkwardly</u>.
(A) smoothly   (C) merrily
(B) clumsily   (D) gracefully

9. She <u>prided</u> herself on her graceful walk.
(A) was proud   (C) was happy
(B) was pricked   (D) was sorry

10. She was slow and never seemed to <u>drag</u>.
(A) dread to move   (C) walk fast
(B) dress carelessly   (D) move too slowly

11. A woman who marries for money, not love, is indeed <u>mercenary</u>.
(A) loving money   (C) frigid
(B) disinterested   (D) meticulous

C. VOCABULARY BUILDING

Words That Describe People

The following list includes words that describe people and their behavior. Look up any words you do not understand. Underline and define those words that especially apply to Arabella Trefoil as Trollope describes her in the selection from *The American Senator*.

1. aura _____

2. charlatan _____

3. debonair _____

4. enticing _____

5. frivolous _____

6. personable _____

7. superficial _____

8. unerring _____

9. urbane _____

10. frugal _____

Here is a list of words that describe the protagonist in an adventure movie or novel. Beside the word write the definition. All of these words are adjectives.

Superman is a hero to his fans because he is

tenacious _____

invincible _____

diligent _____

impetuous _____

relentless _____

pugnacious _____

uncompromising _____

resilient _____

On the other hand, a shrew is a bad-tempered woman who can be described with these words:

obnoxious _____

vindictive _____

grudging _____

scolding _____

loquacious _____

petulant _____

garrulous _____

volatile _____

A cynic shares the shrew's unpopularity. A person who finds fault with everyone, the cynic can be described with these adjectives:

cynical _____

sardonic _____

skeptical _____

imperious _____

critical _____

captious _____

censorious _____

carping _____

Mr. Milquetoast was a comic-strip character whose name now represents a person who is unassertive. These additional adjectives describe that type of person:

timid _____

meek _____

passive _____

pusillanimous _____

vague _____

vapid _____

inept _____

evasive _____

laconic _____

listless _____

phlegmatic _____

nonchalant _____

Now that you have written the definitions for these adjectives that describe people, see if you can match the synonym in Column B with the word in Column A. Put the number from Column B in the blank in Column A.

A	B
_____ a. loquacious	1. timid
_____ b. pugnacious	2. hateful
_____ c. tenacious	3. revengeful
_____ d. imperious	4. fault finding
_____ e. pusillanimous	5. unconquerable
_____ f. censorious	6. talkative
_____ g. obnoxious	7. dictatorial
_____ h. impetuous	8. persistent
_____ i. invincible	9. quarrelsome
_____ j. vindictive	10. hotheaded

Quiz 5

Choose the alternative that has the *same meaning* as the underlined word.

1. Before you can take calculus, you need more than a rudimentary knowledge of algebra.
   (A) rude
   (B) thorough
   (C) elementary
   (D) superficial

2. The augmentation in the population has created a fuel shortage.
   (A) augury
   (B) increase
   (C) demand
   (D) necessity

3. Detective Smith used various means to <u>elicit</u> a confession from the murderer.
    (A) make
    (B) force
    (C) frame
    (D) draw out

4. It seems <u>inevitable</u> that the world will end from natural causes.
    (A) invariable
    (B) unavoidable
    (C) impressionable
    (D) inestimable

5. Dr. Salk was <u>lauded</u> for his work with polio vaccine.
    (A) rewarded
    (B) merited
    (C) praised
    (D) heralded

6. The spacecraft <u>orbited</u> the earth many times.
    (A) circled
    (B) viewed
    (C) returned
    (D) overlooked

7. Dick met Jane at a secluded <u>rendezvous</u> overlooking the avenue.
    (A) restaurant
    (B) park
    (C) meeting place
    (D) picnic ground

8. <u>Dauntless</u> men and women crossed America in covered wagons.
    (A) foreign
    (B) fearless
    (C) adventuresome
    (D) penniless

9. The pilot miraculously survived the crash <u>unscathed</u>.
    (A) unsurprised
    (B) unhurt
    (C) unhappy
    (D) undeterred

10. A week's <u>sojourn</u> in Paris can be very expensive.
    (A) shopping
    (B) sightseeing
    (C) journey
    (D) stay

11. A younger sister is <u>obnoxious</u> to have around when a young lady's boyfriend comes to call.
    (A) welcome
    (B) too much
    (C) objectionable
    (D) talkative

12. You should try to avoid <u>clichés</u> if you want to be a creative writer.
    (A) ungrammatical sentences
    (B) improper language
    (C) plagiarized sections
    (D) trite phrases

13. He <u>devised</u> a folding toothbrush for travelers.
    (A) sold
    (B) bought
    (C) invented
    (D) described

14. The Sphinx was an <u>enigma</u> to all but Oedipus.
    (A) mystery
    (B) problem
    (C) enemy
    (D) entity

15. As an <u>alumnus</u> of Harvard, he felt compelled to contribute to the building fund.
    (A) student
    (B) professor
    (C) supporter
    (D) graduate

Try to do this crossword puzzle; it is a review of the vocabulary used in Part II.

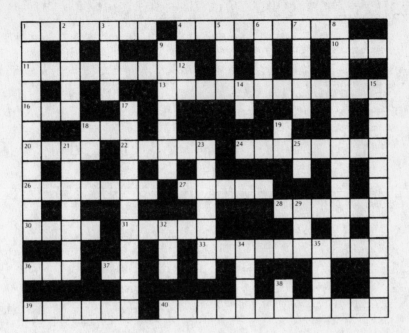

Across

1. Studies or looks at again
4. Make more beautiful
10. Prefix meaning *eight*
11. Delegated
13. Works together
16. Short form of *middle*
18. Hexa
20. Bends the head to show agreement
22. Confusion
24. Ability
26. Friendly, pleasant
28. Kidnap
30. Possessive adjective
31. Salary increase
33. Avoid by going around
36. Past of *sit*
37. Abbreviation for *saint*
38. Indefinite article
39. Property
40. Threat, making someone act through fear

Down

1. Elementary
2. Dull, uninteresting
3. Consumes
5. Deep, round container
6. Animal used for wool
7. Prefix meaning *between*
8. Science of growing fruit, vegetables, and flowers
9. Antonym of *give*
12. Auxiliary verb
14. Preposition: ____ school
15. Irrational belief
17. Excites
18. Abbreviation for *Social Security*
19. Neuter pronoun
21. Fail, as in payments
23. Join together
25. ____ I were you. . .
29. Vagabond
32. Suffix indicating *someone who practices*
34. Wander aimlessly
35. Very large
38. Classified ____

PART III.
UNDERSTANDING
CONTEMPORARY
READING PASSAGES

It is impossible to open a newspaper or magazine today without finding information pertaining to our health. Changes and developments in almost every area, from the social sciences and economics to science, medicine, and technology, are related to the condition of the human body and mind.

In this section you will encounter various styles of writing about contemporary health issues. Note that you will be given the opportunity to review a great many of the concepts you have learned thus far.

Reading 1

Drug abuse is the taking of any substance for any purpose other than the one for which it was intended and in any way that could damage the user's health. The most generally used drugs are the most generally abused. Many people treat aspirin, for example, as if it were candy. On the principle that if two aspirins are recommended to make them feel better, four will give them even more relief, people exceed the recommended dosage—no more than two tablets every four hours and eight within twenty-four hours. Without question, aspirin is a widely abused drug.

Cold capsules, laxatives, cough syrups—all the drugs sold in drugstores and supermarkets—are frequently abused, but their use, when compared to that of other drugs, does not incur the public's concern. The major source of drug abuse is alcohol, a common and easily acquired drug. A group of prohibitionists once asked Abraham Lincoln to support their cause. Sagely, he refused, replying that drunkenness is rooted not in the use of a bad thing, but in the abuse of a good thing.

A. DETAILED COMPREHENSION

Choose the correct answer.

1. A person who exceeds the recommended dosage of aspirin
   (A) is guilty of drug abuse
   (B) likes candy
   (C) is taking aspirin for a headache
   (D) is in for a treat

2. If a person takes a dozen aspirins within twenty-four hours, he or she
   (A) is aiding the aspirin manufacturers
   (B) can relieve the pain
   (C) is endangering his or her health
   (D) is concerned with his or her health

3. The author's reference to Abraham Lincoln
   (A) shows that Lincoln was a wise man
   (B) emphasizes the relation between alcohol and alcoholism
   (C) conveys the idea that alcohol may be harmless
   (D) indicates that alcohol leads to drunkenness

4. True or false? The public is not concerned with addiction to non-prescription drugs. _____

5. Presumably, this selection comes from a
   (A) scientific journal   (C) drug company advertisement
   (B) health book   (D) psychology textbook

B. VOCABULARY BUILDING

This list contains a group of miscellaneous verbs whose noun, adjective, or adverb forms do not follow any particular pattern. Use your dictionary if you do not understand the meaning of any of the words.

Verb	Noun	Adjective	Adverb
abuse	abuse	abusive	abusively
acquire	acquisition		
compare	comparison	comparative	comparatively
damage	damage		
exceed	excess	excessive	excessively
intend	intention	intentional	intentionally
prohibit	prohibition	prohibitive	prohibitively
question	question	questionable	
recommend	recommendation	recommendable	recommendably
refuse	refusal		
reply	reply		
require	requirement		
treat	treatment		
use	use, usage	useful	usefully

Use the correct form of a word from the list above to complete these sentences.

1. With the President's _____, the bill was passed by Congress.

2. I do not object to the use of alcohol in moderation but, rather, to the _____ use of it.

3. There is a(n) _____ between aspirin and alcohol in this passage.

4. Lincoln's _____ to help the prohibitionists incurred their wrath.

5. Send me a list of your _____s for entrance to college.

6. Drug _____ is the subject of this passage.

7. It was not his _____ to take too much aspirin.

8. He had a(n) _____ to ask the professor about the examination.

9. If we have guests for dinner on Saturday, we will _____ our budget for this week.

10. Since the package was insured, the _____ was paid for.

11. _____ was a period in American history when laws prevented legal consumption of alcohol.

12. He was so preoccupied with the _____ of property that he neglected his other interests.

13. There is nothing wrong with the _____ of drugs if you take the proper dosage.

14. His _____ to my letter was short and amusing.

15. Her motives in accepting his proposal are _____.

Reading 2

Vitamins are complex compounds that the body requires to function normally. The word *vitamin* was coined in this century, but the therapeutic value of certain foods in combating disease was recognized as early as 3000 years ago by the ancient Egyptians. They knew that night blindness could be circumvented by eating liver, a source of vitamin A. In the 1700s an Austrian doctor discovered that eating citrus fruits sufficed to cure scurvy, a disease that affects the blood. In 1795 the British Navy began to give sailors lime juice to prevent scurvy. The term *limey* for an Englishman grew out of this use of the humble lime. The Japanese Navy learned that too much polished rice in the diet causes beriberi, a painful nerve disease, and that meat and vegetables, which contain thiamine, prevent the disease.

In the early 1900s, as the causes of an increasing number of diseases were identified as vitamin deficiencies, vitamins were labeled with the letters of the alphabet. Researchers discovered more than twenty-six vitamins, which are now referred to by both letter and chemical names. For example, the vitamin B complex includes twelve vitamins.

A. DETAILED COMPREHENSION

Choose the best alternative, or answer the questions with a few words.

1. True or false? Vitamin deficiencies first developed in the twentieth century.

   _____

2. If you were planning to cross the ocean in your own boat, what would you take with you to prevent beriberi? _____

   _____

3. What is a limey? _____

4. Name a food other than liver that will prevent night blindness because it contains vitamin A. _____

5. True or false? Some diseases are caused by vitamin deficiencies.

   _____

B. VOCABULARY WORK

Put the number of the definition in Column B beside the correct word in Column A.

	<u>A</u>		<u>B</u>
_____	a. complex	1.	insignificant
_____	b. therapeutic	2.	fight
_____	c. combat	3.	shortage
_____	d. circumvent	4.	complicated
_____	e. citrus	5.	genus of a tree or shrub
_____	f. humble	6.	invent
_____	g. diet	7.	check or escape
_____	h. coin	8.	habitual nourishment
_____	i. deficiency	9.	describe
_____	j. label	10.	relating to disease treatment

Reading 3

1)   Stage fright disconcerts even the most experienced performers whether they be professional or not. The minute they open their mouths, they begin to tremble, they forget their lines or act, and their performance is beset by an aura of misery. If the Food and Drug Administration gives its approval, a new drug is going to be provided for the cure of stage fright.

2)   Propranolol is a drug used in the treatment of hypertension. Recent studies indicate that the drug relieves the anxiety of performers. An experiment with students at the Juilliard School of Music in New York and at the University of Nebraska was conducted. After taking propranolol, subjects gave solo perfor-

mances during which their hearts were monitored by an electrocardiograph. Afterward, their blood pressure was taken. Not only were the symptoms of stage fright ameliorated, but also their heart rates were relatively normal and their critics pleased by their performances.

3)   However beneficial propranolol may appear, it must nevertheless be employed judiciously. Used to control high blood pressure and angina and to help prevent heart attacks, the drug is dangerous for sufferers of asthma, hay fever, and various types of diabetes and heart conditions. The drug cannot be imprudently marketed. Scrupulous care must be taken to limit its sale.

A. REVIEW

Topic sentences state the main idea of a paragraph. The topic sentence may appear any place in the paragraph, or it may be merely understood.

Answer these questions about topic sentences and supporting details.

1. What is the topic sentence in paragraph 1? Is it stated or implied? _____

_____

2. What is the topic sentence in paragraph 2? Is it stated or implied? _____

_____

3. What is the topic sentence in paragraph 3? Is it stated or implied? _____

_____

4. List the supporting details for the main idea in paragraph 2.

(A) _____

(B) _____

(C) _____

(D) _____

(E) _____

5. List the supporting details in paragraph 3.

(A) _____

(B) _____

(C) _____

(D) _____

B. DETAILED COMPREHENSION

Choose the best alternative.

1. Before a drug can be marketed, it must have
   (A) no bad side effects   (C) provided a cure
   (B) the FDA's approval   (D) limitless uses

2. True or false? Experienced performers do not suffer from stage fright.

   _____

3. Propranolol has been widely used
   (A) to cure stage fright
   (B) in schools of music
   (C) with great caution
   (D) in the treatment of heart disease

4. One of the effects of taking propranolol is
   (A) decreased anxiety
   (B) very slow heartbeat
   (C) an electrocardiogram
   (D) an inferior performance

5. A person who has _____ could not take propranolol.
   (A) angina
   (B) an aura of misery
   (C) the shakes
   (D) hay fever

6. Presumably the prefix *hyper* in the word *hypertension* means
   (A) high
   (B) too much
   (C) insufficient
   (D) dangerous

7. Give another word that uses *hyper* as its prefix. _____

8. The students who took propranolol before their performance
   (A) performed very well
   (B) were not as nervous as they usually were
   (C) were not disconcerted by performing publicly
   (D) all of the above

9. Propranolol may be marketed for
   (A) a limited public
   (B) all performers
   (C) general use
   (D) an experimental period

10. Presumably an electrocardiograph is
    (A) an X ray
    (B) an experiment
    (C) a machine
    (D) a graph

C. VOCABULARY WORK

Write the number of the definition in Column B beside the word in Column A.

A	B
____ a. disconcert	1. attack without ceasing
____ b. dais	2. offer for sale
____ c. beset	3. platform or stage
____ d. aura	4. cause to become better
____ e. monitor	5. showing good judgment
____ f. ameliorate	6. a feeling that seems to come from a person or place
____ g. judicious	7. correct in every detail, exact
____ h. imprudent	9. keep track of
____ i. market	10. throw into confusion
	11. unwise

Reading 4

1)   Joan is fourteen years old, a bright student, and suffering from self-imposed starvation. She has anorexia nervosa. *Anorexia* means "without appetite," and *nervosa* means "of nervous origin." One morning six months ago Joan looked at herself in the mirror and decided she needed to lose a few pounds. Then five feet three inches tall and weighing 110 pounds, she presently weighs 81 pounds and is in the hospital where she is undergoing psychiatric treatment and being fed intravenously.

2)   What happened to Joan? Why has she ruthlessly starved herself nearly to death? Joan is a typical anorexic—an adolescent girl who refuses to eat for the purpose of rebelling against the pressures imposed upon her by the adult environment. Family members—sometimes the mother, sometimes the father, sometimes both—require her to achieve more than they have in their lives. In her mind, school unites with her family to push her forward. Submissive for years, what does she finally do? She refuses food, says no to the two forces that are pushing her. Instead of growing into a mature woman, she holds back her physical growth by self-imposed starvation. In fact, she regresses to childhood, to the stage when she lacked curves, no one expected much from her, and she was dependent upon adults who gave her love and approval without demanding anything from her in return.

3)   Anorexia nervosa, formerly not recognized as a disease, has become common among adolescent girls. Today the cure is prolonged treatment by a psychiatrist who initiates discussion among family members and the patient to determine the causes and ways to eliminate them in the future.

A. REVIEW

Recognizing Main Ideas and Supporting Details

1. The main purpose of paragraph 1 is to
   (A) define and describe anorexia nervosa
   (B) tell what caused Joan's starvation
   (C) give Joan's past and present weight
   (D) suggest a cure for anorexia nervosa

2. The main idea of paragraph 2 is
   (A) an anorexic is most likely to be an adolescent
   (B) an anorexic is in rebellion against pressures in her environment
   (C) Joan regressed to childhood
   (D) Joan's parents wanted her to succeed

3. The main idea of paragraph 3 is
   (A) an anorexic can cure herself
   (B) the family of an anorexic must agree to seeing a psychiatrist
   (C) the cure of anorexia involves time, discussion, and professional help
   (D) anorexia is now considered a disease

4. List the details in paragraph 2 that support the main idea.

   (A) _____

   (B) _____

(C) _____

(D) _____

(E) _____

5. Describe Joan before and after she developed anorexia nervosa.

_____

_____

_____

B. DETAILED COMPREHENSION

Respond to the following according to the nature of the item.

1. What is anorexia nervosa? _____

_____

2. *Self-imposed* means to
   (A) fool oneself
   (B) starve oneself
   (C) force oneself
   (D) impress oneself

3. The root of anorexia nervosa is
   (A) lack of appetite
   (B) psychological problems
   (C) adolescence
   (D) physical deficiencies

4. The prefix *intra* means
   (A) without
   (B) withdraw
   (C) withhold
   (D) within

5. Give another word beginning with *intra*. _____

6. Give another word like *self-imposed*. _____

7. Give a word like *undergoing*, using the prefix *under*. _____

8. True or false? Excessive pressure from parents can destroy their children's health. _____

9. True or false? Joan wanted to become a young child again. _____
   How did you get your answer?
   (A) It was stated.
   (B) It was implied.
   (C) No information was given.

10. Against what two forces did Joan rebel? _____

_____

11. Anorexia nervosa is currently recognized as a
    (A) mystery
    (B) cure
    (C) disease
    (D) regression

12. The cure for anorexia nervosa is
   (A) forced feeding
   (B) psychiatric treatment
   (C) intense discussion
   (D) dependence upon the family

C. VOCABULARY WORK

For each underlined word in the following phrases, choose the alternative that is closest in meaning.

1. a bright student
   (A) shiny
   (B) brash
   (C) intelligent
   (D) inferior

2. ruthlessly starved herself
   (A) mercilessly
   (B) carefully
   (C) intensely
   (D) rarely

3. a mature woman
   (A) matronly
   (B) intelligent
   (C) thoughtful
   (D) grown-up

4. fed intravenously
   (A) in the veins
   (B) simultaneously
   (C) forcefully
   (D) on the surface

5. a submissive girl
   (A) substitute
   (B) obedient
   (C) tame
   (D) rebellious

6. regresses to childhood
   (A) returns
   (B) yearns
   (C) turns away
   (D) forces

7. dependent upon adults
   (A) relying
   (B) disputing
   (C) insignificant
   (D) pendant

8. formerly not recognized
   (A) fondly
   (B) previously
   (C) only
   (D) formally

9. initiates discussion
   (A) initials
   (B) begins
   (C) continues
   (D) imitates

10. she lacked curves
   (A) lost
   (B) liked
   (C) didn't have
   (D) detested

D. VOCABULARY BUILDING

Whatever your physical or mental problem, there is a specialist to take care of you. Various types of medical people are listed on page 114. Write the specialty of each. Use your dictionary if necessary.

1. chiropodist _____

2. dermatologist _____

3. gynecologist _____

4. obstetrician _____

5. oculist _____

6. ophthalmologist _____

7. optometrist _____

8. orthodontist _____

9. pediatrician _____

10. psychiatrist _____

Now fill in the blanks in the following sentences with the correct word from the above list.

1. Little Jenny's teeth were so crooked that we had to take her to a(n) _____

2. The first year of a baby's life, you should take him or her to a(n) _____ for regular checkups.

3. The _____, the _____, and the _____ treat conditions related to your vision.

4. Several _____s testified at his sanity trial.

5. Jogging made my feet hurt, so I went to the _____.

6. Adolescents troubled with skin problems are the _____'s most frequent patients.

7. The _____ arrived in time to deliver the baby.

Reading 5

Fortunately there are still a few tasty things for us gourmands to enjoy in relative security. Their numbers, however, are depleted almost daily, it seems, by ruthless proclamations from the ever-vigilant Food and Drug Administration and its allies, our doctors. The latest felon to face prosecution is the salt of life, sodium chloride.

Ostensibly, overuse of salt causes high blood pressure and hypertension, the cause of half the deaths in the United States every year. A few years ago the anti-salt campaigners raised such a rumpus that salt was banned from baby food. Currently pressure is being applied to food manufacturers to oblige them to label their products to show sodium content. Because doing so would cost mercenary manufacturers money, they argue that they have no idea how much salt remains on such things as potato chips and how much sticks to the bag. Furthermore, salt isn't the only harmful ingredient in food. If the manufacturer has to provide sodium content, why not require him to list every ingredient and specify which are detrimental to our health? Cigarettes have a warning printed on them. Shouldn't the same type of warning appear on canned foods that are notoriously oversalted?

There are endless ifs and buts in the controversy, but the most telling of these is the questionable proof of salt's diabolic effect upon the blood pressure. True, people who cut their salt intake lowered their blood pressure, but where is the scientific proof that something other than salt didn't do the trick? The most common means of providing dubious proof that salt causes hypertension is to compare societies that use little salt with those that use mountains of salt in their daily diets. Which group has the higher rate of hypertension? Whose blood pressure is lower? What happens when salt is introduced into a group where salt is a novelty? Does the blood pressure rise significantly? Studies of the Japanese indicate that as the world's greatest salters, they suffer the most from hypertension. On the other hand, the simple, salt-free cuisine of several tribes in the Solomon Islands has kept older tribesmen and women from developing hypertension and high blood pressure, ailments traditionally killing their peers in America. No account is taken of the effects of inflation, recession, pollution, crime, and sundry other ills to which Americans, unlike people on primitive islands, are exposed.

To salt or not to salt? That is the question. Now that the question has arisen, it must not be treated with levity but, rather, with searching scientific investigation so that those of us who are preoccupied with both savory food and longevity may decide which of the two is worth its salt.

A. DETAILED COMPREHENSION

Respond to the following according to the nature of the item.

1. The attitude of the author of this passage toward the salt controversy is that
   (A) we must stop eating salt immediately
   (B) she is not convinced that salt is harmful
   (C) the Food and Drug Administration works well with doctors
   (D) soon there won't be anything tasty left to eat

2. The author's approach to the topic is
   (A) angry
   (B) humorous
   (C) scientific
   (D) sympathetic

3. Presumably a gourmand is a
   (A) person
   (B) theory
   (C) food
   (D) protest

4. Food manufacturers don't want to label packages with sodium content because
   (A) they disagree with the FDA
   (B) salt doesn't stick to potato chips
   (C) they would have to spend more money
   (D) it isn't important to single out salt

5. True or false? At present baby food contains salt. _____

6. Canned goods should have the same type of warning as cigarettes because
   (A) both contain salt
   (B) the author likes to smoke and eat
   (C) the cigarette warning reduces smoking
   (D) both are harmful to your health

7. True or false? Comparing societies is a scientific means of determining the
   dangers of salt consumption. _____

8. According to the passage, the Japanese use a lot of salt
   (A) but they suffer from hypertension
   (B) and they suffer from hypertension
   (C) because they suffer from hypertension
   (D) when they suffer from hypertension

9. True, false, or information not given? People in societies that use little salt
   never have high blood pressure. _____

10. The author suggests that Americans suffer from hypertension as a result of
    (A) too much salt   (C) salt-free cuisine
    (B) emotional stress   (D) ailments

B. VOCABULARY WORK

Prefixes and Suffixes

Find a word in the reading that uses either the prefix or suffix given and write it on the first line. Then try to think of another word with the same prefix or suffix. Make sure you understand the meaning of all of the words that you write. If you don't, look them up in your dictionary.

1. -less: (A) _____; (B) _____
2. -ers: (A) _____; (B) _____
3. anti-: (A) _____; (B) _____
4. -ful: (A) _____; (B) _____
5. over-: (A) _____; (B) _____
6. hyper-: (A) _____; (B) _____
7. ex-:   (A) _____; (B) _____
8. -ious: (A) _____; (B) _____

Synonyms

Choose the synonym for the underlined word.

1. The barbarians' treatment of their captives was <u>ruthless</u>.
   (A) rash   (C) rational
   (B) without mercy   (D) liberal

2. The police hunted through the forest for the escaped <u>felon</u>.
   (A) criminal   (C) fugitive
   (B) fellow   (D) hunter

3. Liz is <u>currently</u> appearing on Broadway in a hit show.
   (A) carefully   (C) once
   (B) now   (D) successfully

4. He's so <u>mercenary</u> that he never stops working.
   (A) humane   (C) mad for money
   (B) temporary   (D) worthy

5. <u>Ostensibly</u>, he married for love, but it was really for money.
   (A) really   (C) apparently
   (B) obviously   (D) last year

6. Do you think that coffee is really <u>detrimental</u> to your health?
   (A) harmful   (C) providential
   (B) desperate   (D) determined

7. The James brothers were <u>notorious</u> bank robbers.
   (A) popular   (C) famous
   (B) infamous   (D) ambitious

8. The public is very <u>dubious</u> about the governor's plans for a tax cut.
   (A) debit   (C) delirious
   (B) delightful   (D) doubtful

9. Every Friday night we eat at Lin Chou's because I am crazy about Chinese <u>cuisine</u>.
   (A) restaurants   (C) cooking
   (B) chow mein   (D) customs

10. Adolescents need the approval of their <u>peers</u>.
    (A) principals   (C) equals
    (B) parents   (D) seers

11. Instead of being serious about his work, he treats it with <u>levity</u>.
    (A) leverage   (C) concentration
    (B) lightness   (D) carelessness

C. VOCABULARY BUILDING

There are several common idioms used or hinted at in this passage. They are given below with their definitions. Study them. Then use the idioms to complete the sentences.

(A) the salt of life: reference to the spice of life, the flavor added to make life more exciting
(B) raise a rumpus: create a noisy disagreement
(C) do the trick: accomplish a certain result
(D) mountains of (something): a large quantity
(E) worth its (his/her) salt: worth its (his/her) pay

1. Try putting lemon juice on the stain to see if it will _____.

2. Variety is commonly considered _____.

3. John has had _____ laundry to do for himself since his wife went to visit her mother.

4. If an assistant is _____, he or she will make your work easier for you.

5. The two gangs _____ in the park every night.

Reading 6

1)   Most people are unaware of the fact that a new ailment has developed among subway users. Called "subway syndrome," it causes people to turn pale and cold and even to faint. Commuters misdiagnose the symptoms—acute chest pains and nausea—and rush to hospital emergency rooms in the belief that they are about to succumb to a heart attack. Hearing that their heart attack is only a case of nerves makes them feel better.

2)   What makes people get sick on subways? Various and sundry things. One is that they rush off to work in the morning without having eaten a proper breakfast. Sudden dizziness attacks them. A second cause is the overcrowding and ensuing feeling of claustrophobia, which brings on stress and anxiety. In addition, they are so afraid of mechanical failure, fire, and/or crime that they show signs of panic—men by having chest pains and women by becoming hysterical. Contributing especially to their stress are other factors: overcrowding of both sexes, continual increase in the numbers of passengers, and people's inability to avoid interacting with strangers.

3)   Noise, lack of space, summer heat, fear of entrapment underground—it is a wonder that more people don't have subway syndrome. What therapeutic measures can a commuter take to inoculate himself or herself from the disease? Eat a good breakfast, concentrate on pleasant thoughts as you stand surrounded, bounce a bit on your toes, and roll your head. Thus, mind and body will be restored to a semblance of normality despite the adverse conditions of subway transportation.

A. REVIEW

Main Ideas and Supporting Details

Answer the questions.

1. What is the main idea of paragraph 1? Is it stated in a specific sentence or is it implied? _____

_____

2. List the supporting details of the main idea in paragraph 1.

(A) _____

(B) _____

(C) _____

3. What is the main idea of paragraph 2? Is it stated or implied?

_____

_____

4. List the supporting details in paragraph 2.

(A) _____

(B) _____

(C) _____

(D) _____

(E) _____

5. What is the main idea of paragraph 3? _____

_____

6. List the supporting details in paragraph 3.

(A) _____

(B) _____

(C) _____

(D) _____

B. DETAILED COMPREHENSION

Answer the following questions according to the nature of the item.

1. True or false? Subway syndrome is probably a new name for an old ailment.

_____

2. What does the prefix *mis* in the word *misdiagnose* mean? _____

3. Give another word with the prefix *mis*. _____

4. Why do subway riders think they might be having a heart attack?
   (A) They are overcrowded.   (C) They suffer from chest pains.
   (B) They are afraid.   (D) They don't eat breakfast.

5. True or false? The reading claims that subway riders have frequent heart

attacks. _____

6. True or false? Overcrowding is a cause of subway syndrome. _____

7. The prefix *inter* in the word *interacting* means
   (A) interrupt   (C) bury
   (B) between   (D) enter

8. Give another word like *interacting* with the prefix *inter*. _____

9. Presumably the word *commuter* refers to
   (A) a vehicle   (C) an animal
   (B) a person   (D) an emotion

10. What does the prefix *sub*, as in the word *subway*, mean? _____

11. Give another word that uses *sub* as its prefix. _____

12. According to the passage, if you don't have a good breakfast, you might get
    (A) cold   (C) afraid
    (B) pale   (D) dizzy

13. The author suggests that subway riders will feel better if they
    (A) exercise a little   (C) eat breakfast
    (B) think about pleasant things   (D) all of the above

14. The word *semblance* must be related to the word
    (A) blanch   (C) balance
    (B) resemblance   (D) stimulate

15. A good title for this passage might be
    (A) How to Ride the Subway   (C) The Subway Syndrome
    (B) A Case of Nerves   (D) Overcrowding on the Subways

C. VOCABULARY WORK

Put the number of the definition in Column B beside the correct word in Column A. There are more definitions than there are words to match.

A	B
_____ a. succumb	1. beneath the earth
_____ b. sundry	2. relating to treatment of disease
_____ c. ensuing	3. various
_____ d. underground	4. go up and down
_____ e. therapeutic	5. following
_____ f. inoculate	6. bend the upper part of the body
_____ g. bounce	7. abnormal fear of enclosed space
_____ h. adverse	8. die
_____ i. despite	9. participate
_____ j. claustrophobia	10. inject
	11. unfavorable
	12. in spite of

D. VOCABULARY BUILDING

The following is a list of words that add the prefixes *in-* and *im-* to make them negative. Can you put the correct prefix before the word? The rule for negative prefixes is *il* before *l;* *im* before *b,m,* or *p; ir* before *r;* and *in* before other letters.

1. _____active	11. _____accurate	21. _____calculable
2. _____adequate	12. _____possible	22. _____cessant
3. _____capable	13. _____mobile	23. _____coherent
4. _____ability	14. _____perfect	24. _____controvertible
5. _____competent	15. _____partial	25. _____equitable
6. _____judicious	16. _____disputable	26. _____flexible
7. _____prudent	17. _____discreet	27. _____subordinate
8. _____secure	18. _____eradicable	28. _____passe
9. _____modest	19. _____polite	29. _____probable
10. _____proper	20. _____practical	30. _____potent

Reading 7

1)   Not since Americans crossed the continent in covered wagons have they exercised and dieted as strenuously as they are doing today. Consequently, they do not only look younger and slimmer, but feel better. Because of increased physical fitness, life expectancy in the nation has risen to seventy-three years, with fewer people suffering from heart disease, the nation's number one killer.

2)   Jogging, the easiest and cheapest way of improving the body, keeps over 30 million people of all ages on the run. For the price of a good pair of running shoes, anyone anywhere can join the race.

3)   Dieting, too, has become a national pastime. Promoters of fad diets that eliminate eating one thing or another, such as fats or carbohydrates, promise as much as 20-pound weight losses within two weeks. Books describing such miraculous diets consistently head up the best-seller lists because every corpulent person wants to lose weight quickly and easily.

4)   Nevertheless, both jogging and dieting, carried to extremes, can be hazardous. Many confused joggers overdo and ultimately suffer from ankle and foot damage. Fad dieting, fortunately, becomes only a temporary means for shedding a few pounds while the body is deprived of the balanced nutrition it requires, so most dieters cannot persevere on fad diets. Above all, common sense should be the keystone for any dieting and exercise scheme.

A. GENERAL COMPREHENSION

Choose the alternative that *best completes* the sentence.

1. The main idea of paragraph 1 is
   (A) Americans got exercise when they crossed the continent in covered wagons
   (B) exercise and diet are more widespread in America than ever before
   (C) heart disease is the number one killer among Americans
   (D) Americans live longer than they did before

2. The main idea of paragraph 2 is
   (A) jogging as an exercise appeals to a large number of Americans
   (B) joggers have to buy special shoes
   (C) joggers must be a certain age
   (D) jogging is inexpensive

3. The main idea of paragraph 3 is
   (A) people are so eager to lose weight that they will try any kind of diet
   (B) fad diets are so popular because they are on the best-seller lists
   (C) eliminating fats or carbohydrates will cause drastic weight loss
   (D) diet books guarantee 20-pound weight losses

4. The main idea of paragraph 4 is
   (A) it's good for you to jog and restrict your eating
   (B) improperly controlled, diet and exercise harm rather than benefit your health
   (C) jogging can damage the body because it is too strenuous an exercise
   (D) in the long run, dieting doesn't reduce people because they don't stay on a diet

5. You can infer from this passage that
   (A) a person's life expectancy depends upon diet
   (D) inactive and corpulent people are prone to heart disease
   (C) more people succumb to heart disease than to any other ailment
   (D) all of the above

B. RESTATING

Choose the alternative sentence that is *closest in meaning* to the given sentence.

1. Life expectancy in the nation has risen to seventy-three years.
   (A) Americans now live to be 73 years old.
   (B) The nation is 73 years old.
   (C) Hopefully, with exercise and improved diet, Americans may live to be 73 years old.
   (D) Americans can expect to live to be at least 73 years old.

2. Both jogging and dieting can be hazardous.
   (A) People should not jog or diet.
   (B) Both jogging and dieting can improve your health.
   (C) It's possible that dieting and jogging can damage your health.
   (D) Jogging and dieting are harmful.

3. Fad dieting, fortunately, becomes a temporary scheme for shedding a few pounds.
   (A) Fad dieting is only a temporary scheme.
   (B) It's too bad that people lose only a few pounds on fad diets.
   (C) People should try to stay on fad diets.
   (D) It's a good thing that people don't stay on fad diets.

C. VOCABULARY WORK

Synonyms

Match the words in Column A with the synonyms in Column B. Write the number of the word in Column B on the line provided in Column A.

A	B
____ a. strenuously	1. carry on to excess
____ b. consequently	2. withheld
____ c. ultimately	3. regularly
____ d. cheapest	4. get rid of
____ e. pastime	5. however
____ f. eliminate	6. impermanent
____ g. consistently	7. as a result
____ h. overdo	8. amusement
____ i. deprived	9. least expensive
____ j. temporary	10. with vigorous exertion
____ k. keystone	11. temporary, irrational pursuit
____ l. nevertheless	12. supporting thing
____ m. fad	13. finally

Now choose the alternative that has the *same meaning* as the underlined word.

1. Mary joined a health club in order to use the swimming pool.
   - (A) visited
   - (B) coordinated
   - (C) bought a share in
   - (D) became a member of

2. Your fitness obviously depends upon the amount of food, exercise, and rest you get.
   - (A) readiness
   - (B) eligibility
   - (C) health
   - (D) preparation

3. This product is hazardous to the eyes and should be kept out of reach of children.
   - (A) dangerous
   - (B) liquified
   - (C) hazing
   - (D) arduous

4. Unfortunately, he didn't see the curve in the road.
   - (A) unfavorably
   - (B) unluckily
   - (C) disparately
   - (D) dangerously

5. Corpulent people are constantly trying new diets.
   - (A) slim
   - (B) lazy
   - (C) unfit
   - (D) fat

D. INFERRING AND FINDING SPECIFIC INFORMATION

Which of the following statements can be *inferred* from the passage? Circle *True* or *False;* then show how you got the information needed to answer each question.

1. A very large number of Americans are exercising to get into shape.
   True   or   False
   The information you needed
   (A) was stated in the passage
   (B) was implied but not stated in the passage
   (C) did not appear in the passage

2. Jogging is good for everyone of every age.
   True   or   False
   The information you needed
   (A) was stated in the passage
   (B) was implied but not stated in the passage
   (C) did not appear in the passage

3. Fad diets are extremely popular in the United States.
   True   or   False
   The information that you needed
   (A) was stated in the passage
   (B) was implied but not stated in the passage
   (C) did not appear in the passage

4. Americans live longer than their predecessors did.
   True   or   False
   The information you needed
   (A) was stated in the passage
   (B) was implied but not stated in the passage
   (C) did not appear in the passage

5. The weight lost on a fad diet is a temporary loss.
   True   or   False
   The information you needed
   (A) was stated in the passage
   (B) was implied but not stated in the passage
   (C) did not appear in the passage

6. People who jog and diet sensibly will be healthier than those who do not.
   True   or   False
   The information you needed
   (A) was stated in the passage
   (B) was implied but not stated in the passage
   (C) did not appear in the passage

Reading 8

The statistics relating to the skyrocketing costs of treating the sick indicate that there is no easy cure for inflation in America. Health costs rose 15.1% in 1981, whereas the inflation rate was only 8.9%. The entire nation spent approximately $287 billion on health care, an average of $1,225 per person. Since 85% of all Americans are covered by health insurance and get reimbursements of up to 75%, there are no incentives for reducing costs. Medicare and Medicaid, programs for the poor and the elderly, paid out $73 billion in 1981, an increase of $30 billion over the cost in 1976.

Between 1972 and 1982, hospital care costs quadrupled to $118 billion; doctors' services tripled to $54.8 billion; and nursing home costs quadrupled to $24.2 billion. A day in a hospital cost $133 in 1975; in 1982 the price was $250.

There are multiple causes for soaring medical costs. New construction, particularly when special highly technical areas like burn centers are required, has escalated in cost. To keep a patient alive with modern mechanisms like the kidney dialysis machine costs an added $9 million a year nationwide. The more highly technical treatment becomes, for example for heart and other organ transplants, the more impossible it becomes to halt the inflationary rise of medical costs.

The cost of medical services has a direct influence upon the cost of other things Americans purchase. Large companies provide health plans for their employees, and, as the premiums rise for those plans, the manufacturers must cover their expenses by increasing the sales price of their products. One automobile manufacturer, for example, estimates that the soaring costs of health insurance have added $350 to the cost of a car. Health costs are not isolated but, rather, have had an increasingly appalling effect upon the rate of inflation.

A. SCANNING

Scan the passage as quickly as possible to get the information required to fill in the blanks in the following sentences.

1. _____of all Americans have health insurance.

2. The rate of inflation in 1981 was _____.

3. Medical costs in 1981 rose _____.

4. The average cost per person in the United States for medical care was

    _____.

5. Medical costs in 1981 totaled _____.

6. Medical plans pay up to _____ in reimbursements to participants.

7. A day in the hospital in 1975 cost _____.

8. A day in the hospital cost _____ in 1982.

9. Nursing home care costs _____ times more than it did ten years ago.

10. Hospital care accounted for $_____ in 1982.

11. Physicians were paid _____ in 1982.

12. In ten years physicians' fees have increased _____.

13. Nursing home care cost a total of _____ in 1982.

14. In 1982 hospital care costs rose to _____ times more than they were ten years before.

15. Medicare and Medicaid paid a total of _____ in 1981.

B. CAUSE AND EFFECT

Anything that happens has a cause; the happening is the effect. Read the following sentences and determine what part of the sentence is the cause and what part is the effect. Put brackets around each part and label it *cause* or *effect*.

                            effect   cause

Example: [I took my umbrella] because [it looked like rain.]

1. With soaring medical costs, inflation is difficult to control.
2. Manufacturers are paying so much for employees' health insurance that prices for their products are increasing.
3. New construction of hospital facilities is very expensive, and so medical expenses have risen.
4. With no incentive to cut medical expenses, there has been no effort expended to cut costs.
5. Since a large percentage of Americans have health insurance that pays about 75% of their health care bills, medical costs have continued to rise.
6. Modern technology and more sophisticated equipment have increased medical costs.
7. Because insurance companies are paying their bills, people are taking advantage of the high-quality medical services available.
8. Patients with serious illnesses that formerly would have killed them are now kept alive as a result of organ transplants.
9. Equipping a new intensive care unit adds millions of dollars to the cost of medical services.
10. Escalating construction costs raise medical costs.

C. VOCABULARY WORK

Choose the alternative that *means the same* as the underlined word.

1. If you know in advance that the examination is going to be easy, you have no underline incentive to study very much.
   (A) incidence   (C) time
   (B) motive   (D) interest

2. When there are severe shortages of fuel, prices soar.
   (A) tower   (C) fall
   (B) slow   (D) rise

3. Geraniums thrive if you <u>transplant</u> them from indoors to your garden in the hot weather.
   (A) transfer
   (B) substitute
   (C) trade
   (D) dig

4. The refugees were obliged to <u>halt</u> at the border to have their papers verified.
   (A) hurry
   (B) disrobe
   (C) surrender
   (D) stop

5. Everything I read about costs has the word <u>skyrocketing</u> in it.
   (A) flying in space
   (B) celestial
   (C) writing in the sky
   (D) rapidly increasing

Quiz 6

Choose the alternative that has the *same meaning* as the underlined word.

1. Nutritionists believe that vitamins <u>circumvent</u> disease.
   (A) defeat
   (B) nourish
   (C) treat
   (D) feed

2. After his heart attack, Joe went on a <u>therapeutic</u> diet.
   (A) vegetable
   (B) stringent
   (C) curative
   (D) weight-losing

3. Efforts to <u>ameliorate</u> housing conditions for the poor were halted because government funds were cut off.
   (A) add to
   (B) develop
   (C) study
   (D) improve

4. I think your decision to buy the house was <u>judicious</u>.
   (A) extravagant
   (B) wise
   (C) careful
   (D) joyful

5. I have an appointment this afternoon with my <u>chiropodist</u>.
   (A) eye doctor
   (B) skin specialist
   (C) baby doctor
   (D) foot specialist

6. Usually <u>submissive</u>, little Andy suddenly turned rebellious.
   (A) quiet
   (B) obedient
   (C) permissive
   (D) timid

7. Sometimes <u>hyperactive</u> children are given drugs.
   (A) excessively lively
   (B) slow-moving
   (C) very intelligent
   (D) physically disabled

8. Taking college entrance tests with <u>levity</u> is impossible.
   (A) notes
   (B) care
   (C) lightness
   (D) levitation

9. He was <u>notorious</u> among the women for his fickleness.
   - (A) infamous
   - (B) courted
   - (C) famous
   - (D) noxious

10. Manufacturers are <u>dubious</u> about predictions of an economic recovery.
    - (A) dumbfounded
    - (B) delighted
    - (C) driven
    - (D) doubtful

11. <u>Ostensibly</u>, she enjoys her vacations in Nova Scotia, but she really would prefer someplace warmer.
    - (A) probably
    - (B) obviously
    - (C) seemingly
    - (D) definitely

12. Because children are <u>inoculated</u> against measles, there are currently very few cases of the disease in the United States.
    - (A) treated
    - (B) injected
    - (C) isolated
    - (D) subjected

13. Pat cannot take elevators because she has <u>claustrophobia</u>.
    - (A) unreasonable fear of heights
    - (B) unreasonable fear of closed spaces
    - (C) unreasonable fear of elevators
    - (D) unreasonable fear of people

14. The doctor told him to keep his arm <u>immobile</u> for a few days.
    - (A) in a sling
    - (B) encased in ice
    - (C) motionless
    - (D) exercised

15. The hurricane caused <u>incalculable</u> damage in New England.
    - (A) very great
    - (B) very little
    - (C) very calculating
    - (D) very abusive

Now try this crossword puzzle; it is a review of some of the vocabulary practiced in Part III.

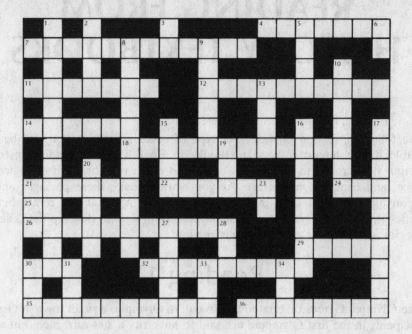

Across

3. Indefinite article
4. Doubtful
7. Very great
11. Cooking
12. Passive, obedient
14. Go up and down
18. Uncertain
21. Very small
22. Beginner
24. Also
25. Indefinite article
26. Someone who takes part
29. Bring up (children)
30. Past of *feed*
32. Antonym of *permanent*
35. Shortage
36. Merciless

Down

1. Disobedient
2. Stage, platform
3. Suffix meaning *relating to*
5. Antonym of *girls*
6. Abbreviation for *saint*
8. Result
9. Divide into two parts
10. Sickness
13. Signify
15. Equal
16. Death notice
17. Suggests
19. Bother
20. Prefix meaning *many*
21. Traveler's tool
23. Suffix meaning *one who*
27. Joyous song
28. Also
30. Temporary pursuit
31. Abbreviation of *definition*
33. Salary
34. Decay

PART IV. TACTICS FOR READING FROM HISTORY TEXTBOOKS

The following section provides the type of reading practice that will be very valuable if you intend to read textbooks in English. When reading historical material, it is crucial to understand cause and effect relations, chronological sequence, and comparison/contrast. As you work through these passages and accompanying exercises, keep in mind that it is not necessary to remember the specific information given here. Your purpose should be to develop the skills and strategies necessary for effective study reading.

Reading 1

The Olympic Games originated in 776 B.C. in Olympia, a small town in Greece. Participants in the first Olympiad are said to have run a 200-yard race, but as the Games were held every four years, they expanded in scope. Only Greek amateurs were allowed to participate in this festival in honor of the god Zeus. The event became a religious, patriotic, and athletic occasion where winners were honored with wreaths and special privileges. There was a profound change in the nature of the Games under the Roman emperors. After they became professional circuses and carnivals, they were banned in 394 A.D. by Emperor Theodosius.

The modern Olympic Games began in Athens in 1896 as a result of the initiative of Baron Pierre de Coubertin, a French educator whose desire was to promote international understanding through athletics. Nine nations participated in the first Games; over 100 nations currently compete.

The taint of politics and racial controversy, however, has impinged upon the Olympic Games in our epoch. In 1936 Hitler, whose country hosted the Games, affronted Jesse Owens, a black American runner, by refusing to congratulate Owens for the feat of having won four gold medals. In the 1972 Munich Games, the world was appalled by the deplorable murder of eleven Israeli athletes by Arab terrorists. The next Olympic Games in Montreal were boycotted by African nations; in addition, Taiwan withdrew. In 1980, following the Soviet invasion of Afghanistan, sixty-two nations caused great consternation to their athletes by refusing to participate in the Games. The consensus among those nations was that their refusal would admonish the Soviets. What may occur in 1984?

A. SCANNING PRACTICE

Scan the passage as quickly as possible and write the event beside the following dates.

1. 776 B.C. _____

2. 394 A.D. _____

3. 1896 _____

4. 1936 _____

5. 1972 _____

6. 1976 _____

7. 1980 _____

B. DETAILED COMPREHENSION

Choose the alternative that best completes the sentence or answers the question.

1. The first Olympic Games were held
    (A) for political reasons
    (B) as an international competition
    (C) as a religious festival
    (D) as a professional athletes' competition

2. Why were the Games discontinued?
    (A) They had ceased to be sports events.
    (B) The Romans did not enjoy them.
    (C) The emperors hated athletes.
    (D) Winners were getting special privileges.

3. Olympic Games are held
    (A) every decade
    (B) biannually
    (C) every four years
    (D) perennially

4. The Greek Olympic Games were _____ in nature.
    (A) religious
    (B) national
    (C) athletic
    (D) all of the above

5. The Games were resumed in modern times for the purpose of
    (A) giving amateur athletes a chance to participate
    (B) promoting goodwill among nations
    (C) creating a political arena
    (D) none of the above

6. You can infer that Hitler's refusal to congratulate Jesse Owens indicated
    (A) national pride
    (B) jealousy
    (C) personal preference
    (D) racial discrimination

7. You can infer that the athletes in sixty-two nations in 1980 were
    (A) terribly disappointed
    (B) very happy
    (C) participants
    (D) boycotted

8. The last three Olympic Games are notorious for their
    (A) racial discrimination
    (B) triumphant victories
    (C) fidelity to the goals of the Olympic Games
    (D) political controversy

C. VOCABULARY WORK

Choose the synonym for the underlined word.

1. The first man to reach the summit of Mt. Everest won worldwide acclaim for his feat.
   (A) climb   (C) courage
   (B) deed   (D) stamina

2. They boycotted the Olympic Games because they disapproved of the politics of some of the participants.
   (A) shunned   (C) attended
   (B) cursed   (D) braved

3. The refusal of many nations to participate in the Olympic Games in Moscow was an admonishment to the Soviets.
   (A) admission   (C) rebuke
   (B) admiration   (D) stigma

4. The consensus among the judges was that Miss Puerto Rico was the most beautiful girl in the universe.
   (A) congress   (C) choice
   (B) agreement   (D) dissension

5. The social worker was appalled by the squalor of their living conditions.
   (A) dismayed   (C) tired
   (B) surprised   (D) excited

6. We tried in vain to wake him from a profound sleep.
   (A) proper   (C) drowsy
   (B) light   (D) deep

7. Politics should not impinge upon athletic events.
   (A) imply   (C) encroach
   (B) enlist   (D) demand

8. When the refrigerator broke down during the heat wave, all of our meat was tainted.
   (A) warmed   (C) humid
   (B) contaminated   (D) frozen

9. The bride's mother was affronted by her brother's appearance at the wedding in tennis gear.
   (A) approached   (C) angered
   (B) excited   (D) insulted

10. My understanding of basic mathematics puts advanced physics beyond my scope.
    (A) range   (C) view
    (B) telescope   (D) hollow

Getting the Meaning from Context

Fill in each blank with one of the following words.
deplorable   detrimental   currently   acclaim   initiative   epoch

1. If someone doesn't take the _____ and plan for the trip, we will never leave home.

2. _____ the tax on automobiles is higher than ever.

3. This is the _____ of travel in space.

4. Child abuse is one of the most _____ crimes.

5. Your sore knee indicates that jogging is _____ to your health.

Reading 2

When Christopher Columbus landed on America's shores, he encountered copper-skinned people whom he promptly called "Indians." Mistaken in his geography, he believed he had reached India. Current estimates indicate that there were over a million Indians inhabiting North America then. There are approximately 800,000 Indians today, of whom about 250,000 live on reservations.

The early settlers had an amicable relationship with Indians, who shared their knowledge of hunting, fishing, and farming with their uninvited guests. The stereotyped stealthy, diabolical Indian of modern Western movies was created by callous, treacherous white men; the Indian was born friendly.

Antipathy developed between the Indians and the settlers, whose encroachment on Indian lands provoked an era of turbulence. As early as 1745, Indian tribes coalesced to drive the French off their land. The French and Indian War did not end until 1763. The Indians had succeeded in destroying many of the Western settlements. The British, superficially submissive to the Indians, promised that further migrations west would not extend beyond a specified boundary. However, there was no holding back ardent adventurers like Daniel Boone, who ignored the British covenant with the Indians and blazed a trail westward.

Evicted from their lands or, worse still, ingenuously ceding their property to the whites for a few baubles, Indians were ruthlessly pushed west. Tempestuous wars broke out, but lacking their former stamina and large numbers, the Indians were doomed to capitulatation. The battle in 1876 at Little Big Horn River in Montana, in which Sitting Bull and the Sioux tribes massacred General Custer's cavalry, caused the whites to intensify their campaign against the redmen. The battle at Wounded Knee, South Dakota, in 1890 rescinded the last vestige of hope for amity between Indians and whites. Thenceforth Indians were relegated to their own reservations, lands allotted to them by the federal government.

Although the Bureau of Indian Affairs has operated since 1824, presumably for the purpose of guarding Indians' interests, Indians on reservations lead notoriously deprived lives. Poverty, unemployment, high infant mortality, and deficient medical care have maimed a once proud race. In recent times irate Indians have taken a militant stand and have appealed to the courts and the American people to ameliorate their substandard living conditions.

A. DETAILED COMPREHENSION

Choose the alternative that best completes the sentence.

1. You can infer that the author of this passage
   (A) works for the Bureau of Indian Affairs
   (B) thinks the Indians were ferocious savages
   (C) admires the settlers for their endurance
   (D) sympathizes with the Indian

2. The early settlers in America
   (A) had to fight Indians
   (B) found the Indians very helpful
   (C) went hunting and fishing
   (D) thought the Indians were sly and mean

3. The French and Indian War
   (A) was quickly terminated
   (B) caused great destruction among the French forces
   (C) lasted eighteen years
   (D) led to westward migration

4. The British made an agreement with the Indians to
   (A) fool the Indians
   (B) get the Indians' land
   (C) stop westward migration
   (D) send Daniel Boone across the continent

5. The Indians sold their land
   (A) for huge profits
   (B) for a few trinkets
   (C) because they didn't understand the language
   (D) thinking it was infertile

6. At Little Big Horn River the Indians were
   (A) defeated   (C) obliged to retreat
   (B) the victors   (D) massacred

7. The battle at Wounded Knee
   (A) marks the end of the Indian wars
   (B) occurred on the Indian reservation
   (C) caused great hope among the Indians
   (D) was won by the Indians

8. Apparently the author feels that the Bureau of Indian Affairs
   (A) has been of great help to the Indians
   (B) was established in the nineteenth century
   (C) deprived the Indians
   (D) has never done much for the Indians

9. The Indians have recently begun to
   (A) rebel against the Bureau of Indian Affairs
   (B) stand up for their rights as a people
   (C) suffer from extreme deprivation
   (D) live on reservations

10. You can infer that Indian reservations
    (A) are on fertile land
    (B) would appeal to American tourists
    (C) offer little opportunity for agriculture
    (D) are happy hunting grounds

B. RESTATING

Choose the alternative that has the same meaning as the statement given.

The stereotyped stealthy, diabolic Indian of modern Western movies was created by callous, treacherous white men, not born.

(A) The Indian depicted in the movies was born, not made.

(B) The type of Indian depicted in the movies became a reality because settlers treated them so heartlessly.

(C) Modern Western movies picture the type of person the Indian was when the settlers arrived in America.

(D) Callous, treacherous white men depicted the Indian as stealthy and sly in the movies.

C. VOCABULARY WORK

Prefixes and Suffixes

Find the word in the reading passage that completes the prefix or suffix given below. Write the meaning of the prefix or suffix on the line provided.

1. _____ers   _____
2. _____ment   _____
3. _____ous   _____
4. _____tion   _____
5. _____less(ly)   _____
6. ex_____   _____
7. e_____   _____
8. _____ity   _____
9. de_____   _____
10. sub_____   _____
11. un_____   _____
12. super_____   _____

Synonyms

Choose the alternative that has the same meaning as the underlined word.

1. <u>Current</u> affairs are meticulously discussed on television.
   (A) customary
   (B) cursory
   (C) stream
   (D) present

2. Dick and Jane made an <u>amicable</u> divorce settlement by dividing their property equally.
   (A) avaricious
   (B) friendly
   (C) flimsy
   (D) terrible

3. With his swarthy complexion and squinty eyes, he was the <u>stereotyped</u> movie villain of the 1920s.
   (A) lacking originality
   (B) ugly
   (C) evil-doing
   (D) stern

4. I didn't hear his <u>stealthy</u> footsteps coming up the stairs.
   (A) strident
   (B) sneaking
   (C) hidden
   (D) flat-footed

5. His plan to exterminate the Indians was <u>diabolical</u>.
   (A) devious
   (B) different
   (C) dragging
   (D) devilish

6. <u>Callous</u> treatment of the Indians caused widespread suffering.
   (A) confused
   (B) unfeeling
   (C) hazardous
   (D) poor

7. Friendship changed to <u>antipathy</u> when the settlers took the Indians' land.
   (A) amity
   (B) fright
   (C) aversion
   (D) heat

8. The settlers' steady <u>encroachment</u> on the Indians' territory ultimately left the Indians homeless.
   (A) endearment
   (B) infringement
   (C) enchantment
   (D) enforcement

9. The era was marked by the <u>turbulence</u> of Indian wars against the settlers.
   (A) termination
   (B) trap
   (C) trial
   (D) turmoil

10. The tribes <u>coalesced</u> to withstand the forces that were destroying their livelihood.
    (A) divided
    (B) met
    (C) united
    (D) cohabitated

11. She had cleaned the apartment <u>superficially</u>, but a close look at the furniture showed she had done very little.
    (A) on the surface
    (B) in the corners
    (C) inside
    (D) from a distance

12. Indians have never been <u>submissive</u> to aggression.
    (A) complaining
    (B) comfortable
    (C) compliant
    (D) commanding

13. After he failed to pay his rent for three months, he was <u>evicted</u> from his apartment.
    (A) put out
    (B) avoided
    (C) evidence
    (D) evinced

14. I am an <u>ardent</u> tennis fan.
    (A) archaic
    (B) eager
    (C) enervated
    (D) busy

15. His response to my question was so <u>ingenuous</u>, one would think he was ten years old instead of fifty.
    (A) youthful
    (B) tired
    (C) ingenious
    (D) naive

16. They refused to <u>cede</u> their rights to the land and declared war.
    (A) see
    (B) legalize
    (C) plant
    (D) yield

17. The enemy's <u>ruthless</u> advance through the countryside left the village in ruins.
    (A) speedy
    (B) careful
    (C) merciless
    (D) pitiful

18. The French saw <u>tempestuous</u> times during the Revolution.
    (A) violent
    (B) vibrant
    (C) virulent
    (D) veracious

19. At the end of the race, his <u>stamina</u> gave out, so he lost the race.
    (A) place
    (B) stand
    (C) memory
    (D) vigor

20. After the riot the prison officials <u>rescinded</u> the prisoners' privileges.
    (A) relegated
    (B) removed
    (C) added to
    (D) changed

21. In truth, the land the government <u>allotted</u> to them had been theirs from the beginning.
    (A) apportioned
    (B) aligned
    (C) offered
    (D) extorted

22. Despite repeated attempts to <u>ameliorate</u> their living conditions, slum dwellers continue to suffer.
    (A) annihilate
    (B) encourage
    (C) investigate
    (D) improve

23. That new cleaner is so effective that there is no <u>vestige</u> of chocolate on the dress now.
    (A) stain
    (B) trace
    (C) vexation
    (D) brown

24. The terrorists <u>maimed</u> twenty bystanders during the shooting.
    (A) shot
    (B) massacred
    (C) wounded
    (D) killed

25. Scrooge was <u>notorious</u> for his reluctance to part with his money.
    (A) well-known
    (B) notarized
    (C) keen
    (D) stingy

Reading 3

On July 4, 1776, a conclave of insurgent colonists in America passed the Declaration of Independence. War against the British had already been going on for over a year, so the Declaration came as the culmination of years of tempestuous events in America.

The impetus for the American Revolution was the Treaty of Paris in 1763, which ended the struggle between the British and the French for control over North America. Since the colonists no longer were intimidated by the French, they ceased to rely upon the British for protection and were not as submissive as they were formerly. On the other hand, the British regarded the colonies as a source of revenue and began to impose inequitable taxes upon them. The Sugar Act in 1764 and the Stamp Act in 1765 were so vehemently opposed by disgruntled colonists that rioting broke out. The Stamp Act was repealed in 1766 as a result of the riots.

The British continued their policy of taxation without collaboration with their once docile subjects. The Townshend Acts (a series of taxes on glass, lead, paper, and tea) created such antipathy that the citizens of Boston attacked British soldiers who fired upon them. That was the Boston Massacre of 1770. After the repeal of the Townshend Acts, a new tea tax in 1773 again consolidated Boston residents' dissension. About fifty men disguised as Indians boarded British ships and jettisoned their cargo of tea in protest against the tea tax. That was the famous Boston Tea Party. In reprisal, the British abolished the Bostonians' right to self-rule, and by passing what were referred to as Intolerable Acts in Boston, they infuriated all of the colonies and caused them to unite in protest.

Representatives from twelve colonies gathered in Philadelphia in 1774 to plan a stratagem to circumvent British interference in trade and to protest the infamy of taxation without representation. The British responded that the colonies were in rebellion, and, since nothing would appease either side, both sides prepared for war.

A. DETAILED COMPREHENSION

Choose the alternative that best completes each sentence.

1. The author's intent in this passage is to
    (A) tell about the American Revolution
    (B) describe the temperament of the colonists
    (C) give the causes of the American Revolution
    (D) describe the effects of the American Revolution

2. You may infer that the Treaty of Paris
   (A) gave the French control of Canada
   (B) gave the control of North America to the British
   (C) made the colonists in America very angry
   (D) had an immediate effect upon colonists' desire for independence

3. The colonists after the Treaty of Paris did not need the British because they
   (A) were independent
   (B) didn't like to pay taxes
   (C) didn't need protection from an enemy
   (D) made a treaty with the French

4. The Sugar Act and Stamp Act were
   (A) passed in 1765   (C) repealed
   (B) taxes upon the colonists   (D) equitable

5. The first violent protest against the British was made in
   (A) 1764   (C) 1770
   (B) 1765   (D) 1773

6. You can infer that in the Boston Massacre in 1770
   (A) Boston was a battlefield
   (B) Boston residents wanted independence
   (C) colonists were killed
   (D) British soldiers sided with Boston residents

7. The Boston Tea Party was
   (A) a celebration in Boston
   (B) an Indian rebellion
   (C) held on board a British ship
   (D) an act of aggression by the colonists

8. You can infer that the Intolerable Acts
   (A) were repealed
   (B) infringed upon colonists' rights
   (C) displeased the British
   (D) were entirely related to taxes

9. You can infer that the meeting in Philadelphia in 1774
   (A) was a very important social event
   (B) took place to discuss taxes
   (C) was a conclave of the British and the colonists
   (D) was the first time the colonists united to protest British injustice

10. The British and their colonists went to war because
    (A) the colonists wanted independence from their rulers
    (B) the British fired at the Bostonians in the Boston Massacre
    (C) the Bostonians dumped tea in the sea at the Boston Tea Party
    (D) the colonists objected to taxation without representation

B. RESTATING

Choose the alternative that means the same as the sentence given.

War against the British had been going on for over a year, so the Declaration of Independence culminated years of tempestuous events.

(A) The Declaration of Independence began the American Revolution after a year.

(B) The Declaration of Independence was the culmination of years of tempestuous events that had led to war the previous year.

(C) Tempestuous events led to the passing of the Declaration of Independence.

(D) When the war for independence began, it had been preceded by tempestuous events and the Declaration of Independence.

C. VOCABULARY WORK

Getting the Meaning from Context

From the context of the underlined word, choose its synonym from the alternatives given.

1. They sat in <u>conclave</u> to decide upon a course of action against the British.
   (A) a building
   (B) a secret meeting
   (C) an opposition
   (D) an accord

2. The government sent its army against the <u>insurgent</u> villagers.
   (A) interested
   (B) friendly
   (C) rebellious
   (D) faithless

3. His life of crime <u>culminated</u> in a long prison sentence.
   (A) climaxed
   (B) prosecuted
   (C) started
   (D) congregated

4. The <u>tempestuous</u> sea drove the ship into the reef.
   (A) temperate
   (B) lightning
   (C) terrific
   (D) stormy

5. An invitation to a party may be the needed <u>impetus</u> to get her out in society.
   (A) interpretation
   (B) stimulus
   (C) greeting
   (D) implication

6. The novice player is usually <u>intimidated</u> by the tennis champion's reputation.
   (A) intimated
   (B) beaten
   (C) chastened
   (D) frightened

7. Goliath expected David to be <u>submissive</u>, but David was too stubborn.
   (A) gentle
   (B) gregarious
   (C) greedy
   (D) obedient

8. The colonists protested against inequitable taxes.
   (A) uneven
   (B) unjust
   (C) unpublished
   (D) unlikely

9. The temperamental tennis player was known for his vehement dislike of linesmen.
   (A) concealed
   (B) crazy
   (C) noisy
   (D) passionate

10. The disgruntled tenants complained to the landlord about their recent rent increase.
    (A) disappointed
    (B) disarmed
    (C) displeased
    (D) disgraced

11. Because of the close collaboration of architect and builder, the building was completed ahead of schedule.
    (A) joint work
    (B) termination
    (C) collage
    (D) affinity

12. Young children learn to ride on docile ponies.
    (A) ferocious
    (B) galloping
    (C) gentle
    (D) dormant

13. There seems to be a natural antipathy between a dog and a cat.
    (A) anticipation
    (B) anxiety
    (C) aversion
    (D) antic

14. Following the consolidation of their two businesses, the Smith brothers' profits increased.
    (A) dispersal
    (B) unification
    (C) declaration
    (D) convention

15. During the storm at sea, the captain gave orders for the crew to jettison the cargo to lighten the ship.
    (A) throw overboard
    (B) consume
    (C) jostle lightly
    (D) transfer

Synonyms

Put the number from Column B beside the word in Column A which means the same.

	A		B
_____	a. infuriate	1.	soothe
_____	b. stratagem	2.	disgrace
_____	c. circumvent	3.	retaliation
_____	d. infamy	4.	enrage
_____	e. appease	5.	scheme
_____	f. reprisal	6.	thwart

Reading 4

In Britain in the middle of the eighteenth century, requisite conditions were in evidence for making that nation the first great industrial country, "the workshop of the world." Already enjoying a vigorous commercial economy, Britain experienced a tremendous population growth and increasing trade at home and abroad.

The population boom is attributed to several circumstances in Britain at that time. Good harvests had produced abundant and therefore cheaper food. The plague years were over, probably as a result of improved water supplies and the availability of soap. With opportunities for work in industry, people were marrying younger and producing larger families for whom they could earn the means to provide. The death rate dropped, and the population increased. Labor was thus accessible for the development of an industrial society.

Industry's need for fuel sparked expansion in coal mining. Production of iron depended upon coal smelting, which produced cheap iron for machines and buildings. The iron industry moved to the central and northern sections of Britain for coal. Following the invention and improvement of the steam engine, water power was supplanted by steam power with its ensuing requirement of access to coal fields.

Britain's foremost industries were wool and cotton weaving. Between 1733 and 1789, a series of ingenious labor-saving machines were invented. They would dispense with water power and rely on steam for increased production. Kay's flying shuttle made it possible to widen cloth and doubled production as well. Hargreaves' spinning jenny, a cotton-spinning machine that replaced the spinning wheel, and Cartwright's power loom rejuvenated both the cotton and wool industries. Once the countryside was dotted with mills beside rivers and streams, but the need for coal drove the textile industry into the North where it continues to operate to this day.

Industrialization was complemented by a dynamic approach to cheap transportation. A network of canals was constructed and covered 2,000 miles by 1815. The canal system reduced coal prices and provided easier access to raw materials and markets. Furthermore, a man named Macadam had the idea of solidifying roads with small stones, so road traffic was made easier.

This period of British industrial expansion is called the Industrial Revolution. The rapid change in the nation's economy was effected by the steam engine and various power-driven machines. Never again would England be an agricultural nation.

A. CAUSE AND EFFECT

The following statements have a cause and effect relationship. Put brackets around each part and label it *cause* or *effect*.

effect   cause

Example: [The game was called] [because of rain.]

1. A vigorous commercial economy, expanding trade, and a population boom were the conditions requisite for making Britain the first industrial nation.
2. The population boom is attributed to good harvests, the end of the plague, youthful marriages, and greater opportunities for work.
3. The plague ended after water supplies were improved and soap became more readily available.

4. With the drop in the death rate and the increase in the birth rate, more labor was available for industry.
5. Industry's need for fuel sparked expansion in coal mining.
6. Production of iron depended upon coal.
7. The iron industry moved to the Midlands and the North for coal.
8. Following the invention of the steam engine, water power was supplanted by steam power.
9. Steam power required access to coal fields.
10. Labor-saving machinery dispensed with water power.
11. The flying shuttle made it possible to widen cloth and double production.
12. The spinning jenny and the power loom rejuvenated the cotton and wool industries.
13. The need for coal pushed the textile industry north.
14. Cheap transporation was needed to complement industrialization.
15. The canal system reduced coal prices.

B. RESTATING

Choose the alternative that has the same meaning as the statement given.

Between 1733 and 1789, a series of ingenious labor-saving machines that would dispense with water power and rely on steam were invented.

(A) Labor-saving machines invented a method of relying on water power between 1733 and 1789.

(B) Water power and steam power dispensed with labor-saving machines between 1733 and 1789.

(C) The invention of labor-saving machines between 1733 and 1789 caused a change from water to steam power.

(D) Water power and steam power relied upon labor-saving machines between 1733 and 1789.

C. VOCABULARY WORK

Put the number from Column B beside the synonym in Column A.

A	B
_____ a. rejuvenate	1. replace
_____ b. access	2. clever
_____ c. requisite	3. necessary
_____ d. dispense with	4. complete
_____ e. supplant	5. follow
_____ f. attribute	6. approach
_____ g. complement	7. renew
_____ h. ingenious	8. accomplish
_____ i. ensue	9. do without
_____ j. effect	10. ascribe

Reading 5

The *Titanic* was the last "unsinkable" ship ever to set sail. Built in 1912 for the British White Star Line, she was a colossal ship for the times—882 feet long, 46,328 tons, and capable of doing 25 knots an hour. Acclaimed as the zenith of luxury liners, the ship had been fitted out with palatial accoutrements. Her sixteen watertight compartments, her builders claimed, guaranteed that nothing could sink her.

April 10, 1912, was a glittering occasion as the *Titanic* began her maiden voyage from England to New York with 2,207 people on board, some of whom were American tycoons whose estimated worth was over $250 million.

At 11:40 on April 14, many of the sleeping passengers were awakened by a slight jolt. The ship had struck an iceberg, incurred a 300-foot gash in her side, and five compartments were flooded. "Unsinkable," however, meant the ship could float if two, not five, compartments were inundated. Ten miles away from the *Titanic* was another ship, the *Californian,* which had stopped because of ice fields and which had wired six explicit warnings to nearby ships. Unfortunately, the *Titanic*'s wireless, a new invention on shipboard, was being employed for frivolous messages to and from the passengers. The tired wireless operator had worked long hours and impatiently told the *Californian*'s operator to shut up and stop annoying him.

By 12:05 A.M. officers and crew fully comprehended that something was seriously amiss. Lifeboats were uncovered, and passengers and crew were mustered to the boat deck. Ten minutes later a "CQD" sent out to summon help was received by ships too distant to be of immediate help. The *Californian* might as well have been in the South Seas for all the assistance she ever gave. Her wireless operator, unfamiliar with the new equipment, had failed to wind up the mechanism that kept the set running. At about 11:40 he tuned in, heard nothing from his dead set, and went to bed.

Secure in the knowledge that their ship was unsinkable, the White Star Line had provided enough lifeboat space for only 1,178 people. There were sixteen wooden lifeboats and four collapsible canvas boats on board for 2,207 people. The crew's efforts to load the lifeboats in the midst of chaos and bitterly cold weather were heroic but disorganized. Women and children were supposed to be first in the lifeboats, but no matter how chivalrous the men, the women were querulous about leaving the ship for a cold, open boat and had to be cajoled into the boats. At 12:45 the *Californian* crew watched the *Titanic*'s rockets overhead and regarded them as "strange." The first boat was being lowered into the icy sea at the same moment; with a capacity for forty, it contained twelve. Throughout the fiasco of lifeboat loading, the ship's orchestra played ragtime, the lights blazed, and the *Titanic* continued to slip downward at the bow.

Meanwhile, three ships had received an SOS, the first time that signal had ever been used, and they were confused. All had been advised that the *Titanic* was sinking. The *Carpathia* was fifty-eight miles away. The *Californian* watched the last rocket go off at 1:40. At 2:05 the last boat was lowered as the band played an Episcopal hymn, "Autumn," not "Abide with Me," as is usually believed. With the ship standing at a 90° angle, perpendicular in the water, at 2:10 the last SOS was sent out. At 2:20 A.M. on April 15, 1912, the *Titanic* sank. The crew of the *Californian* believed that the disappearing lights indicated that the ship was leaving the area.

At 4:10 the *Carpathia* was the first ship to reach the scene. The *Californian* arrived at 5:40, too late to rescue any survivors. From eighteen boats 705 people were rescued. Following inquiries regarding the disaster, it was revealed that very few of the third class passengers had been saved. Of 143 women in first class, 4 were lost; of 93 women in second class, 15 were lost; of 179 women in third class, 81 were lost. All but one child in first and second class were saved, but of the 76 children in third class, only 23 survived.

A. CHRONOLOGY

Write the date or time for the events listed below.

1. _____ *Titanic* set sail for New York

2. _____ *Titanic* hit iceberg (date)

3. _____ *Titanic* hit iceberg (hour)

4. _____ lifeboats uncovered

5. _____ first call for help

6. _____ rockets sent up

7. _____ last rocket went off

8. _____ last lifeboat lowered

9. _____ last SOS sent

10. _____ *Titanic* sank (date)

11. _____ *Titanic* sank (hour)

12. _____ first rescue ship arrived

13. _____ *Californian* arrived

B. STATISTICS

Fill in the numbers required below.

1. _____ *Titanic*'s weight

2. _____ *Titanic*'s length

3. _____ *Titanic*'s speed

4. _____ people on board *Titanic*

5. _____ number of compartments flooded by iceberg impact

6. _____ size of cut in *Titanic*'s side

7. _____ estimated worth of passengers on board

8. _____ number of spaces available in lifeboats

9. _____ total number of lifeboats

10. _____ *Californian*'s distance from *Titanic*

11. _____ *Carpathia*'s distance from *Titanic*

12. _____ passengers saved

13. _____ number of lifeboats actually used

14. _____ number of women in first class saved

15. _____ number of women in second class saved

16. _____ number of women in third class saved

17. _____ number of children in first and second class lost

18. _____ number of children in third class lost

C. DETAILED COMPREHENSION

Choose the alternative that best completes the sentence or that best answers the question.

1. You can infer that "the *Titanic* was the last 'unsinkable' ship" means that
   (A) the *Titanic* was not unsinkable
   (B) the *Titanic* would not have sunk if only two compartments had been flooded
   (C) nobody ever believed in an "unsinkable" ship after the *Titanic* disaster
   (D) nobody ever built a ship like the *Titanic* again

2. You can infer from the statistics regarding the number of third class passengers who survived that
   (A) they did not know the ship was sinking
   (B) they ignored the crew's calls to the lifeboats
   (C) they courteously allowed the first and second class passengers to leave the ship first
   (D) there was class distinction in the filling of the lifeboats

3. You can infer that the *Californian* crew
   (A) callously ignored the *Titanic*'s plight
   (B) could have saved many if it had heeded the rockets
   (C) didn't want to lose any sleep
   (D) did its best to aid the *Titanic*

4. You can infer that many of the *Titanic*'s male passengers
   (A) succumbed quickly in the icy sea
   (B) were frivolous
   (C) saved themselves instead of the women and children
   (D) were very rich

5. The author implies that the crew of the *Californian*
   (A) acted like idiots
   (B) worked long hours
   (C) tried to help the *Titanic*
   (D) was too far away to help the *Titanic*

6. The *Titanic* would not have sunk if
   (A) it had had a wireless
   (B) it had been smaller
   (C) only two compartments had flooded
   (D) the crew had been better trained

7. The first SOS signal was called
   (A) a wireless
   (B) a warning
   (C) CQD
   (D) a message

8. True or false? The band played "Abide with Me" just before the ship sank.

   _____

   How did you get your answer?
   (A) It was stated.
   (B) It was implied
   (C) No information was given.

9. The number of people lost in the disaster was
   (A) half the number of passengers
   (B) 705
   (C) more than double the number saved
   (D) less than the number saved

10. The number of third class women and children lost was
    (A) 255
    (B) 134
    (C) 76
    (D) 81

D. RESTATING

Choose the alternative that means the same as the statement given.

The *Californian* might as well have been in the South Seas for all the help she ever gave.

(A) The *Californian* was in the South Seas, so she couldn't help.

(B) The *Californian* gave all her help in the South Seas.

(C) The *Californian* went to the South Seas to help the *Titanic*.

(D) The *Californian* did not help at all, even though she was nearby.

E. VOCABULARY WORK

Choose the synonym for the underlined word.

1. The *Titanic* struck a <u>colossal</u> iceberg.
   - (A) cold
   - (B) huge
   - (C) awesome
   - (D) fatal

2. The ship sank on her <u>maiden</u> voyage.
   - (A) chaste
   - (B) virgin
   - (C) first
   - (D) new

3. He began his business career in a very small way but died a multimillionaire <u>tycoon</u>.
   - (A) powerful businessman
   - (B) civic leader
   - (C) type
   - (D) politician

4. The ship's luxurious <u>accoutrements</u> appealed to the very rich.
   - (A) costs
   - (B) equipment
   - (C) accesses
   - (D) dress

5. Illness struck him at the <u>zenith</u> of his career.
   - (A) beginning
   - (B) zealousness
   - (C) makeshift
   - (D) summit

6. The lifeboat was <u>inundated</u> by a huge wave.
   - (A) flooded
   - (B) capsized
   - (C) involved
   - (D) lifted

7. He gave <u>explicit</u> instructions to the office staff, so they should have understood him.
   - (A) courteous
   - (B) crucial
   - (C) definite
   - (D) uncertain

8. The <u>querulous</u> old lady at the check-out counter in the supermarket annoyed the clerk.
   - (A) sick
   - (B) bold
   - (C) meek
   - (D) fretful

9. A <u>chivalrous</u> gentleman helped the frightened woman into the lifeboat.
   - (A) childish
   - (B) courteous
   - (C) callous
   - (D) ridiculous

10. They never noticed that something was <u>amiss</u> until water began to cover the cabin floor.
    - (A) leaky
    - (B) wet
    - (C) faulty
    - (D) open

11. It took millions of years for order to grow out of the <u>chaos</u> of the universe.
    - (A) adjustment
    - (B) change
    - (C) confusion
    - (D) oscillation

12. Some of the survivors had risked their lives to save <u>frivolous</u> things like photographs and dolls.
    (A) frightening
    (B) trivial
    (C) important
    (D) inexpensive

13. The fireman tried to <u>coax</u> the cat down from the top branch of the tree.
    (A) push
    (B) shoot
    (C) cajole
    (D) force

14. The captain of the militia <u>mustered</u> his troops under the oak tree at Bunker Hill.
    (A) trained
    (B) gathered
    (C) nursed
    (D) mumbled

15. After I read his fifty-page report, I began to <u>comprehend</u> the nature of the project.
    (A) follow
    (B) contend
    (C) embrace
    (D) understand

Reading 6

When Franklin D. Roosevelt was elected President of the United States in 1932, not only the United States but also the rest of the world was in the throes of an economic depression. Following the termination of World War I, Britain and the United States at first experienced a boom in industry. Called the Roaring Twenties, the 1920s ushered in a number of things—prosperity, greater equality for women in the work world, rising consumption, and easy credit. The outlook for American business was rosy.

October 1929 was a month that had catastrophic economic reverberations worldwide. The American stock market witnessed the "Great Crash," as it is called, and the temporary boom in the American economy came to a standstill. Stock prices sank, and panic spread. The ensuing unemployment figure soared to 12 million by 1932.

Germany in the postwar years suffered from extreme deprivation because of onerous reparations it was obliged to pay to the Allies. The country's industrial capacity had been greatly diminished by the war. Inflation, political instability, and high unemployment were factors conducive to the growth of the embryonic Nazi party. Germans had lost confidence in their old leaders and heralded the arrival of a messiah-like figure who would lead them out of their economic wilderness. Hitler promised jobs and, once elected, kept his promise by providing employment in the party, in the newly expanded army, and in munitions factories.

Roosevelt was elected because he promised a "New Deal" to lift the United States out of the doldrums of the depression. Following the principles advocated by Keynes, a British economist, Roosevelt mustered the spending capacities of the federal government to provide welfare, work, and agricultural aid to the millions of down-and-out Americans. Elected President for four terms because of his innovative policies, Roosevelt succeeded in dragging the nation out of the Depression before the outbreak of World War II.

A. DETAILED COMPREHENSION

Choose the alternative that best completes the sentence.

1. A good title for this selection would be
   (A) The Twenties
   (B) The End of World War I
   (C) The Great Crash
   (D) The Depression

2. The 1920s were called the Roaring Twenties because
   (A) social and economic affairs were prospering
   (B) women were advancing in the fight for equal rights
   (C) there was little unemployment
   (D) people were celebrating the end of World War I

3. When Roosevelt was elected,
   (A) the nation was in a deep depression
   (B) there were 12 million unemployed workers
   (C) the nation needed help from the federal government
   (D) all of the above

4. The "Great Crash" refers to
   (A) the end of World War I
   (B) the Great Depression
   (C) a slump in the stock market
   (D) high unemployment figures

5. In the postwar years, Germany
   (A) had a booming industrial program
   (B) had difficulty paying reparations
   (C) was optimistic about the future
   (D) none of the above

6. You can infer that the author of this selection
   (A) thinks the Depression could have been avoided
   (B) blames the Depression on the "Great Crash"
   (C) thinks that the appeal of Roosevelt and Hitler was similar
   (D) disapproves of Roosevelt's "New Deal"

7. Both Roosevelt and Hitler were successful in their bids for leadership because
   (A) they had dynamic leadership qualities
   (B) their nations needed innovative economic policies
   (C) their nations were suffering from a depression
   (D) all of the above

8. Hitler is compared to
   (A) the Nazis
   (B) the old leaders of Germany
   (C) Jesus
   (D) an army general

9. Roosevelt's "New Deal" advocated
   (A) government spending to provide employment
   (B) providing support for the poor and unemployable
   (C) government aid to farmers
   (D) all of the above

10. Four terms of office as President of the United States would mean
    (A) eight years   (C) sixteen years
    (B) four years   (D) until he dies

B. RESTATING

Choose the alternative that means the same as the statement given.

Germans had lost confidence in their old leaders and heralded the arrival of a messiah-like figure who would lead them out of their economic wilderness.

(A) Because Germany was in the depths of a depression that the nation's leaders could not ameliorate, the Germans welcomed Hitler as though he were their savior.

(B) The old leaders in Germany lost confidence because the depression in the nation could not be ended until a messiah was found.

(C) The economic depression in Germany had so bad an effect on the old leaders that they looked for a messiah in the wilderness.

(D) A messiah led the German nation out of its economic wilderness when the Germans lost confidence in their old leaders.

C. VOCABULARY WORK

Choose the correct synonym for the underlined word from the alternatives given.

1. The Great Crash in the stock market ended the <u>boom</u> in American industry.
   (A) loud noise   (C) expansion
   (B) boon   (D) boor

2. A nation in the <u>throes</u> of revolution will not welcome outside interference.
   (A) wars   (C) agonies
   (B) fights   (D) enmities

3. The hurricane that hit Florida in 1926 had a <u>catastrophic</u> effect because so many homes were constructed of wood.
   (A) categories   (C) frightening
   (B) disastrous   (D) blowing

4. Lady Donna's butler <u>ushered in</u> the guests during the cocktail party.
   (A) introduced   (C) pushed
   (B) conducted   (D) entered

5. The <u>reverberations</u> of the shot that killed the Crown Prince of Austria were heard around the world.
   (A) echoes   (C) trials
   (B) reverses   (D) reviews

6. After winning the football game and drinking too much at the ensuing party, Hector felt terrible.
   (A) issuing
   (B) entering
   (C) victorious
   (D) following

7. Many of the unemployed suffered extreme deprivation during the Great Depression.
   (A) depression
   (B) dislocation
   (C) discrimination
   (D) privation

8. The country parson in the nineteenth century didn't find his duties onerous.
   (A) easy
   (B) enjoyable
   (C) heavy
   (D) rosy

9. Germany after the war had no industry to enable the nation to make reparations to the Allies.
   (A) recompense
   (B) rewards
   (C) returns
   (D) reasons

10. You need an atmosphere conducive to study if you want to succeed in college.
    (A) customary
    (B) promotive
    (C) conforming
    (D) ornamental

11. His embryonic genius developed in his adolescent years.
    (A) great
    (B) embroidered
    (C) incipient
    (D) mature

12. The audience heralded his appearance on stage with thunderous applause.
    (A) hailed
    (B) rewarded
    (C) clapped
    (D) protested

13. Mary has been in the doldrums ever since she broke up with her boyfriend.
    (A) despondent
    (B) tired
    (C) elated
    (D) diverted

14. Jack mustered all his energy to win the marathon.
    (A) extolled
    (B) lost
    (C) arranged
    (D) gathered

15. Millions of Americans were down and out in 1932.
    (A) illiterate
    (B) imprudent
    (C) divided
    (D) impoverished

Reading 7

On September 2, 1945, the Communist Viet Minh party took over Vietnam and declared the country autonomous. The French, however, backed by the British, returned to Vietnam and forced the Viet Minh to attend the Fountainebleau Conference in 1946. Ho Chi Minh, the Viet Minh leader, was inflexible in his demands for unification of his country. The French had divided it into three parts:

Cochin China in the south, Tonkin in the middle, and Annam in the north. A French decree making Cochin China a separate republic closed the door on any possible negotiations at the conference. War broke out between the French and the Viet Minh.

In the conflict the United States supported the French, while the Chinese and the Soviets backed the Viet Minh. By 1954 public disapproval of the war and its financial burden forced the French to withdraw. At a peace conference in Geneva, Vietnam was divided with the proviso that reunification would take place by elections two years later.

The Communists in North Vietnam and the anti-Communists in South Vietnam refused to collaborate. Led by Ngo Dinh Diem, whose regime was backed by the United States, the South Vietnamese prevented unification elections and persecuted Communists in their region. In January 1959, militant Hanoi Communists again declared war, this time against their own neighbors in the south.

The United States' involvement in Vietnam's internal affairs increased as President Kennedy sent military advisers in 1961 to assist the South Vietnamese. The war continued. President Johnson ordered American bombing of North Vietnam on February 8, 1965. Ground fighting intensified early in 1968. Neither side appeared to have gained ascendancy over the other, and the American people were fed up with human and financial losses in Vietnam. President Johnson ordered a cutback in the bombing. His successor Richard Nixon continued to support South Vietnam but ordered the withdrawal of American combat troops.

Peace negotiations between the United States and North Vietnam began in Paris in May 1968, but were not terminated until January 27, 1973. Fighting had reached a deadlock, and the Americans had renewed their bombing offensive in December 1972.

With Communist forces remaining in South Vietnam after the American withdrawal, the fighting was renewed immediately after the peace conference. South Vietnam was defeated on April 30, 1975. The following year Hanoi united North and South Vietnam. The conflict had lasted thirty chaotic years. The United States had supported the losing side with over half a million troops and billions of dollars.

A. DATES AND NUMBERS

Fill in the blank with the correct date or number for the information given.

1. _____ First Communist takeover of Vietnam

2. _____ Fontainebleau Conference

3. _____ French withdrawal from Vietnam war

4. _____ Date specified for unification elections

5. _____ American military advisers in Vietnam

6. _____ American bombing of North Vietnam began

7. _____ Peace negotiations began

8. _____ Peace negotiations ended

9. _____ Americans renewed bombing

10. _____ Expense to Americans

11. _____ Number of American troops in Vietnam

12. _____ Total years of conflict

13. _____ Final defeat of South Vietnam

B. DETAILED COMPREHENSION

Choose the alternative that best completes the sentence.

1. You can infer from the fact that the United States supported South Vietnamese leader Ngo Dinh Diem that
   (A) he was a poor leader
   (B) he was anti-Communist
   (C) he was supportive of French colonization
   (D) the United States opposed the French

2. The author's final statement in this passage implies that
   (A) Americans ought to have stayed out of Vietnam
   (B) Americans should have put more effort into winning the war
   (C) Americans have a tendency to interfere in other nations' affairs
   (D) the cost to the Americans was worthwhile

3. The French withdrew from Vietnam because
   (A) they were weak
   (B) the people at home did not sanction fighting the war
   (C) they wanted to divide the country
   (D) the Vietnamese hated them

4. Negotiations at the Fontainebleau Conference broke down because the
   (A) Viet Minh attended it
   (B) French couldn't make up their minds
   (C) Americans interfered
   (D) French made Cochin China a separate state

5. The apparent cause of the entire Vietnam conflict was
   (A) French refusal to allow unification
   (B) Communists' demands for possession of North Vietnam
   (C) South Vietnam's withdrawal from the northern leaders
   (D) social upheaval throughout Vietnam

6. In 1959 the war in Vietnam was
   (A) an international struggle for power
   (B) expected to last a long time
   (C) almost over
   (D) an internal struggle

7. When neither side seems to be winning, we say they are
   (A) losing
   (B) winning
   (C) deadlocked
   (D) neutral

8. After seven years of conflict in Vietnam, the American people
   (A) favored increased efforts to win the war
   (B) paid little attention to the war
   (C) protested against the waste of the war
   (D) supported the South Vietnamese

9. You can infer that the renewed bombing of North Vietnam at the end of 1972
   (A) destroyed North Vietnam's forces
   (B) contributed to ending the conflict
   (C) made the Americans seek peace
   (D) caused very little damage

10. At the end of thirty years, the Viet Minh
    (A) defeated the French
    (B) defeated the purpose of the conflict
    (C) achieved their 1945 purpose
    (D) defeated the Americans

C. VOCABULARY WORK

Choose the alternative that is the synonym for the underlined word.

1. He was inflexible in his determination to unite his country.
   (A) inflatable
   (B) infernal
   (C) infantile
   (D) inexorable

2. By the time peace was negotiated, the affairs of the nation were in a chaotic state.
   (A) confused
   (B) exotic
   (C) disputable
   (D) obscure

3. Because the author and the artist refused to collaborate, the book was never finished.
   (A) confide
   (B) collate
   (C) provide proof
   (D) work together

4. After World War II, the Vietnamese believed that the French would allow them to be an autonomous people.
   (A) self-respecting
   (B) self-governing
   (C) self-reliant
   (D) self-supporting

5. He took a militant stand against the opposition and won the point.
   (A) mild
   (B) aggressive
   (C) positive
   (D) awkward

6. The Communist regime favored unification of the country.
   (A) leader
   (B) government
   (C) regiment
   (D) register

7. The North Vietnamese gained <u>ascendancy</u> over the south after many years of warfare.
   (A) defeat
   (B) rising
   (C) ascription
   (D) power

   Now do this crossword puzzle to review some of the vocabulary practiced in Part IV.

Across

1. Yield
6. Eager
8. Angry
12. Piece of land, as in parking ____
13. Preposition: ____ the same time
14. Negative word
15. Prefix meaning *against*
16. Unmoving
17. Inter
19. Have you ____ Tom?
20. Cause
23. Very valuable object
25. Ability

Down

1. Unfeeling
2. Harmful
3. Abbreviation for *kitchen*
4. Abbreviation for *street*
5. Quality, characteristic
6. Equipment
7. Poison
8. Wounds
9. Careless and impolite
10. Prefix meaning *before*
11. Antonym of *yes*
15. Entrance, means of reaching
18. Neither/____

Across

26. Use the eyes
28. Informal word for *friend*
29. Conclave
31. What is expected, usual, or average
33. Scold, rebuke
36. Wrong, faulty
39. Abbreviation for *North America*
40. Suffix used to form a noun from *occur*
41. Atmosphere
42. An infant is totally ____ upon its mother.

Down

20. Subject pronoun
21. Has the sun always ____ in the east?
22. Vigor
24. Clear and definite
25. Soothe, relieve
27. Circum, peri
30. Conjunction
32. Prefix meaning *two*
34. Uni, mono
35. Feminine pronoun
36. Indefinite article
37. Abbreviation for *medium*
38. Abbreviation for *separate*

Quiz 7

Choose the word from the alternatives that has the *same meaning* as the underlined word.

1. The union members boycotted the meeting because they didn't want to strike.
   (A) attended
   (B) protested
   (C) picketed
   (D) shunned

2. Mrs. Smith was appalled by her daughter's latest boyfriend.
   (A) amused
   (B) surprised
   (C) dismayed
   (D) thrilled

3. The school bus driver admonished the noisy children.
   (A) rebuked
   (B) drove
   (C) admitted
   (D) struck

4. By now we all know that smoking is detrimental to your health.
   (A) fundamental
   (B) harmful
   (C) lethal
   (D) deplorable

5. Hitler initiated a diabolical program for extermination.
   (A) deplorable
   (B) devastating
   (C) devilish
   (D) damaging

6. Mother and her daughter-in-law have been on amazingly amicable terms for years.
   (A) equal
   (B) hostile
   (C) happy
   (D) friendly

7. All attempts to evict him from his house failed.
   (A) evade
   (B) expel
   (C) expiate
   (D) call

8. The king's council sat in <u>conclave</u> to discuss taxes.
   (A) a quiet place
   (B) a rendezvous
   (C) parliament
   (D) a secret meeting

9. Kristina objected <u>vehemently</u> to eating spinach.
   (A) strongly
   (B) noisily
   (C) verbosely
   (D) heavily

10. Increased population was a <u>potent</u> factor in the nation's industrial expansion.
    (A) inhibiting
    (B) influential
    (C) powerful
    (D) strengthening

11. If you cannot get to work on time, I shall have to <u>dispense with</u> your services.
    (A) disperse
    (B) do without
    (C) charge for
    (D) time

12. Universal Studios built a <u>colossal</u> set in order to film the adventure story.
    (A) fantastic
    (B) beautiful
    (C) colorful
    (D) huge

13. The bankruptcy of the gold mining company had <u>reverberations</u> in the currency market.
    (A) strains
    (B) echoes
    (C) failures
    (D) decreases

14. Without assistance from government, the elderly would suffer extreme <u>deprivation</u>.
    (A) privation
    (B) problems
    (C) necessities
    (D) tremblings

15. Economists forecast a <u>boom</u> in the stock market this year.
    (A) cannon noise
    (B) crash
    (C) bonus
    (D) expansion

PART V.
INTERPRETATION OF
SCIENTIFIC READING
MATERIALS

As you read the following passages, you will notice that the writing is particularly clear and precise because of the many technical terms employed. This is characteristic of science materials. Owing to the complexity of scientific concepts, it is important for the author to present ideas in such a way that the reader can establish relationships between details and facts. As in the previous section, we will concentrate on some of the study skills taught earlier: note taking, scanning, understanding relationships, and locating specific information.

Reading 1

PREQUESTIONS

Scan the passage quickly and answer these questions.

1. What is the text related to?
   (A) astronomy
   (B) biology
   (C) physiology
   (D) archaeology

2. What does the text concentrate on?
   (A) the earth
   (B) the sun
   (C) the moon
   (D) space exploration

3. What type of reader was this text written for?
   (A) a scientist
   (B) an average adult
   (C) a young child
   (D) an astronaut

1) The moon goes around the earth in an average time of 27 days, 7 hours, and 43.2 minutes. This is called the sidereal period. The lunar month, the period from one new moon to the next, covers a span of 29 days, 12 hours, and 44.05 minutes. This is the moon's synodical period.

2) The moon is 238,857 miles from the earth. This is considered the mean distance because the moon's path is elliptical, not circular. The maximum distance the moon travels from earth is 252,710 miles, whereas the minimum is 221,463 miles. These distances are measured from the center of earth to the center of the moon.

3) The diameter of the moon is 2,160 miles. Deducting the radius of the moon, 1,080 miles, from the radius of the earth, a minimum of 3,963 miles, we get the closest figure of the bodies' surfaces, 216,420 miles.

4)   The moon's rotation on its axis is exactly equal to its sidereal circuit around the earth—27.321666 days. Although the moon's circuit is irregular because of its elliptical course, its rotation is nevertheless regular. The regular rotation and the irregular rotation create "libration in longitude," which makes it possible for us to see first farther around the east side and then farther around the west side of the moon. On the other hand, "libration in latitude" enables us to see farther over either the north or the south pole. These two librations allow us to see over 60% of the moon's surface at one time or another. The first time the other side of the moon was photographed was in 1959, by the Soviet spaceship *Lunik III*. Since then, United States spaceships have taken many pictures of the moon's surface.

A. NOTE TAKING

Readers are often confused when confronted with a large quantity of facts and figures within a passage. Go back to the reading and jot down the important numbers given there.

1. sidereal period	
2. synodical period	
3. distance moon–earth	
4. moon's diameter	
5. earth's radius	
6. moon's radius	
7. surface areas of the earth and the moon	
8. first photographs of the moon	

B. DETAILED COMPREHENSION

Answer according to the nature of the question.

1. What is the meaning of sidereal period? _____

_____

2. What is the meaning of synodical period? _____

_____

3. In paragraph 2 what is the meaning of the word *mean*? _____
_____

4. True or false? The moon's path around the earth is circular. _____

5. In this passage the word *rotation* presumably means
   (A) by rote   (C) planting different crops
   (B) complete turn around a point   (D) balance

6. Revolution of the moon refers to
   (A) the moon's elliptical path around earth
   (B) the moon's turning on its axis
   (C) the turmoil in the composition of the moon
   (D) changes in the moon's surface

7. Librations of the moon cause
   (A) it to turn slowly
   (B) us to view it from different sides at various times
   (C) its irregular course
   (D) its distance from earth

8. True or false? The Russians took the first pictures of the dark side of the
   moon. _____

9. True or false? Sixty percent of the moon's surface is hidden from us.
   _____

10. How do we determine the distances the moon travels? _____
_____

11. Why are two different times given for the moon's circuit of the earth? _____
_____

12. What has given us a clearer concept of the moon? _____
_____

13. Why are two distances given for the moon's distance from earth? _____
_____

14. What do latitude and longitude mean? _____
_____

15. Libration in latitude means that
   (A) the moon's diameter is smaller than the earth's latitude
   (B) we see farther over the north and south poles
   (C) the moon's rotation is irregular
   (D) the moon's circuit is regular

Reading 2

PREQUESTIONS

Skim the three paragraphs as quickly as you can and answer these questions.

1. Can you guess where this passage came from?
   (A) a chemistry book
   (B) a science fiction story
   (C) an encyclopedia
   (D) a medical article

2. What are the period and eras referred to in the passage? Which is longer, a

   period or an era? _____

   _____

   _____

1)   About a billion years after the earth had formed, the first signs of life appeared. Three billion years elapsed before creatures became complex enough to leave fossils their descendants could recognize and learn from. These were shelled creatures called trilobites, followed by jawless fish, the first vertebrates. During the Devonian period, great upheavals occurred in the earth's crust, resulting in the formation of mountains and in the ebb and flow of oceans. In the aftermath, beds of mud rich in organic matter nourished vegetation, and insects, scorpions, and spiders appeared. Next developed the amphibians, descendants of fish that had crawled out of fresh water.

2)   Between 225 and 65 million years ago, reptiles developed from which many new forms grew until finally evolved the mammal. Dinosaurs were overgrown reptiles. Although some were as small as chickens, others grew to be the largest animals on earth, as long as 82 feet and as heavy as 50 tons, with long necks and a liking for a vegetarian diet. Current theory suggests that dinosaurs were warm-blooded and behaved more like mammals than like reptiles.

3)   The end of the Mesozoic Era (middle life) saw the inexplicable demise of dinosaurs and large swimming and flying birds. Geological changes were converting the giant land mass into separate continents. The beginning of a new era, called Cenozoic (recent life), saw the marked predominance of mammals that would ultimately become man's ancestors.

A. DETAILED COMPREHENSION

Answer the following according to the nature of the question.

1. What would be a good title for this reading?
   (A) How Reptiles Became Dinosaurs
   (B) The Ages of Man
   (C) The Evolution of Life
   (D) The Formation of the Earth

2. How much time elapsed after the earth had formed before fossils formed?

   _____

3. What were the first vertebrates? _____

4. What preceded insects? _____

5. True or false? Dinosaurs were carnivorous beasts. _____

6. True or false? Trilobites had shells. _____

7. True or false? All dinosaurs were huge. _____

8. What is required for vegetation?
   (A) dinosaurs
   (B) oceans
   (C) organic matter
   (D) mud

9. What must an amphibian be?
   (A) a spider
   (B) a person
   (C) a creature
   (D) a body of water

10. By inference, what would you say insects need?
    (A) water
    (B) vegetation
    (C) mud
    (D) organic matter

11. What does the prefix *Meso* mean in *Mesozoic?*
    (A) mixed
    (B) middle
    (C) median
    (D) mean

12. What does *zoic,* as in *Mesozoic,* mean? _____

13. Presumably *over* in the word *overgrown* means
    (A) above
    (B) often
    (C) on top of
    (D) excessively

14. The suffix *less,* as in *jawless,* means
    (A) full of
    (B) not many
    (C) fewer
    (D) without

15. Why did the dinosaur disappear?
    (A) It was undernourished.
    (B) It was a reptile.
    (C) No one knows.
    (D) Large birds killed it.

16. What must *demise* mean?
    (A) death
    (B) appearance
    (C) change
    (D) evolution

17. The prefix *in,* as in *inexplicable,* changes a word to
    (A) an adjective
    (B) the negative
    (C) an interior
    (D) the comparative

18. Presumably the word *elapsed* is the same as
    (A) elated
    (B) evaporated
    (C) passed
    (D) formed

19. The suffix *est* is added to an adjective and makes it
    (A) an adverb
    (B) the superlative form
    (C) easier to read
    (D) clearer in meaning

20. The word *marked,* as in *marked predominance,* must mean
    (A) watched
    (B) having marks on it
    (C) signed
    (D) noticeable

Reading 3

PREQUESTIONS

Skim the reading as quickly as possible to find the paragraph that tells you about the following.

1. defensive measures being taken in California _____

2. an earthquake in Japan _____

3. the effects of geologists' predictions _____

4. the location of the San Andreas Fault _____

5. an explanation of why earthquakes occur _____

1) Earthquakes are the most lethal of all natural disasters. What causes them? Geologists explain them in terms of a theory known as plate tectonics. Continents are floating apart from each other; this is referred to as the continental drift. About sixty miles below the surface of the sea, there is a semimolten bed of rock over which plates, or slabs, carry continents and sea floors at a rate of several inches a year. As the plates separate from each other, a new sea floor is formed by the molten matter that was formerly beneath. Volcanic islands and large mountain ranges are created by this type of movement. The collision of plates causes geological instability such as that in California called the San Andreas Fault, located between the Pacific and North American plates. The plates there are constantly pushing and pulling adjacent plates, thereby creating constant tremors and a potential for earthquakes in the area.

2) Geologists would like to be able to predict earthquakes accurately. Using laser beams, seismographs, gravity-measuring devices, and radio telescopes, they are presently studying the San Andreas Fault to determine the rate of strain and the amount of ground slippage. Calculations indicate that sometime within the next ten years, California will be struck by a major earthquake.

3) In spite of the geologists' theory of plate tectonics, there are still gaps in man's understanding and knowledge of the causes of earthquakes. Powerful earthquakes have occurred in places where plate boundaries are hundreds of miles away. In the 1800s New Madrid, Missouri and Charleston, South Carolina, were shaken by earthquakes that no one had foreseen.

4) Certain areas of the world are quake prone. Italy, Yugoslavia, and Algeria have experienced many quakes. In November 1980, Naples was struck by an especially devastating quake. China and Japan have also been hit by horrendous quakes. In 1923, Tokyo and Yokohama were reduced to rubble by gigantic tremors that were followed by fires, tornadoes, and finally a thirty-four-foot *tsunami,* or tidal wave, which was caused by the earth's drop into the waters of Tokyo Bay. More than 150,000 people died in that earthquake.

5)   What effects have geologists' predictions of earthquakes had? The Chinese in Haicheng in 1974 were warned that an earthquake might occur within the next year or two. With the help of amateur seismologists' observations of animal behavior and the rise and fall of water in wells and measurements of quantities of radioactive gas in water, professional geologists were able, in January 1975, to predict an earthquake within the next six months. On February 4, Haicheng was destroyed, but because its residents had been evacuated, very few people were killed. In California, where earthquake is an ever-present menace, building codes now require quakeproof structures, and Civil Defense units have intensified their training in how to deal with disaster should it strike or, perhaps more accurately, when it strikes. Should predictions of a quake within the next ten years be accurate, many Californians may be able to save both their lives and their property.

A. DETAILED COMPREHENSION

Choose the correct answer according to the reading.

1. Continental drift is the concept that
    (A) continents are drawing nearer to each other
    (B) continents are separating
    (C) continents are 60 miles apart from each other
    (D) new continents are developing beneath the sea

2. If predictions are correct, California
    (A) will be struck by an earthquake in the next decade
    (B) will be saved from an earthquake within ten years
    (C) is unstable as a result of the San Andreas Fault
    (D) has nothing to fear

3. Geologists are using modern technology to
    (A) help predict earthquakes
    (B) enhance their reputations
    (C) measure the accuracy of earthquakes
    (D) control ground slippage

4. An earthquake may be followed by
    (A) wind, fire, and tidal waves   (C) radioactive gas
    (B) predictions   (D) strange behavior by animals

5. The Chinese predicted an earthquake by
    (A) employing amateur seismologists
    (B) observing professional geologists
    (C) watching animals, wells, and radioactive gas
    (D) evacuating the population

6. Californians are preparing for an earthquake by
    (A) saving their property
    (B) building stronger houses and practicing techniques to handle emergencies
    (C) ignoring the San Andreas Fault
    (D) moving to another state

7. No one had foreseen quakes in Missouri because
   (A) the area is not quake prone
   (B) geologists do not understand the area
   (C) there are gaps in the area
   (D) the theory of plate tectonics is incorrect

8. Geologists have been able to predict an earthquake
   (A) with unerring accuracy
   (B) within months
   (C) by measuring tremors
   (D) by knowing about continental drift

9. Volcanic islands are formed by
   (A) the separation of plates and the consequent uncovering of the molten sea floor beneath them
   (B) the constant pushing and pulling of adjacent plates
   (C) constant tremors
   (D) huge mountain ranges

10. Naples was
   (A) not damaged much by an earthquake
   (B) struck by a horrendous earthquake
   (C) struck by an earthquake a long time ago
   (D) prepared for an earthquake

B. VOCABULARY WORK

Synonyms

These words or phrases have approximately the same meaning as words that appear in the reading. The numbers indicate the paragraph where the synonym can be found. Write each synonym on the line provided.

1. deadly (1) _____

2. falling away (2) _____

3. destructive (4) _____

4. lack of firmness (1) _____

5. possibility (1) _____

6. dreadful (4) _____

7. particularly (4) _____

8. limiting lines (3) _____

9. threat (5) _____

10. unfortunate event (5) _____

11. seen beforehand (3) _____

12. free from error (2) _____

13. liquified by heat (1) _____

14. neighboring (1) _____

15. vacant spaces (3) _____

16. having a natural tendency to something (4) _____

C. VOCABULARY BUILDING

Study the pairs of words below, then fill in the sentence with the correct form. If you do not know the meaning of any of the words and cannot understand the word from the context of the reading, look it up in your dictionary.

Verb	Noun
1. behave	behavior
2. calculate	calculation
3. create	creation
4. devastate	devastation
5. form	formation
6. measure	measurement
7. observe	observation
8. occur	occurrence
9. predict	prediction
10. refer	reference
11. separate	separation
12. tremble	tremor
13. warn	warning

1. The geologists in California _____ an earthquake within ten years. Their _____ may be correct.

2. The _____ of plates from each other causes a new sea floor to be formed. When the plates _____, they uncover molten matter.

3. To feel the earth _____ is a terrifying experience. Such _____s indicate an earthquake.

4. Earthquakes _____ cities. Buildings are destroyed, and many lives are lost in the _____ left behind by an earthquake.

5. Geologists _____ that California will have another earthquake. Some Californians have heeded their _____ and are preparing for the disaster.

6. Scientists _____ certain phenomena, and as a result of their _____s, they can often predict earthquakes.

7. It is difficult to _____ the exact time that an earthquake may occur, but it is possible to judge from scientific _____s that an earthquake *will* occur.

8. The _____ of volcanic islands is the result of the uncovering of molten matter on the sea floor. When plates move, they _____ a new floor.

9. Scientists _____ to the movement of continents as continental drift. They use the term in _____ to the movements of continents away from each other.

10. Huge mountains _____ in the same manner as volcanic islands. Their _____ is explained by the theory of plate tectonics.

11. Earthquakes usually _____ in certain areas of the world. Their _____ has been observed, however, in unexpected places like New England.

12. The _____ of an earthquake is fairly predictable. Panic makes people _____ unpredictably.

13. Scientists have instruments to _____ gravity. Their _____s assist in predicting earthquakes.

Reading 4

There is a growing concern that mankind is heading toward self-destruction. What are some of the causes of this fear? Think of as many examples as you can.

_____

_____

_____

The following article describes a coal-mining technique that has proven dangerous to the environment. Did you list other environmental threats?

1) The Federal Surface Mining Act was passed in 1977 for the laudable purpose of protecting the environment from the ravages of strip-mining of coal. For many years environmentalists had fought to get the bill passed. Strip-mining menaces the habitat of wildlife and causes incalculable damage to the environment. The law is explicit on such matters as where strip-mining is prohibited, the disposal of toxic waste, the placement of power lines, and the rights of the public to take part in the control of strip-mining. However, the Secretary of the Interior has recently incurred the wrath of environmentalists by advocating numerous proposals that repudiate the existing law.

2)   According to the law, strip-mining is prohibited in national forests, national wildlife refuges, public parks, historic places, and within a specified number of feet from roads, cemeteries, parks, houses, and schools. The exception to this prohibition is stated in the words *valid existing rights,* referring to those miners who had rights in protected lands before the law was passed. By redefining "valid existing rights," the Secretary now intends to infringe upon the law by opening over a million acres of national forest and wildlife refuges to strip-mining. Naturally, the National Wildlife Federation is appalled. This new proposal does not augur well for wildlife, which will be destroyed by such latent killers as power lines and tainted ponds near strip-mines.

3)   Why is the Secretary attempting to jettison the regulations so tempestuously gained only a few years ago? He claims that mining companies are losing money and that the new proposals would make mining more lucrative. Irate ecologists repudiate that theory on the basis of a study made by the Department of Energy that estimates that the savings to mining companies would be less than five cents per ton of coal.

4)   It doesn't require a sage to foresee the wrangle that is forthcoming between proponents of conservation and the Interior Department. The consensus among environmentalists is that unless they obstruct the Secretary's new regulations, this land will be ravaged and our wildlife severely maimed by strip-mining companies for the sake of a few pennies' profit.

A. GENERAL COMPREHENSION

Answer the following according to the nature of the item.

1. From the context of the article, the meaning of strip-mining is
   - (A) the mining of coal on public lands
   - (B) surface mining
   - (C) shaft mining
   - (D) illegal mining

2. The Federal Surface Mining Act
   - (A) limits coal production
   - (B) prohibits strip-mining
   - (C) restricts strip-mining to specific locations
   - (D) menaces wildlife

3. The Secretary of the Interior has
   - (A) rescinded the law
   - (B) angered the environmentalists
   - (C) been in office for five years
   - (D) destroyed wildlife

4. The Secretary of the Interior plans to
   - (A) fight the environmentalists
   - (B) break the law
   - (C) open up public lands to strip-miners
   - (D) protect the environment

5. The expression *existing valid rights* refers to
   - (A) mining rights in existence before 1977
   - (B) miners' rights that cannot be violated
   - (C) the right to mine coal any place in the United States
   - (D) the right to mine on protected land

6. Wildlife is endangered by
   (A) coal mining
   (B) the Secretary of the Interior
   (C) toxic waste in bodies of water
   (D) migration paths

7. The proposed new regulations will
   (A) curtail the rights of environmentalists
   (B) increase the area of strip-mining
   (C) help clean up the environment
   (D) cost miners a lot of money

8. The purpose of the new regulations is to
   (A) create a ravaged land
   (B) kill wildlife
   (C) increase coal miners' profits
   (D) anger environmentalists

9. Without the present regulations on strip-mining, profits would increase
   (A) tremendously
   (B) a little bit
   (C) not at all
   (D) by leaps and bounds

10. The main idea of this article is that
    (A) changes in the present law would be detrimental to the environment
    (B) a powerful government official can change laws
    (C) environmentalists protect our land
    (D) laws are made to be broken

11. To whom would this article appeal?
    (A) government officials
    (B) the President
    (C) conservationists
    (D) weathermen

B. VOCABULARY WORK

Getting the Meaning from Context

Scan paragraph 4 and choose the correct answer.

1. To what does the word *sage* refer?
   (A) a spice
   (B) a person
   (C) an event
   (D) a book

2. What must a *wrangle* be?
   (A) a man
   (B) a mine
   (C) an argument
   (D) a wreck

3. What must a *proponent* be?
   (A) an issue
   (B) a person
   (C) a cause
   (D) a priority

4. The word *obstruct* must mean
   (A) approve
   (B) block off
   (C) disapprove
   (D) consent

5. What must *maimed* mean?
   (A) managed
   (B) wounded
   (C) cared for
   (D) endangered

6. What does *for the sake of* mean?
   (A) for the purpose of
   (B) to help
   (C) in spite of
   (D) by any means

7. The word *forthcoming* refers to
   (A) a disagreement
   (B) the past experience
   (C) the future
   (D) new arrivals

C. PREFIX AND SUFFIX REVIEW

Choose the best answer.

1. The prefix *pro* in the word *proponent* means
   (A) professional
   (B) property
   (C) against
   (D) for

2. The prefix in *redefining* means
   (A) clearly
   (B) later
   (C) informally
   (D) again

3. The suffix *ist* in *environmentalist* and *ecologist* indicates
   (A) an area
   (B) a thing
   (C) a person
   (D) a time

4. The prefix *fore* in *foresee* means
   (A) at the same time
   (B) before
   (C) in favor of
   (D) beside

D. VOCABULARY BUILDING

Find the correct meaning in Column B for each word in Column A. Write the number of the meaning in the space at the left of each word.

A	B
_____ a. laudable	1. the natural home of a plant or animal
_____ b. ravage	2. poisonous
_____ c. menace	3. deserving praise
_____ d. habitat	4. to receive as the result of certain actions
_____ e. incalculable	5. to encroach
_____ f. explicit	6. to threaten
_____ g. toxic	7. to show mercy
_____ h. incur	8. very great
_____ i. repudiate	9. to ruin and destroy
_____ j. infringe	10. to set a value on
	11. clear and fully expressed
	12. being expelled
	13. to refuse to recognize

E. RESTATING

Select the option that has the same meaning as the sentence given.

1. Miss Truerite was appalled by her students' grammar.
   (A) She thought their grammer was very good.
   (B) She was shocked that her students' grammar was so bad.
   (C) She was thoughtful of her students' grammar.
   (D) She tried to teach them good grammar.

2. The lack of rain augurs trouble for the farmers.
   (A) No rain is a sign of trouble in the future.
   (B) Without rain nothing will grow.
   (C) Lack of rain causes trouble for the farmers.
   (D) Trouble comes to farmers when it rains.

3. Since Einstein didn't begin to talk until he was three years old, no one realized that he was a latent genius.
   (A) Even though he was a genius, it wasn't noticeable because he was late in beginning to talk.
   (B) He talked late, so he must not have been a genius.
   (C) Geniuses begin talking when they are three years old.
   (D) No one knows when a genius will begin to talk.

4. I ended up in the hospital after eating tainted fish.
   (A) I had to go to the hospital after eating fresh fish.
   (B) Eating poisoned fish made me exceedingly sick.
   (C) The hospital served bad fish.
   (D) Canned fish made me so sick that I had to go to the hospital.

5. The argument grew so tempestuous that they punched each other.
   (A) It was a quiet argument, but they had a fist fight later.
   (B) They had an argument in a storm and began to fight.
   (C) The argument was so violent that they hit each other.
   (D) The argument grew temperate when they punched each other.

Reading 5

PREQUESTIONS

1. People are becoming more aware of the need for alternative sources of energy. Can you name some of the most common energy sources (and some that are not so common)? _____

   _____

   _____

2. Nuclear energy is a point of controversy in the United States and in many other countries around the world. Why? List some of the reasons for the rising antinuclear movement. _____

   _____

   _____

3. Now skim the reading and find the words that mean approximately the same as *fiasco* (paragraph 2).

paragraph 2   ——————

                 ——————

paragraph 4   ——————

                 ——————

paragraph 5   ——————

1)   The nuclear industry is beset by controversy and mischance. Partially constructed plants have been closed down for several reasons. Construction costs have escalated, the demand for power has decreased, and the number of antagonists to nuclear plants has increased tremendously. Nuclear energy, once hailed with hope for a future with cheap, plentiful power, is currently reaching an impasse.

2)   The major cause of the deterioration in the nuclear industry is the fiasco at Three Mile Island in 1979. Ordinary machines break down, and humans are prone to error, but a nuclear power plant accident can cause widespread catastrophe. Salvage operations and cleanup of debris at Three Mile Island are going to take twenty years and more than a billion dollars (more than the plant cost to construct). The most significant factor about the accident is, however, that it has jeopardized the whole future of nuclear energy. Public dissent, present though dormant when the first nuclear plants were constructed, has solidified after the deplorable chaos at Three Mile Island.

3)   Nevertheless, the nuclear plants built twenty and thirty years ago continue to operate safely and economically. Smaller than more recently built plants, they have produced power that is consistently less expensive than power from coal or oil. Newer plants were larger, less safe, and managed and run by less qualified personnel. Many of these plants were designed and constructed so negligently that they are now closed down.

4)   The investigaton of the Three Mile Island accident revealed that supervisors and management alike were inadequately trained to cope with a crucial mechanical failure in the nuclear system. Training programs today are developed more precisely. Now prospective operators take two years of classroom work and spend three months under supervision in a control room and two more months at the simulator, a computer programmed to recreate the Three Mile Island disaster, before returning to another two months in the classroom. The Nuclear Regulatory Commission administers oral and written exams before licensing new operators. Every six weeks compulsory refresher courses are given. Presumably, more scrupulous training requisites will reduce the chances of another Three Mile Island debacle.

5)   One solution to the nuclear power plant dilemma may be to standardize facilities, as the French have done. Because France has neither oil nor coal, nuclear power is clearly the solution to its energy demands. The government constructs and operates plants that produce 44% of the nation's electricity. The French envisage that by 1990 they will have facilities to produce 75% of their power.

6)   Standardization, however, would never be acceptable in the United States, but there are more palatable alternatives. Plants would have to be standardized to some degree. Nuclear wastes must somehow be disposed of more safely than they are at present. Most important of all, safety must be assured to appease the fears of a potent antinuclear coalition of the American public.

A. DETAILED COMPREHENSION

Answer the following according to the nature of each item.

1. What is the public's biggest objection to nuclear plants?
   (A) their cost
   (B) the length of time it takes to construct them
   (C) the amount of electricity they generate
   (D) their danger

2. Why has construction on new nuclear plants been stopped?
   (A) They cost too much to build.
   (B) People are using less electricity.
   (C) The plants are unsafe.
   (D) All of the above

3. Why has the Three Mile Island accident jeopardized the future of nuclear energy?
   (A) The public saw the potential danger of nuclear plants and has united to protest their use.
   (B) It will cost more than a billion dollars to clean up the debris.
   (C) It will take twenty years to get the plant running again.
   (D) Nuclear energy is too expensive.

4. Why are the older plants still in operation?
   (A) They were built twenty years ago.
   (B) They have better supervision than the new plants.
   (C) They are cheap to operate.
   (D) They are relatively safe, produce cheap electricity, and have efficient personnel.

5. Why have new plants been shut down?
   (A) Too much time was spent building them.
   (B) They were designed and built too carelessly.
   (C) The public objected to them.
   (D) Their operators were not well enough trained.

6. Who or what is to blame for the Three Mile Island accident?
   (A) poor design
   (B) inadequately trained personnel
   (C) leaks in the reactor
   (D) a faulty computer

7. How long is the training course for nuclear plant operators?
   (A) a year
   (B) long enough to enable them to take exams
   (C) thirty-one months
   (D) six weeks

8. After being licensed, what further training do power plant operators get?
   (A) They get experience on the job.
   (B) They take frequent refresher courses.

(C) None

(D) They have to take exams.

9. Why are the French committed to nuclear power?

    (A) They have nationalized their nuclear plants.

    (B) They have government control of plants and equipment.

    (C) They have no alternatives.

    (D) Their plants are producing 44% of their electricity.

10. What must the United States do before nuclear plants can be considered acceptable to their antagonists?

    (A) Nuclear plants must be nationalized.

    (B) Nuclear plants must be less expensive to build.

    (C) Waste disposal and safety must be assured.

    (D) Antinuclear groups must conceal their fears.

B. VOCABULARY WORK

Synonyms and Antonymns

Find the sentences in the reading that contain each of these words. Then choose the correct answer based upon the meaning of the word *as it is used in the reading*. For questions 1–5, choose the lettered word that means most nearly the *same* as the numbered word.

1. crucial

    (A) decisive   (C) necessary

    (B) cross   (D) cruel

2. dormant

    (A) dreadful   (C) incapable

    (B) important   (D) inactive

3. scrupulous

    (A) honest   (C) integral

    (B) private   (D) careful

4. impasse

    (A) failure   (C) impiety

    (B) deadlock   (D) process

5. chaos

    (A) disagreement   (C) confusion

    (B) accident   (D) mismanagement

For questions 6–10, choose the lettered word that is most nearly *opposite* in meaning to the numbered word.

6. anti

    (A) against   (C) after

    (B) pro   (D) before

7. antagonist
   (A) friend
   (B) relative
   (C) believer
   (D) goner

8. dissent
   (A) question
   (B) disapproval
   (C) agreement
   (D) reach

9. fiasco
   (A) party
   (B) success
   (C) fracas
   (D) explosion

10. negligent
    (A) denying
    (B) negative
    (C) careful
    (D) partial

For questions 11–16, complete each sentence by adding a verb from the following list.

beset	solidify	envisage
escalate	administer	appease

11. It is predicted that the price of real estate will continue to _____ before it goes down.

12. The plan was _____ with difficulties from the beginning.

13. The courts _____ the law.

14. You can sometimes _____ an angry man by saying you are sorry.

15. Put the jelly in the refrigerator to help it _____.

16. Let us _____ a day when nuclear power plants are safe.

Now try to complete this crossword puzzle as a review of the vocabulary practiced in Part V.

Across

1. Careful; honest
6. Inactive
11. Consume
12. Preposition: ____ the table
14. Vacant space
16. Prefix meaning *wrong*
19. Rudimentary
21. Indefinite article
22. Abbreviation for *streets*
24. Existing but not yet active
28. Encroach
30. Preposition: ____ home
31. Masculine pronoun
32. Prefix meaning *out*

Down

1. Wise
2. Do again
3. You're very ____; are you sick?
4. Names of things written to keep them in order
5. Remain
6. Auxiliary verb
7. Prefix meaning *again*
8. Wounding
9. See 30 Across
10. Antonym of *from*
13. Careless
15. Suffix used to change *arrive* to a noun

Across

33. Where are you ____?
34. Poisonous
35. First word of letter salutation
36. Past participle of *be*
37. Fights, argues
39. Container used to carry groceries
41. Superlative ending
42. Eager, enthusiastic
44. Convince
46. Money charged for a service
48. Period of time
49. Conjunction
50. United States of America
51. Incalculable
53. Soothe, relieve
54. Very close, next to

Down

16. Title for a married woman
17. Draws toward
18. Antonym of *give*
20. Type of bomb
23. Unclear, vague
24. Deserving praise
25. See 9 Down
26. Prefix meaning *beyond*
27. Antonym of *catch*
29. Antonym of *come*
34. Number of events in a decathlon
36. However
38. Destroy
40. Number of people or things put together
41. Prefix meaning *out*
43. Legal document
45. Preposition in 50 Across
46. Succeed
47. Way out
50. See 50 Across
52. Advertisement

Quiz 8

Choose the word from the alternatives that has the same meaning as the underlined word.

1. A gun is a <u>lethal</u> weapon.
   (A) dangerous   (C) deadly
   (B) modern   (D) light

2. A soothsayer can <u>foresee</u> events.
   (A) see after   (C) see before
   (B) see behind   (D) see now

3. In order to save a ship in a storm, in the old days the crew <u>jettisoned</u> the
   cargo.
   (A) loaded   (C) threw overboard
   (B) ate   (D) tied down

4. Constant <u>wrangles</u> over money disturbed the harmony of their marriage.
   (A) discussions   (C) bills
   (B) problems   (D) arguments

5. Many civilians were <u>maimed</u> in the air raid.
   (A) killed   (C) evacuated
   (B) wounded   (D) molested

6. The beaver dam <u>obstructed</u> the flow of the river.
   (A) observed   (C) assisted
   (B) endangered   (D) blocked off

7. <u>Toxic</u> waste disposal is a major concern at a nuclear power plant.
   (A) poisonous   (C) metallic
   (B) superfluous   (D) liquid

8. The neighbors' swimming pool <u>infringed</u> upon my property.
   (A) remained   (C) implicated
   (B) threatened   (D) encroached

9. Following the <u>fiasco</u> at the nuclear plant, the public protested against its
   reopening.
   (A) partial breakdown (C) boycott
   (B) complete failure   (D) destructive fire

10. The negotiations reached an <u>impasse</u> because the union representatives
    walked out of the meeting.
    (A) solution   (C) rejection
    (B) impossibility   (D) deadlock

11. The Red Cross arrived at the <u>disaster</u> area within twenty-four hours.
    (A) calamity   (C) departure
    (B) destruction   (D) hurricane

12. The earthquake caused great <u>devastation</u> in California.
    (A) ruin
    (B) confusion
    (C) movement
    (D) gaps

13. Nestor's <u>sage</u> suggestions saved the Greeks from calamity.
    (A) repeated
    (B) wise
    (C) helpful
    (D) ingenious

14. <u>Proponents</u> of conservation oppose the new laws.
    (A) antagonists
    (B) properties
    (C) advocates
    (D) proposals

15. The President's former supporters have <u>repudiated</u> his current economic plan.
    (A) rejected
    (B) supported
    (C) hailed
    (D) divorced

Introduction to Practice Tests

The following three tests simulate the Reading Comprehension and Vocabulary section of the TOEFL. In order to take these practice tests under conditions most nearly like those of the real TOEFL, use the answer sheets that are provided to record your answers. Each test is designed to be completed in 65 minutes. Make sure to set a timer or ask a friend to time you. After completing these tests, check your answers with the answer keys at the end of the book.

Answer Sheet for Reading Comprehension and Vocabulary Practice Test A

1 Ⓐ Ⓑ Ⓒ Ⓓ	19 Ⓐ Ⓑ Ⓒ Ⓓ	37 Ⓐ Ⓑ Ⓒ Ⓓ	55 Ⓐ Ⓑ Ⓒ Ⓓ	73 Ⓐ Ⓑ Ⓒ Ⓓ
2 Ⓐ Ⓑ Ⓒ Ⓓ	20 Ⓐ Ⓑ Ⓒ Ⓓ	38 Ⓐ Ⓑ Ⓒ Ⓓ	56 Ⓐ Ⓑ Ⓒ Ⓓ	74 Ⓐ Ⓑ Ⓒ Ⓓ
3 Ⓐ Ⓑ Ⓒ Ⓓ	21 Ⓐ Ⓑ Ⓒ Ⓓ	39 Ⓐ Ⓑ Ⓒ Ⓓ	57 Ⓐ Ⓑ Ⓒ Ⓓ	75 Ⓐ Ⓑ Ⓒ Ⓓ
4 Ⓐ Ⓑ Ⓒ Ⓓ	22 Ⓐ Ⓑ Ⓒ Ⓓ	40 Ⓐ Ⓑ Ⓒ Ⓓ	58 Ⓐ Ⓑ Ⓒ Ⓓ	76 Ⓐ Ⓑ Ⓒ Ⓓ
5 Ⓐ Ⓑ Ⓒ Ⓓ	23 Ⓐ Ⓑ Ⓒ Ⓓ	41 Ⓐ Ⓑ Ⓒ Ⓓ	59 Ⓐ Ⓑ Ⓒ Ⓓ	77 Ⓐ Ⓑ Ⓒ Ⓓ
6 Ⓐ Ⓑ Ⓒ Ⓓ	24 Ⓐ Ⓑ Ⓒ Ⓓ	42 Ⓐ Ⓑ Ⓒ Ⓓ	60 Ⓐ Ⓑ Ⓒ Ⓓ	78 Ⓐ Ⓑ Ⓒ Ⓓ
7 Ⓐ Ⓑ Ⓒ Ⓓ	25 Ⓐ Ⓑ Ⓒ Ⓓ	43 Ⓐ Ⓑ Ⓒ Ⓓ	61 Ⓐ Ⓑ Ⓒ Ⓓ	79 Ⓐ Ⓑ Ⓒ Ⓓ
8 Ⓐ Ⓑ Ⓒ Ⓓ	26 Ⓐ Ⓑ Ⓒ Ⓓ	44 Ⓐ Ⓑ Ⓒ Ⓓ	62 Ⓐ Ⓑ Ⓒ Ⓓ	80 Ⓐ Ⓑ Ⓒ Ⓓ
9 Ⓐ Ⓑ Ⓒ Ⓓ	27 Ⓐ Ⓑ Ⓒ Ⓓ	45 Ⓐ Ⓑ Ⓒ Ⓓ	63 Ⓐ Ⓑ Ⓒ Ⓓ	81 Ⓐ Ⓑ Ⓒ Ⓓ
10 Ⓐ Ⓑ Ⓒ Ⓓ	28 Ⓐ Ⓑ Ⓒ Ⓓ	46 Ⓐ Ⓑ Ⓒ Ⓓ	64 Ⓐ Ⓑ Ⓒ Ⓓ	82 Ⓐ Ⓑ Ⓒ Ⓓ
11 Ⓐ Ⓑ Ⓒ Ⓓ	29 Ⓐ Ⓑ Ⓒ Ⓓ	47 Ⓐ Ⓑ Ⓒ Ⓓ	65 Ⓐ Ⓑ Ⓒ Ⓓ	83 Ⓐ Ⓑ Ⓒ Ⓓ
12 Ⓐ Ⓑ Ⓒ Ⓓ	30 Ⓐ Ⓑ Ⓒ Ⓓ	48 Ⓐ Ⓑ Ⓒ Ⓓ	66 Ⓐ Ⓑ Ⓒ Ⓓ	84 Ⓐ Ⓑ Ⓒ Ⓓ
13 Ⓐ Ⓑ Ⓒ Ⓓ	31 Ⓐ Ⓑ Ⓒ Ⓓ	49 Ⓐ Ⓑ Ⓒ Ⓓ	67 Ⓐ Ⓑ Ⓒ Ⓓ	85 Ⓐ Ⓑ Ⓒ Ⓓ
14 Ⓐ Ⓑ Ⓒ Ⓓ	32 Ⓐ Ⓑ Ⓒ Ⓓ	50 Ⓐ Ⓑ Ⓒ Ⓓ	68 Ⓐ Ⓑ Ⓒ Ⓓ	86 Ⓐ Ⓑ Ⓒ Ⓓ
15 Ⓐ Ⓑ Ⓒ Ⓓ	33 Ⓐ Ⓑ Ⓒ Ⓓ	51 Ⓐ Ⓑ Ⓒ Ⓓ	69 Ⓐ Ⓑ Ⓒ Ⓓ	87 Ⓐ Ⓑ Ⓒ Ⓓ
16 Ⓐ Ⓑ Ⓒ Ⓓ	34 Ⓐ Ⓑ Ⓒ Ⓓ	52 Ⓐ Ⓑ Ⓒ Ⓓ	70 Ⓐ Ⓑ Ⓒ Ⓓ	88 Ⓐ Ⓑ Ⓒ Ⓓ
17 Ⓐ Ⓑ Ⓒ Ⓓ	35 Ⓐ Ⓑ Ⓒ Ⓓ	53 Ⓐ Ⓑ Ⓒ Ⓓ	71 Ⓐ Ⓑ Ⓒ Ⓓ	89 Ⓐ Ⓑ Ⓒ Ⓓ
18 Ⓐ Ⓑ Ⓒ Ⓓ	36 Ⓐ Ⓑ Ⓒ Ⓓ	54 Ⓐ Ⓑ Ⓒ Ⓓ	72 Ⓐ Ⓑ Ⓒ Ⓓ	90 Ⓐ Ⓑ Ⓒ Ⓓ

Answer Sheet for Reading Comprehension and Vocabulary Practice Test B

1 Ⓐ Ⓑ Ⓒ Ⓓ	19 Ⓐ Ⓑ Ⓒ Ⓓ	37 Ⓐ Ⓑ Ⓒ Ⓓ	55 Ⓐ Ⓑ Ⓒ Ⓓ	73 Ⓐ Ⓑ Ⓒ Ⓓ
2 Ⓐ Ⓑ Ⓒ Ⓓ	20 Ⓐ Ⓑ Ⓒ Ⓓ	38 Ⓐ Ⓑ Ⓒ Ⓓ	56 Ⓐ Ⓑ Ⓒ Ⓓ	74 Ⓐ Ⓑ Ⓒ Ⓓ
3 Ⓐ Ⓑ Ⓒ Ⓓ	21 Ⓐ Ⓑ Ⓒ Ⓓ	39 Ⓐ Ⓑ Ⓒ Ⓓ	57 Ⓐ Ⓑ Ⓒ Ⓓ	75 Ⓐ Ⓑ Ⓒ Ⓓ
4 Ⓐ Ⓑ Ⓒ Ⓓ	22 Ⓐ Ⓑ Ⓒ Ⓓ	40 Ⓐ Ⓑ Ⓒ Ⓓ	58 Ⓐ Ⓑ Ⓒ Ⓓ	76 Ⓐ Ⓑ Ⓒ Ⓓ
5 Ⓐ Ⓑ Ⓒ Ⓓ	23 Ⓐ Ⓑ Ⓒ Ⓓ	41 Ⓐ Ⓑ Ⓒ Ⓓ	59 Ⓐ Ⓑ Ⓒ Ⓓ	77 Ⓐ Ⓑ Ⓒ Ⓓ
6 Ⓐ Ⓑ Ⓒ Ⓓ	24 Ⓐ Ⓑ Ⓒ Ⓓ	42 Ⓐ Ⓑ Ⓒ Ⓓ	60 Ⓐ Ⓑ Ⓒ Ⓓ	78 Ⓐ Ⓑ Ⓒ Ⓓ
7 Ⓐ Ⓑ Ⓒ Ⓓ	25 Ⓐ Ⓑ Ⓒ Ⓓ	43 Ⓐ Ⓑ Ⓒ Ⓓ	61 Ⓐ Ⓑ Ⓒ Ⓓ	79 Ⓐ Ⓑ Ⓒ Ⓓ
8 Ⓐ Ⓑ Ⓒ Ⓓ	26 Ⓐ Ⓑ Ⓒ Ⓓ	44 Ⓐ Ⓑ Ⓒ Ⓓ	62 Ⓐ Ⓑ Ⓒ Ⓓ	80 Ⓐ Ⓑ Ⓒ Ⓓ
9 Ⓐ Ⓑ Ⓒ Ⓓ	27 Ⓐ Ⓑ Ⓒ Ⓓ	45 Ⓐ Ⓑ Ⓒ Ⓓ	63 Ⓐ Ⓑ Ⓒ Ⓓ	81 Ⓐ Ⓑ Ⓒ Ⓓ
10 Ⓐ Ⓑ Ⓒ Ⓓ	28 Ⓐ Ⓑ Ⓒ Ⓓ	46 Ⓐ Ⓑ Ⓒ Ⓓ	64 Ⓐ Ⓑ Ⓒ Ⓓ	82 Ⓐ Ⓑ Ⓒ Ⓓ
11 Ⓐ Ⓑ Ⓒ Ⓓ	29 Ⓐ Ⓑ Ⓒ Ⓓ	47 Ⓐ Ⓑ Ⓒ Ⓓ	65 Ⓐ Ⓑ Ⓒ Ⓓ	83 Ⓐ Ⓑ Ⓒ Ⓓ
12 Ⓐ Ⓑ Ⓒ Ⓓ	30 Ⓐ Ⓑ Ⓒ Ⓓ	48 Ⓐ Ⓑ Ⓒ Ⓓ	66 Ⓐ Ⓑ Ⓒ Ⓓ	84 Ⓐ Ⓑ Ⓒ Ⓓ
13 Ⓐ Ⓑ Ⓒ Ⓓ	31 Ⓐ Ⓑ Ⓒ Ⓓ	49 Ⓐ Ⓑ Ⓒ Ⓓ	67 Ⓐ Ⓑ Ⓒ Ⓓ	85 Ⓐ Ⓑ Ⓒ Ⓓ
14 Ⓐ Ⓑ Ⓒ Ⓓ	32 Ⓐ Ⓑ Ⓒ Ⓓ	50 Ⓐ Ⓑ Ⓒ Ⓓ	68 Ⓐ Ⓑ Ⓒ Ⓓ	86 Ⓐ Ⓑ Ⓒ Ⓓ
15 Ⓐ Ⓑ Ⓒ Ⓓ	33 Ⓐ Ⓑ Ⓒ Ⓓ	51 Ⓐ Ⓑ Ⓒ Ⓓ	69 Ⓐ Ⓑ Ⓒ Ⓓ	87 Ⓐ Ⓑ Ⓒ Ⓓ
16 Ⓐ Ⓑ Ⓒ Ⓓ	34 Ⓐ Ⓑ Ⓒ Ⓓ	52 Ⓐ Ⓑ Ⓒ Ⓓ	70 Ⓐ Ⓑ Ⓒ Ⓓ	88 Ⓐ Ⓑ Ⓒ Ⓓ
17 Ⓐ Ⓑ Ⓒ Ⓓ	35 Ⓐ Ⓑ Ⓒ Ⓓ	53 Ⓐ Ⓑ Ⓒ Ⓓ	71 Ⓐ Ⓑ Ⓒ Ⓓ	89 Ⓐ Ⓑ Ⓒ Ⓓ
18 Ⓐ Ⓑ Ⓒ Ⓓ	36 Ⓐ Ⓑ Ⓒ Ⓓ	54 Ⓐ Ⓑ Ⓒ Ⓓ	72 Ⓐ Ⓑ Ⓒ Ⓓ	90 Ⓐ Ⓑ Ⓒ Ⓓ

Answer Sheet for Reading Comprehension and Vocabulary Practice Test C

1 Ⓐ Ⓑ Ⓒ Ⓓ   19 Ⓐ Ⓑ Ⓒ Ⓓ   37 Ⓐ Ⓑ Ⓒ Ⓓ   55 Ⓐ Ⓑ Ⓒ Ⓓ   73 Ⓐ Ⓑ Ⓒ Ⓓ

2 Ⓐ Ⓑ Ⓒ Ⓓ   20 Ⓐ Ⓑ Ⓒ Ⓓ   38 Ⓐ Ⓑ Ⓒ Ⓓ   56 Ⓐ Ⓑ Ⓒ Ⓓ   74 Ⓐ Ⓑ Ⓒ Ⓓ

3 Ⓐ Ⓑ Ⓒ Ⓓ   21 Ⓐ Ⓑ Ⓒ Ⓓ   39 Ⓐ Ⓑ Ⓒ Ⓓ   57 Ⓐ Ⓑ Ⓒ Ⓓ   75 Ⓐ Ⓑ Ⓒ Ⓓ

4 Ⓐ Ⓑ Ⓒ Ⓓ   22 Ⓐ Ⓑ Ⓒ Ⓓ   40 Ⓐ Ⓑ Ⓒ Ⓓ   58 Ⓐ Ⓑ Ⓒ Ⓓ   76 Ⓐ Ⓑ Ⓒ Ⓓ

5 Ⓐ Ⓑ Ⓒ Ⓓ   23 Ⓐ Ⓑ Ⓒ Ⓓ   41 Ⓐ Ⓑ Ⓒ Ⓓ   59 Ⓐ Ⓑ Ⓒ Ⓓ   77 Ⓐ Ⓑ Ⓒ Ⓓ

6 Ⓐ Ⓑ Ⓒ Ⓓ   24 Ⓐ Ⓑ Ⓒ Ⓓ   42 Ⓐ Ⓑ Ⓒ Ⓓ   60 Ⓐ Ⓑ Ⓒ Ⓓ   78 Ⓐ Ⓑ Ⓒ Ⓓ

7 Ⓐ Ⓑ Ⓒ Ⓓ   25 Ⓐ Ⓑ Ⓒ Ⓓ   43 Ⓐ Ⓑ Ⓒ Ⓓ   61 Ⓐ Ⓑ Ⓒ Ⓓ   79 Ⓐ Ⓑ Ⓒ Ⓓ

8 Ⓐ Ⓑ Ⓒ Ⓓ   26 Ⓐ Ⓑ Ⓒ Ⓓ   44 Ⓐ Ⓑ Ⓒ Ⓓ   62 Ⓐ Ⓑ Ⓒ Ⓓ   80 Ⓐ Ⓑ Ⓒ Ⓓ

9 Ⓐ Ⓑ Ⓒ Ⓓ   27 Ⓐ Ⓑ Ⓒ Ⓓ   45 Ⓐ Ⓑ Ⓒ Ⓓ   63 Ⓐ Ⓑ Ⓒ Ⓓ   81 Ⓐ Ⓑ Ⓒ Ⓓ

10 Ⓐ Ⓑ Ⓒ Ⓓ   28 Ⓐ Ⓑ Ⓒ Ⓓ   46 Ⓐ Ⓑ Ⓒ Ⓓ   64 Ⓐ Ⓑ Ⓒ Ⓓ   82 Ⓐ Ⓑ Ⓒ Ⓓ

11 Ⓐ Ⓑ Ⓒ Ⓓ   29 Ⓐ Ⓑ Ⓒ Ⓓ   47 Ⓐ Ⓑ Ⓒ Ⓓ   65 Ⓐ Ⓑ Ⓒ Ⓓ   83 Ⓐ Ⓑ Ⓒ Ⓓ

12 Ⓐ Ⓑ Ⓒ Ⓓ   30 Ⓐ Ⓑ Ⓒ Ⓓ   48 Ⓐ Ⓑ Ⓒ Ⓓ   66 Ⓐ Ⓑ Ⓒ Ⓓ   84 Ⓐ Ⓑ Ⓒ Ⓓ

13 Ⓐ Ⓑ Ⓒ Ⓓ   31 Ⓐ Ⓑ Ⓒ Ⓓ   49 Ⓐ Ⓑ Ⓒ Ⓓ   67 Ⓐ Ⓑ Ⓒ Ⓓ   85 Ⓐ Ⓑ Ⓒ Ⓓ

14 Ⓐ Ⓑ Ⓒ Ⓓ   32 Ⓐ Ⓑ Ⓒ Ⓓ   50 Ⓐ Ⓑ Ⓒ Ⓓ   68 Ⓐ Ⓑ Ⓒ Ⓓ   86 Ⓐ Ⓑ Ⓒ Ⓓ

15 Ⓐ Ⓑ Ⓒ Ⓓ   33 Ⓐ Ⓑ Ⓒ Ⓓ   51 Ⓐ Ⓑ Ⓒ Ⓓ   69 Ⓐ Ⓑ Ⓒ Ⓓ   87 Ⓐ Ⓑ Ⓒ Ⓓ

16 Ⓐ Ⓑ Ⓒ Ⓓ   34 Ⓐ Ⓑ Ⓒ Ⓓ   52 Ⓐ Ⓑ Ⓒ Ⓓ   70 Ⓐ Ⓑ Ⓒ Ⓓ   88 Ⓐ Ⓑ Ⓒ Ⓓ

17 Ⓐ Ⓑ Ⓒ Ⓓ   35 Ⓐ Ⓑ Ⓒ Ⓓ   53 Ⓐ Ⓑ Ⓒ Ⓓ   71 Ⓐ Ⓑ Ⓒ Ⓓ   89 Ⓐ Ⓑ Ⓒ Ⓓ

18 Ⓐ Ⓑ Ⓒ Ⓓ   36 Ⓐ Ⓑ Ⓒ Ⓓ   54 Ⓐ Ⓑ Ⓒ Ⓓ   72 Ⓐ Ⓑ Ⓒ Ⓓ   90 Ⓐ Ⓑ Ⓒ Ⓓ

READING COMPREHENSION AND VOCABULARY PRACTICE TEST A
Time—65 Minutes

This test is designed to measure your ability to understand various kinds of reading materials, as well as your ability to understand the meaning and use of words. There are two types of questions in this test, with special directions for each type.

Directions: In questions 1–45 each sentence has a word or phrase underlined. Below each sentence are four other words or phrases, marked (A), (B), (C), and (D). You are to choose the *one* word or phrase that *best keeps the meaning* of the original sentence if it is substituted for the underlined word or phrase. Then, on your answer sheet, find the number of the question and blacken the space that corresponds to the letter you have chosen so that the letter inside the oval cannot be seen.

Example:
The American Revolution was fought to gain autonomy.
(A) self-righteousness   (C) self-rule
(B) self-satisfaction   (D) self-reformation

The best answer is (C), *self-rule*. The Revolution, as you may already know, was the War of Independence, which is the same as *self-rule*.

When you understand the directions, begin work on the vocabulary problems.

1. If the weatherman has predicted <u>accurately</u>, tomorrow will be a perfect day for our picnic.
   (A) astutely   (C) carefully
   (B) correctly   (D) acutely

2. Swarms of locusts <u>ravaged</u> the crops.
   (A) raided   (C) flew over
   (B) landed on   (D) destroyed

3. The earthquake left huge <u>gaps</u> in the city's streets.
   (A) debris   (C) buildings
   (B) crevices   (D) electric lines

185

4. A series of <u>ingenious</u> inventions in Britain provided the impetus for the Industrial Revolution.
   (A) clever
   (B) minor
   (C) mechanical
   (D) intricate

5. All of the <u>tenants</u> in the building complained about the lack of hot water.
   (A) old people
   (B) landlords
   (C) superintendents
   (D) occupants

6. On every pack of cigarettes there is a <u>warning</u> from the Surgeon General.
   (A) caution
   (B) message
   (C) reaction
   (D) price

7. Bruce is such a <u>fanatic</u> jogger that he takes his running shorts and shoes with him on business trips.
   (A) athletic
   (B) excessively enthusiastic
   (C) fantastic
   (D) easily duped

8. Because the jury had reached a <u>deadlock</u>, the judge called for a retrial.
   (A) impasse
   (B) verdict
   (C) disagreement
   (D) reduction

9. The snarling dog on my doorstep <u>disconcerted</u> the potential thief.
   (A) frustrated
   (B) attacked
   (C) bit
   (D) disconnected

10. Car owners who live by the sea are well aware of the <u>havoc</u> salt water causes to a car's finish.
    (A) distortion
    (B) drag
    (C) destruction
    (D) care

11. The royal <u>nuptials</u> captured the attention of the whole world.
    (A) attendance
    (B) wedding
    (C) baptism
    (D) event

12. In spite of the <u>complexity</u> of the problem, the mathematician solved it quickly.
    (A) completeness
    (B) community
    (C) compression
    (D) complication

13. When the former movie star was killed in an automobile accident, her <u>obituary</u> appeared worldwide.
    (A) picture
    (B) death notice
    (C) agent
    (D) beauty

14. After a <u>sojourn</u> of two weeks in Venice, they moved on to Florence.
    (A) vacation
    (B) trip
    (C) hotel
    (D) stay

15. The ship left New York on her <u>maiden</u> voyage.
    (A) first
    (B) final
    (C) fast
    (D) famous

16. I just bought the second part of the <u>trilogy</u>.
    (A) eight-sided thing   (C) three-part novel
    (B) musical score   (D) three-petaled plant

17. The heavy rains <u>inundated</u> our basement.
    (A) undulated   (C) humidified
    (B) flooded   (D) cooled

18. <u>Conservationists</u> are interested in protecting the environment from the pollution of industrial waste.
    (A) conservatives
    (B) people who want to conserve natural resources
    (C) people who enjoy getting out in the country
    (D) people who grow their own produce

19. An old story says that the Indians sold New York for $24 worth of <u>baubles</u>.
    (A) trinkets   (C) jewels
    (B) bubbles   (D) bullets

20. His <u>tenacious</u> personality made him top salesperson in the company.
    (A) tenable   (C) persistent
    (B) explosive   (D) charming

21. Archaeologists have discovered <u>fossils</u> of million-year-old animals in excavations.
    (A) remnants   (C) records
    (B) graves   (D) paws

22. The old car <u>jolted</u> along the country road at a snail's pace.
    (A) rode   (C) honked
    (B) dawdled   (D) bounced

23. Abraham Lincoln was born in a <u>humble</u> log cabin.
    (A) meek   (C) modern
    (B) modest   (D) pretentious

24. Her first year at school away from home, she suffered <u>qualms</u> of homesickness.
    (A) quakes   (C) lapses
    (B) regrets   (D) pangs

25. Prohibition in the United States <u>ushered in</u> an era of crime and corruption.
    (A) introduced   (C) used
    (B) caused   (D) upset

26. His <u>antagonist</u> knocked him out in the first round of the fight.
    (A) boxer   (C) weakness
    (B) hostility   (D) opponent

27. <u>Submissive</u> wives are seldom successful in the business world.
    (A) unassertive   (C) overworked
    (B) substitute   (D) indifferent

28. Man is <u>prone</u> to error, even though he'd like to think he's infallible.
    (A) lying down
    (B) averse
    (C) disposed
    (D) pronounced

29. Vitamin C has a <u>therapeutic</u> effect in the treatment of beriberi.
    (A) thrifty
    (B) medicinal
    (C) deficient
    (D) utilitarian

30. If you ate <u>wholesome</u> food instead of junk food, you would feel a lot better.
    (A) whole
    (B) energy
    (C) fresh
    (D) nutritious

31. Reading a good mystery only <u>whets</u> my appetite for more books by the same author.
    (A) waits
    (B) cajoles
    (C) sharpens
    (D) resolves

32. Some of the expensive house trailers provide all of the <u>amenities</u> of home.
    (A) things conductive to comfort
    (B) things conducive to convenience
    (C) things conducive to pleasantness
    (D) all of the above

33. The family conducted an <u>illicit</u> whiskey business during Prohibition.
    (A) secret
    (B) boundless
    (C) ill-fated
    (D) illegal

34. Some voters are easily swayed by <u>glib</u> politicians.
    (A) smooth-speaking
    (B) handsome
    (C) dishonest
    (D) gray-haired

35. The jury found that the manufacturer had been <u>negligent</u> in installing safety devices.
    (A) carefree
    (B) careless
    (C) careworn
    (D) careful

36. <u>Irate</u> residents of the neighborhood protested the construction of the nuclear power plant.
    (A) irritated
    (B) angry
    (C) nearby
    (D) berated

37. Queen Elizabeth I's coronation <u>heralded</u> an era of exploration in the New World.
    (A) hailed
    (B) preceded
    (C) was the forerunner of
    (D) all of the above

38. During the flight from New York to London, Helen <u>beguiled</u> herself by reading comic books.
    (A) fooled
    (B) tired
    (C) laughed
    (D) amused

39. A good teacher must establish <u>rapport</u> with his or her students.
    (A) report
    (B) acquaintance
    (C) understanding
    (D) conversation

40. Manufacturers spend millions of dollars on advertising to <u>entice</u> people to buy their products.
    (A) entertain
    (B) encounter
    (C) tempt
    (D) force

41. If we had taken his <u>sage</u> advice, we wouldn't be in so much trouble now.
    (A) sturdy
    (B) wise
    (C) willing
    (D) eager

42. The politician's conviction for tax fraud <u>jeopardized</u> his future in public life.
    (A) jettisoned
    (B) penalized
    (C) rejuvenated
    (D) endangered

43. A <u>mediocre</u> student who gets low grades will have trouble getting into an Ivy League college.
    (A) average
    (B) lazy
    (C) moronic
    (D) diligent

44. Last year he was a <u>rookie</u> pitcher with the Yankees.
    (A) mediocre
    (B) first-year
    (C) probationary
    (D) experienced

45. Our host made so many <u>allusions</u> to sleep that we felt obliged to leave the party early.
    (A) illusions
    (B) yawns
    (C) hints
    (D) delusions

Directions: The rest of this test is based on a variety of reading material (single sentences, paragraphs, and the like). For questions 46–90, you are to choose the *one* best answer, (A), (B), (C), or (D), to each question. Then, on your answer sheet, find the number of the question and blacken the space that corresponds to the letter of the answer you have chosen.

Answer all questions following a passage on the basis of what is *stated* or *implied* in that passage.

Read the following passage.

> The shares of the apartment corporation are offered under this plan only to individuals over 18 years of age. Non-individual tenants in occupancy of apartments on the date of presentation of the plan may designate an individual to purchase the shares allocated to such apartment, provided that such individual proposes to purchase the shares for his own account and not as a nominee of any corporation, partnership, association, trust, estate, or foreign government.

Example 1:
To what does this passage refer?
(A) employment wanted
(B) apartment to share
(C) a real estate partnership

(D) sale of an apartment to a non-tenant

You should choose answer (D), because the passage says tenants in occupancy may designate an individual to purchase the shares allocated to the apartment.

Example 2:
The passage says the apartment may *not* be sold to
(A) a corporation
(B) a person under 18
(C) the British Embassy
(D) all of the above

You should choose (D), because the passage prohibits sale to foreign governments (the British Embassy, for example) and (A) and (B) as well.

Questions 46–50 are related to this passage.
   Young people today are very different from their predecessors in the 60s. The 1960s were dominated by activists, long-haired and protesting American intervention in Vietnam. No longer interested in politics and causes, most of the 32 million people from 13 to 21 are preoccupied with issues closer to themselves. Their foremost concern is with training for and finding a job that will support them in these uncertain times. They worry, as do their parents, about the dangers of nuclear destruction. But they seldom do anything about their worries. Protest marches and the like simply do not appeal to them. They are much too busy getting on with the business of living their own self-centered lives. Not surprisingly, excessive drinking among teenagers has become a national concern, with an estimated 5.3 million 14- to 17-year-old problem drinkers.

46. You can infer from this passage that
    (A) teenagers drink to excess because their parents provide a bad example
    (B) excessive drinking among teenagers indicates that they are responding to the stresses of their lives by drinking
    (C) present-day teenagers drink because of their more lighthearted approach to life
    (D) teenagers have more money to buy alcohol than the youth of the 60s did

47. Teenagers today are different from the youth of the 60s in their attitude toward
    (A) government   (C) making a living
    (B) hair styles   (D) all of the above

48. Most young people are
    (A) preoccupied with earning a living
    (B) involved in protest marches
    (C) a national concern
    (D) problem drinkers

49. You can infer that the author's opinion is that people who worry about nuclear destruction
    (A) should keep their worries to themselves
    (B) should tell their parents about their worries
    (C) should be more like the activists of the 60s
    (D) seldom do anything constructive about their worries

50. What is the main idea of this passage?
    (A) Young people in the 1960s were rebellious.
    (B) Young people today drink too much.
    (C) The youth of today have a different attitude toward life from that of the youth of the 60s.
    (D) Young people today are different from and better than the youth of the 1960s.

Questions 51–54 are related to this passage.

Health food addicts have at last gained the support of the National Academy of Sciences in the argument about the relationship between diet and cancer. The National Academy has issued a 500-page report called "Diet, Nutrition and Cancer" that recommends dietary strategies for protecting yourself from cancer. For example, they advise you to reduce your consumption of fat, as in pork and butter, and increase your intake of vitamin C, as in grapefruit and cabbage. More beta-carotene, a type of vitamin A in yellow and green vegetables, should be added to your diet as well.

51. What can you infer that health food addicts have claimed?
    (A) They needed confirmation from the Academy of Sciences.
    (B) People need to eat better.
    (C) People should cut down their consumption of fat and vitamins.
    (D) People who eat nutritious food are less likely to get cancer.

52. What foods apparently fight cancer?
    (A) fat and vitamins A and C
    (B) bacon, grapefruit, and cabbage
    (C) fruits and vegetables
    (D) junk foods

53. The majority of people reading this passage would infer that the Academy of Sciences is
    (A) an association of nutrition professors
    (B) a reliable scientific organization
    (C) a company that manufactures health food
    (D) a publisher of scientific journals

54. You can infer from this passage that
    (A) experiments were performed on groups of people to show the effect of nutrition on cancer
    (B) health food addicts had already proven that good nutrition prevents cancer
    (C) nothing has been proven in regard to the effect of diet upon the development of cancer
    (D) there is no way to prevent cancer

Questions 55–58 relate to this passage.

The condition of your heart is directly related to the amount of stress you regularly experience. Be aware of stress in your life and train yourself to counteract its disastrous effects. These are some of the deliberate steps you may take to reduce stress:

1. Enjoy a lengthy vacation yearly. Don't take your work with you; forget all about the office.
2. Be certain that what you are doing is what you really want to do.
3. Face each challenge realistically. Don't attempt to do more each day than you possibly can do well. You need to feel satisfied with your accomplishments daily.
4. Relax every evening and do the things you enjoy, whether this means strenuous exercise like tennis or curling up in a comfortable chair and reading a mystery.

55. The purpose of this passage is to
   (A) show the effects of stress upon the heart
   (B) describe symptoms of stress
   (C) help you reduce stress
   (D) encourage you to reduce your work load

56. One of the causes of stress is
   (A) loving your work
   (B) playing tennis too strenuously
   (C) attempting to do more than is possible
   (D) a heart condition

57. The passage says that
   (A) strenuous exercise can damage your heart
   (B) your heart can create stress
   (C) reading a mystery can create stress
   (D) no matter what you do, you will regularly encounter stress

58. The passage says that the first thing to do about stress is
   (A) ignore it because it can be alleviated
   (B) talk to your boss about a vacation
   (C) do things you like to do
   (D) be aware of its existence in your life

Questions 59–64 relate to this passage.

A few years ago a shortage of natural gas drove prices sky high. Likewise, gasoline prices rose when demands exceeded supplies. A glut in the oil market drove prices back down. The law of supply and demand functioned according to textbook description in the case of oil, but the situation is otherwise in the current natural gas market. Natural gas consumers are finding their heating bills more of a burden than last year, in spite of a dramatic increase in supplies. There is so much natural gas available that many suppliers are closing down their plants for lack of a market, and it is rumored that some suppliers are even burning off their surplus gas.

59. You can infer that the law of supply and demand means that prices
   (A) rise if supplies are abundant
   (B) fall if supplies are limited
   (C) rise if supplies are limited
   (D) stay even when supplies are abundant

60. The author's purpose is to
    (A) discuss oil prices
    (B) discuss gas shortages
    (C) question high gas prices
    (D) compare gas and oil prices

61. You can infer that gas suppliers are burning their surplus gas in order to
    (A) lower the prices on their product
    (B) create a shortage to sustain high prices
    (C) get rid of an inferior product
    (D) create a glut in the market

62. Many suppliers of natural gas are
    (A) reducing their prices
    (B) going out of business
    (C) running out of gas
    (D) converting to the oil business

63. The cost of heating with natural gas this year
    (A) has risen
    (B) depends on supply and demand
    (C) is easier to bear
    (D) has remained the same as last year

64. The amount of natural gas currently available is
    (A) more than last year's supply
    (B) equal to last year's supply
    (C) less than last year's supply
    (D) none of the above

Questions 65–71 relate to this passage.

Under the Medicare insurance policy, people approaching 65 may enroll during the seven-month period that includes three months before the sixty-fifth birthday, the month in which the birthday falls, and three months after the birthday. However, if they wish the insurance coverage to begin when they reach 65, they must enroll three months before their birthday. People who do not enroll within their first enrollment period may enroll later, during the first three months of each year. Those people, however, must pay 10% additional for each twelve-month period that elapsed since they first could have enrolled. The monthly premium is deducted from social security payments, railroad retirement or civil service retirement benefits.

65. The author's purpose is to
    (A) describe the benefits of Medicare
    (B) stimulate enrollment in Medicare
    (C) tell people when they may enroll in Medicare
    (D) advertise Medicare

66. People would pay 10% more for their insurance if they
    (A) were under 65
    (B) applied seven months before their sixty-fifth birthday
    (C) enrolled after their sixty-fifth birthday
    (D) enrolled in a private plan

67. To start coverage by Medicare on their sixty-fifth birthday, people must apply
    (A) seven months before their birthday
    (B) four months before their birthday
    (C) the month in which their birthday occurs
    (D) three months before their birthday

68. The seven-month period described in this passage includes
    (A) seven months before a subscriber's birthday
    (B) seven months after the subscriber's birthday
    (C) three months before, three months after, and the month during which the subscriber's birthday occurs
    (D) none of the above

69. The period after the sixty-fifth birthday during which people may apply for Medicare is
    (A) one year
    (B) seven months
    (C) one month
    (D) January 1 to March 31 yearly

70. Medicare subscribers' premiums
    (A) are due the first of every month
    (B) are taken out of their salaries
    (C) are subtracted from their pension checks
    (D) come from the federal government

71. You can infer that people over 65 who enroll two years after they could have enrolled pay 10% more for two years and then would
    (A) continue to pay more than people who enrolled before they were 65
    (B) pay less than people who enrolled before 65
    (C) pay the same as people who enrolled before 65
    (D) be excluded from the Medicare plan completely

Questions 72–77 relate to this passage.

Plague is a disease carried by animals, primarily by rodents, and by people. It was widespread in Europe, where in the 1300s, 25 million people died and raging epidemics spread as late as the latter part of the seventeenth century. Once people became aware of the fact that plague was spread by rats that carried the epidemic on ships from one port to another, rodent extermination put an end to the devastating plagues in the world. In the United States, plague occurred in epidemic strength in San Francisco in 1900. Intensive rat control measures were employed immediately, but squirrels in the area had been infected and had to be destroyed too. Descendants of these rodents continue the infection and have transmitted it to other rodents such as prairie dogs in the western and southwestern parts of the United States. The plague is endemic to those areas that are sparsely populated. There have been scattered cases of plague since 1900, but no serious outbreaks.

72. Plague is spread by
    (A) rats
    (B) rodents and people
    (C) ships
    (D) prairie dogs and squirrels

73. You can infer that there were no further raging plague epidemics
    (A) after the 1300s
    (B) in Europe
    (C) after the seventeenth century
    (D) in San Francisco

74. The western and southwestern parts of the United States
    (A) still have serious outbreaks of plague
    (B) are the habitat of infected rodents
    (C) have large populations
    (D) are sparsely populated because of the plague

75. The plague spread in Europe because
    (A) infected rats traveled in ships
    (B) people did not know what caused the disease
    (C) nothing was done to prevent the disease
    (D) all of the above

76. Raging epidemics ended in Europe when
    (A) ships were not allowed in foreign ports
    (B) rats were exterminated
    (C) populations moved out of the big cities
    (D) 25 million people had died

77. You can infer that in the late 1300s
    (A) Europe's population was very small
    (B) intensive rat control measures were applied
    (C) people were extremely poor
    (D) people were accustomed to the plague

Questions 78–80 are related to this passage.

In 1746 Benjamin Franklin decided to convince his peers that lightning was a form of electricity. He flew a kite in a thunderstorm, a foolhardy thing to do, and got sparks from the metal key he had attached to the string at ground level. He shocked his friends into believing his theory.

78. You can infer that Benjamin Franklin
    (A) didn't realize his danger in flying a kite during an electrical storm
    (B) was a very brave scientist
    (C) enjoyed flying kites
    (D) was a great American statesman

79. The sparks from the key were caused by
    (A) the thunder   (C) the string it was attached to
    (B) Franklin   (D) lightning

80. You can infer from this passage that in 1746
    (A) thunderstorms were unusual occurrences
    (B) energy was produced by lightning
    (C) not much had been learned about electricity
    (D) a key on a kite string would give off sparks

Questions 81–85 relate to this passage.

Children who appear intelligent and have normal sight and hearing may nevertheless have learning disabilities such as dyslexia, difficulty in reading; dysgraphia, difficulty in writing; dyscalculia, difficulty with numbers; and auditory-memory problems that prevent the child from remembering what has just been said. Considered an "invisible" handicap, such learning disabilities can be detected by alert parents before the child goes to school. If the child at about thirty months is not developing normal language skills, something is amiss. A child who cannot do puzzles or put pegs in holes lacks perceptual-motor skills. Kindergartners should recognize the *ABCs*. First-graders may commonly reverse their letters, writing a *d* for a *b*, but if they are still doing this at the start of second grade, they should be tested for learning disabilities. Proper and early treatment is essential.

81. The author's intent in this selection is to
    (A) describe the various types of learning disabilities
    (B) explain why some children have dyslexia
    (C) warn parents of the signs of learning disabilities
    (D) describe kindergartners' skills

82. The selection would most likely appear in a
    (A) health book
    (C) medical journal
    (B) parents' magazine
    (D) college yearbook

83. A child who cannot remember a long question might have
    (A) dyslexia
    (C) auditory-memory problems
    (C) dysgraphia
    (D) hyperactivity

84. The author emphasizes the need for
    (A) listening to children
    (B) more learning centers to help the disabled
    (C) trained personnel to prevent learning disabilities
    (D) early detection of learning disabilities

85. A child who reads from right to left may have
    (A) a poor diet
    (C) inadequate teachers
    (B) poor vision
    (D) dyslexia

Questions 86–88 relate to this passage.

Basic Skills Proficiency—Undergraduate Students

Each student must meet standards of proficiency in the basic skills area of reading, writing, and mathematics established by the college. In addition, the board of trustees has mandated that students meet a university-wide minimal level of skills proficiency before entrance to the upper division. Consequently, students will be tested in these areas after admission, but prior to their freshman year, so as to determine whether they meet minimal university standards and the college's standards. Those who fail initially to meet these requirements will be given appropriate remedial instruction to assist them in achieving the required skills-competency levels. Students who fail to achieve the minimal standards of the university by the end of their sophomore year will not be permitted to continue in the university.

86. Students are required to take proficiency tests
    (A) during their first year in college
    (B) before their first year in college
    (C) at the end of their first year in college
    (D) none of the above

87. Students who fail to meet minimal standards upon admission
    (A) are required to take further tests during their freshman year
    (B) must take remedial courses their first year
    (C) are required to take remedial courses for two years
    (D) will have their admission permits revoked

88. Students who do not meet minimal standards at the end of two years will
    (A) be required to take further remedial courses
    (B) have to take additional tests
    (C) have to reapply for admission
    (D) be expelled from the university

Questions 89–90. For each of these questions, choose the answer that is *closest in meaning* to the original sentence. Note that several of the choices may be factually correct, but you should choose the one that is the *closest restatement of the given sentence.*

89. Misguided attempts to make left-handed children use their right hands have made many children stutterers, yet the number of stutterers among lefties appears to be little different from that among right-handed people.
    (A) Forcing lefties to use their right hands can make them stutterers, but there are just as many right-handed as left-handed stutterers.
    (B) People become stutterers because they have been forced to use their right hands when they were by nature left-handed.
    (C) Stutterers are both left- and right-handed because they were forced to use their right hands.
    (D) Many left-handed stutterers blame their stuttering on people who forced them to use their right hands, so the number of lefties and right-handed stutterers is the same.

90. In many homes the water heater ranks second only to the heating system in total energy consumption.
    (A) The water heater uses more energy than the heating system.
    (B) Total energy consumption in many homes includes a water heater and the heating system.
    (C) The largest energy consumption in many homes is by the heating system, and the second largest by the water heater.
    (D) The water heater and the heating system in many homes consume twice as much energy as the other appliances.

READING COMPREHENSION AND VOCABULARY PRACTICE TEST B
Time—65 Minutes

This test is designed to measure your ability to understand various kinds of reading materials, as well as your ability to understand the meaning and use of words. There are two types of questions in this test, with special directions for each type.

Directions: In questions 1–45, each sentence has a word or phrase underlined. Below each sentence are four other words or phrases, marked (A), (B), (C), and (D). You are to choose the *one* word or phrase that *best keeps the meaning* of the original sentence if it is substituted for the underlined word or phrase. Then, on your answer sheet, find the number of the question and blacken the space that corresponds to the letter you have chosen so that the letter inside the oval cannot be seen.

Example:
   The American Revolution was fought to gain autonomy.
   (A) self-righteousness   (C) self-rule
   (B) self-satisfaction   (D) self-reformation

The best answer is (C), *self-rule*. The Revolution, as you may already know, was the War of Independence, which is the same as *self-rule*.
   When you understand the directions, begin work on the vocabulary problems.

1. He had reached the zenith of his career when he became president of General Motors.
   (A) ambition   (C) happiest moment
   (B) zeal   (D) summit

2. The road west gave access to the lake.
   (A) ascendancy   (C) exit
   (B) approach   (D) asset

3. Because Jack defaulted in his alimony payments, his wife took him to court.
   (A) defamed   (C) paid
   (B) erred   (D) failed

4. Alchemists seek a <u>panacea</u> for the world's ills.
   - (A) gold
   - (B) chemical
   - (C) change
   - (D) remedy

5. After years of <u>litigation</u>, the will was settled.
   - (A) illness
   - (B) lawsuits
   - (C) longevity
   - (D) taxes

6. Boutiques cater to a young <u>clientele.</u>
   - (A) dress style
   - (B) customers
   - (C) adolescent
   - (D) class

7. Short skirts were the <u>vogue</u> a few years ago.
   - (A) repute
   - (B) length
   - (C) fashion
   - (D) brevity

8. The builder's <u>conservative</u> estimate of the time required to remodel the kitchen was six weeks.
   - (A) reactionary
   - (B) cautious
   - (C) protective
   - (D) traditional

9. Christian's path was <u>beset</u> by peril.
   - (A) surrounded
   - (B) chased
   - (C) frightened
   - (D) bested

10. A <u>precedent</u> was set in the case by a law passed in 1900.
    - (A) precept
    - (B) example
    - (C) jurisdiction
    - (D) pace

11. Frequent minor <u>ailments</u> kept her home from work.
    - (A) irritations
    - (B) young children
    - (C) sicknesses
    - (D) falls

12. The neighbors' constant <u>wrangles</u> with each other shattered our tranquility.
    - (A) wrecks
    - (B) wraths
    - (C) quarrels
    - (D) conversations

13. The Red Cross made an <u>equitable</u> distribution of the bread to the starving children.
    - (A) just
    - (B) quick
    - (C) nutritious
    - (D) convenient

14. When you apply for a loan, you must show that you have <u>assets</u> to cover the amount of the loan.
    - (A) assessments
    - (B) property
    - (C) legal documents
    - (D) stocks

15. The union members <u>boycotted</u> the meeting because they did not want to go on strike.
    - (A) attended
    - (B) blackmailed
    - (C) shunned
    - (D) left

16. The Industrial Revolution marked the beginning of an epoch of exodus from rural areas to cities.
    (A) episode
    (B) period
    (C) migration
    (D) story

17. Participants from 100 countries go to the Olympic Games.
    (A) people who represent
    (B) people who come
    (C) people who take part
    (D) people who are athletes

18. He got a gold medal for the feat of lifting 500 pounds.
    (A) accomplishment
    (B) fear
    (C) trial
    (D) event

19. We had to list the chronology of events in World War II on our test.
    (A) catastrophe
    (B) time sequence
    (C) disaster
    (D) discrepancy

20. You may find that jogging is detrimental to your health rather than beneficial.
    (A) helpful
    (B) facile
    (C) depressing
    (D) harmful

21. The power failure at dinnertime caused consternation among the city's housewives.
    (A) disability
    (B) deliberation
    (C) dismay
    (D) distaste

22. The hostess was affronted by Bill's failure to thank her for dinner.
    (A) affable
    (B) insulted
    (C) afflicted
    (D) confronted

23. His drunken behavior at the wedding was deplorable.
    (A) intoxicated
    (B) displayed
    (C) delightful
    (D) wretched

24. The tainted meat made him desperately ill.
    (A) contaminated
    (B) touched
    (C) refrigerated
    (D) colored

25. The consensus among the senators was that the bill would not be passed.
    (A) controversy
    (B) gathering
    (C) divided
    (D) agreement

26. I can jog a few miles, but the Boston Marathon is certainly beyond my scope.
    (A) view
    (B) opportunity
    (C) range
    (D) score

27. Militant suffragettes demanded the right to vote.
    (A) feminine
    (B) fighting
    (C) organized
    (D) liberated

28. <u>Currently</u> there are at least four movies playing that deserve the Academy Award.
    (A) downtown
    (B) at the present time
    (C) at the local theater
    (D) frequently

29. The embarrassed young mother <u>admonished</u> her children for having taken the candy from the grocery shelf.
    (A) spanked
    (B) reminded
    (C) rebuked
    (D) hit

30. The dental work made a <u>profound</u> change in her appearance.
    (A) thorough
    (B) provocative
    (C) proper
    (D) interesting

31. The Browns were in a <u>dilemma</u> about whether to buy a house in the country or an apartment in the city where they worked.
    (A) predicament
    (B) discussion
    (C) agreement
    (D) stage

32. <u>Tempestuous</u> times preceded the declaration of war.
    (A) terrible
    (B) turbulent
    (C) trying
    (D) temperate

33. Citizens who <u>collaborated</u> with the enemy during the war were executed after the war.
    (A) resisted
    (B) fought
    (C) lost
    (D) cooperated

34. A <u>versatile</u> material for home construction is wood.
    (A) variable
    (B) durable
    (C) inflammable
    (D) common

35. Current laws protect <u>wildlife</u> from useless slaughter.
    (A) undomesticated animals
    (B) birds
    (C) nature
    (D) predators

36. Her refusal to go out with him <u>infuriated</u> him.
    (A) saddened
    (B) intoxicated
    (C) angered
    (D) frightened

37. Participation in <u>intramural</u> sports is required.
    (A) within the school
    (B) with outsiders
    (C) overly strenuous
    (D) extraordinary

38. On the <u>brink</u> of matrimony, he fled to a desert island.
    (A) ship
    (B) proposal
    (C) edge
    (D) evasion

39. The professor <u>elicited</u> a loud groan from his students with his difficult assignment.
    (A) eluded
    (B) heard
    (C) drew out
    (D) articulated

40. City dwellers are <u>exhilarated</u> by country air.
    (A) amazed   (C) humbled
    (B) fanned   (D) stimulated

41. Ponce de Leon searched for magic waters to <u>rejuvenate</u> the elderly.
    (A) make young again   (C) reject again
    (B) clean again   (D) stimulate again

42. Although they had never met before the party, Dick and Jane felt a strong <u>affinity</u> to each other.
    (A) affability   (C) dislike
    (B) attraction   (D) interest

43. A person who suffers from stage fright is easily <u>intimidated</u> by a large audience.
    (A) inspired   (C) frightened
    (B) applauded   (D) expelled

44. Every other woman at the premiere was envious of the star's <u>ostentacious</u> display of her emeralds.
    (A) wealthy   (C) oscillating
    (B) loud   (D) showy

45. Young people often <u>dispense with</u> the traditional ceremonies of marriage.
    (A) engage upon   (C) destroy
    (B) unite   (D) omit

Directions: The rest of this test is based on a variety of reading material (single sentences, paragraphs, and the like). For questions 46–90, you are to choose the *one* best answer, (A), (B), (C), or (D), to each question. Then, on your answer sheet, find the number of the question and blacken the space that corresponds to the letter of the answer you have chosen.

Answer all questions following a passage on the basis of what is *stated* or *implied* in that passage.

Read the following passage.

> The shares of the apartment corporation are offered under this plan only to individuals over 18 years of age. Non-individual tenants in occupancy of apartments on the date of presentation of the plan may designate an individual to purchase the shares allocated to such apartment, provided that such individual proposes to purchase the shares for his own account and not as a nominee of any corporation, partnership, association, trust, estate, or foreign government.

Example 1:
  To what does this passage refer?
  (A) employment wanted
  (B) apartment to share
  (C) a real estate partnership
  (D) sale of an apartment to a non-tenant

You should choose answer (D), because the passage says tenants in occupancy may designate an individual to purchase the shares allocated to the apartment.

Example 2:
    The passage says the apartment may not be sold to
    (A) a corporation   (C) the British Embassy
    (B) a person under 18   (D) all of the above

You should choose (D), because the passage prohibits sale to foreign governments (the British Embassy, for example) and (A) and (B) as well.

Questions 46–53 are related to this passage.

Yeast is one of nature's most perfect foods, since it contains more nutrients than any other food. B vitamins, choline, inositol, protein, amino acids—yeast has them all. Indisputably, liver and wheat germ are a prime source of protein and B vitamins. But how many people like the taste of liver or wheat germ? For that matter, yeast has a bitter taste, and not many people relish eating it. That's all in the past now. Tasty Mix Yeast Treat, blended with your favorite beverage, tastes so good that children will be clamoring for more. Be creative and add Tasty Mix to your favorite meat or vegetable dish, casserole, bread, soup, practically anything. Easy, convenient Tasty Mix Yeast Treat is one of nature's unique foods. Take advantage of it now. You can find it at any health food store or at your local supermarket.

46. You can infer that this passage can be found in
    (A) a brochure at a health food store
    (B) a health textbook
    (C) a Japanese restaurant
    (D) a TV guide

47. This passage implies that
    (A) there are substitutes equal to yeast in nutrition
    (B) yeast tastes better than liver
    (C) wheat germ doesn't have as much nutrition as liver
    (D) this product will give you more nutrients than any other source

48. According to the passage, wheat germ, liver, and ordinary yeast
    (A) appeal to most people   (C) taste awful
    (B) contain choline and inositol   (D) blend with your favorite drink

49. Tasty Mix Yeast Treat is
    (A) a mixture of tasty yeast in powder form
    (B) an old product on the market for years
    (C) bitter and inedible
    (D) pleasant tasting mixed with other foods

50. You can infer that Tasty Mix Yeast Treat is unique because
    (A) it's readily available
    (B) it contains so much nutrition
    (C) of its good taste and nutritional value
    (D) liver and wheat germ are nutritious foods too

51. You can infer that Tasty Mix Yeast Treat is
    (A) a specialty store product   (C) sold at some health food stores
    (B) a mail order product   (D) easy to obtain

52. Tasty Mix Yeast Treat
    (A) tastes bitter
    (B) is tasteless
    (C) can be combined with many foods
    (D) is creative

53. This passage is
    (A) a classified advertisement   (C) a product advertisement
    (B) a help wanted advertisement   (D) a nutrition description

Questions 54–61 are related to this passage.

Every five years the House Interior Committee reviews the effects of the Strip-Mine Control and Reclamation Act. The time is here. Opposing sides have mustered their forces: James Watt, Secretary of the Interior, and James Harris, Director of the Office of Surface Mining, versus at least six conservationist groups, whose most outspoken proponent is John Seiberling, an Ohio Democrat in the House. Mr. Seiberling denounced Secretary Watt for his efforts to rewrite the federal regulations restraining strip-mining and suggested that "it is one more example of the fox being put in the henhouse to guard the chickens." If Watt succeeds with his revisions of the hard-won legislation, our national parks will be open to strip-mining, and some of the greatest glories of nature will be lost forever.

54. You can infer that the author of this passage
    (A) favors strip-mining
    (B) sides with the conservationists
    (C) has no interest in the strip-mining controversy
    (D) is impartial in discussing this subject

55. The House Interior Committee will review the effects of the Strip-Mine Control and Reclamation Act
    (A) in five years
    (B) after the conservationists concur with the act
    (C) when Watt resigns
    (D) now

56. In the strip-mining controversy
    (A) conservationists and Watt are on the same side
    (B) Watt and Harris are opposed to the House Interior Committee
    (C) Seiberling and the mining companies are united
    (D) groups like the Audubon Society and the National Wildlife Society oppose Watt and Harris

57. The adage "the fox put in the henhouse to guard the chickens" means that
    (A) conservationists protect the land from destruction
    (B) a fox can be trained to be a protector of chickens
    (C) a fox is a natural enemy of chickens, so he is the last one to rely on to protect them
    (D) chickens need a protector like a fox

58. You can infer that strip-mining
    (A) conserves the land   (C) fertilizes the land
    (B) protects the land   (D) disfigures the land

59. What is the subject of this passage?
    (A) the fight to pass the strip-mining law
    (B) the opposition of conservationists to the Secretary of the Interior's proposals to change the existing strip-mining law
    (C) the need for committee hearings on the subject of whether or not to continue with the old law or to change it.
    (D) the denouncing of one official by another

60. Which of the following was *not* a cause of dissension in this passage?
    (A) The old law is good, and proposed changes are bad.
    (B) Strip-mining will ruin national parks.
    (C) The Secretary of the Interior is revising strip-mining regulations.
    (D) The Secretary of the Interior is expected to protect the land from defacement and pollution.

61. It can be inferred that opponents of the Secretary of the Interior hope to
    (A) keep national parks open to the public
    (B) establish new regulations
    (C) uphold the old regulations
    (D) prevent his promotion

Questions 62–64 refer to this passage.
  The federal government is beginning to crack down on college graduates who default on their federally insured school loans. In Philadelphia this week, federal officers impounded thirteen cars, including a Jaguar and a Lincoln, belonging to some of the 500 people in that section of the state who have failed to respond to lending institutions' requests for payment.

62. You can infer that the owner of the Jaguar
    (A) was a good financial risk
    (B) paid for his car with a government loan
    (C) could have repaid his loan
    (D) was destitute

63. You can infer that the federal government is pursuing
    (A) people's cars
    (B) 500 loan defaulters
    (C) people who fail to repay college loans nationwide
    (D) loan defaulters in eastern Pennsylvania

64. You can infer that if graduates don't repay their loans, the federal government
    (A) will repay the lending institutions
    (B) will try to get the value of the loans from the borrowers
    (C) will probably discontinue its support of the college loan program
    (D) all of the above

Questions 65–69 relate to this passage.
  Disney World was constructed a decade ago on 27,400 acres of partially swamp land in central Florida. Eight thousand of these acres constitute a wildlife sanctuary not accessible to the 130 million people from around the world who have been to Disney World since its opening.

The park opens at 9 A.M. and shuts down at various hours, depending upon the time of year—six, nine, or midnight. On a busy day as many as 90,000 visitors may be in the park, but there are so many activities available that there is plenty of room for everybody. The Magic Kingdom is the main section, but there are hotels, restaurants, a lagoon, and a huge lake with four and a half miles of beaches where visitors swim or paddle around in rented boats. A reasonable estimate of the cost per person daily is about $60, excluding transportation costs to Orlando.

65. Disney World was opened
   (A) last year
   (B) currently
   (C) ten years ago
   (D) a decent time ago

66. Disney World has many water attractions because
   (A) the Florida climate is conducive to water sports
   (B) it was built on wet land
   (C) visitors like to swim and rent boats
   (D) they are a lucrative business

67. You can infer that there are 90,000 visitors in Disney World
   (A) daily during the holidays like Thanksgiving and Christmas
   (B) weekly when the park is busy
   (C) normally when the weather is pleasant
   (D) daily throughout the year

68. The average daily cost for a family of four might be
   (A) $60
   (B) $240
   (C) an unlimited amount
   (D) dependent upon transportation costs

69. You can infer that when there are 90,000 people in the park
   (A) people have to wait in lines to get into the attractions
   (B) there are not enough restaurants to feed all of them
   (C) the lake shore is too small to accommodate swimmers
   (D) the best thing to do is to rent a boat to get away from the crowds

Questions 70–74 relate to this passage.

It has been said that to turn a corner in Toledo is to enter another century. The city is a rich blend of the cultures that occupied it after a series of invasions. Strategically nearly impregnable, Toledo is located in the center of Spain and is encircled by the Tagus River. Roman rule lasted 300 years and saw the development of the Spanish language. Having defeated the Romans, the Visigoths established their capital at Toledo and brought Christianity to the city's citizens.

It was the conquest of Toledo in the eighth century by the Moors that created the most dramatic and lasting effects upon the city. Moorish arts and architecture embellished the once predominantly military fortress. Mosques, mansions, and towers were built to last, so they remain to impress the visitor to Toledo with their opulence to this day.

Medieval Toledo sheltered a compatible mixture of Christians, Moslems, and Jews. Scholars from all three religious groups collaborated to make the School of Translators famous throughout Europe for its Aristotelian philosophy.

70. You can infer that if you turn four corners in Toledo, you will
    (A) find four different cultures
    (B) find yourself on the banks of the Tagus River
    (C) see Moorish architecture
    (D) discover relics of 400 years

71. Christianity was brought to Toledo by the
    (A) Romans   (C) Visigoths
    (B) Spanish kings   (D) Moors

72. What kinds of buildings for religious worship would you find in Toledo?
    (A) cathedrals, mosques, and synagogues
    (B) vicarages, churches, and synagogues
    (C) synagogues, spires, and monasteries
    (D) temples, fortresses, and mosques

73. What invader of Toledo left the most lasting impression upon the city's style of building?
    (A) the Romans   (C) the Jews
    (B) Spanish kings   (D) the Moors

74. You can infer from the fact that the School of Translators had scholars from three very different religious groups that
    (A) religious tolerance existed in Toledo for some time
    (B) religious persecution was common in Toledo
    (C) Aristotelian philosophy made scholars logical
    (D) translators were needed to expound their teachings

Questions 75–77 are related to this passage.

  Studies of playground equipment have revealed that of 93,000 injuries sustained in playgrounds and treated in hospital emergency rooms, 21,300 involved metal swings. The Parks Department plans to replace metal swings with rubber-belt swings in several parks to test their durability. The rubber-belt swings will be not only safer but cheaper than the old metal equipment.

75. Swing injuries accounted for
    (A) about 23% of documented playground accidents
    (B) half of the playground accidents treated in hospitals
    (C) a small part of the large number of playground accidents
    (D) all of the playground injuries treated in hospitals

76. The reason for the Parks Department's replacement of metal swings with rubber-belted swings is that
    (A) metal swings are more expensive
    (B) metal swings are hazardous
    (C) rubber-belted swings are cheap
    (D) metal swings are more durable

77. The newer-style swings will appear
    (A) in all of the city's parks
    (B) in only a few parks
    (C) when the old swings wear out
    (D) when the number of accidents increases

Questions 78–80 are related to this passage.

One of the multitude of theories about how our world will end is that in a few billion years the sun will burn itself out. First, however, its supply of hydrogen fuel will give out, leaving it a mammoth red star sending out 100 times more energy than it does now. The planets surrounding the sun will become incredibly hot. Earth will heat up, oceans will boil, and ultimately life on earth will end. The cooling sun will then become a tiny, weak star.

78. The American poet who compared the end of the world to "fire and ice" was
    (A) ignorant of the theories of the end of the world
    (B) knowledgeable about the theories of the end of the world
    (C) a very imaginative writer
    (D) a space scientist

79. When the sun's hydrogen supply fails, the sun will
    (A) burn itself up
    (B) turn red
    (C) burn up its neighboring planets
    (D) all of the above

80. The end of the world is expected
    (A) within the author's lifetime
    (B) when the sun turns to ice
    (C) billions of years from now
    (D) when earth runs out of hydrogen

Questions 81–85 relate to this passage.

From the eleventh to the thirteenth centuries, Christians made eight expeditions to wrest the Holy Land from the Saracens. Of all the crusades, the Children's Crusade was the most pitiful. In 1212 Stephen, a shepherd boy, led 30,000 children who were twelve years old and under. Thousands died as a result of shipwreck and exhaustion. Five shiploads were sold into slavery. Another group of 20,000 led by a German boy, Nicholas, met the same fate a few years later.

81. You can infer that the Children's Crusade
    (A) was led by adults
    (B) succeeded where the adults' crusades had failed
    (C) accomplished nothing at all
    (D) conquered the Saracens

82. The number of children involved in the Children's Crusade was estimated to be
    (A) 30,000
    (B) 20,000
    (C) 5,000
    (D) none of the above

83. The crusades lasted
    (A) until 1212
    (B) until the Children's Crusade
    (C) until the Saracens were defeated
    (D) about 200 years

84. The crusade led by a German boy was
    (A) as great a failure as the first boy's crusade
    (B) considered more successful than the other crusades
    (C) sold into slavery
    (D) eight years in duration

85. Stephen's Crusade was
    (A) a great success
    (B) in the early thirteenth century
    (C) against slavery
    (D) the most pitiful

Questions 86–88 refer to this passage.

The government of China has announced that consumers may soon purchase television sets and other expensive items on the installment plan. No interest will be charged when the plan is initiated. However, should the necessity arise, interest payments may be added later. If the price of the item increases, consumers will pay the original price. If the price decreases, they will pay the cheaper rate.

86. Based upon the information in this passage, you may infer that the
    (A) Chinese buy most of their products on the installment plan
    (B) installment plan is managed by the government
    (C) installment plan will be an innovation in China
    (D) installment plan will decrease prices in China

87. Installment payments will be interest free
    (A) forever
    (B) for the moment
    (C) for the next year
    (D) for the original price

88. A television set bought on the installment plan at a specified price may
    (A) increase, so the cost would increase
    (B) be more expensive
    (C) need necessary repairs
    (D) cost less by the time the payments are concluded

Questions 89–90. For each of these questions, choose the answer that is *closest in meaning* to the original sentence. Note that several of the choices may be factually correct, but you should choose the one that is the *closest restatement of the given sentence.*

89. Faith in human reason and science as a source of truth and a means to improve the environment was bolstered by scientific discoveries in spite of theological opposition.
    (A) Theological opposition made people lose faith in human reason and science as a source of truth and a means to improve the environment.
    (B) Even though the church opposed science, people continued to believe in human reason and science as a source of truth and a means to improve the environment.
    (C) Scientific discoveries supported people's faith in science and reason as a source of truth and a means to improve their lives, and the church agreed.
    (D) People's faith in reason and science was diminished by church opposition and scientific discoveries.

90. After Paris, Montreal is the largest French-speaking capital in the world.
    (A) Montreal is the largest French-speaking city in the world.
    (B) Paris is the second largest French-speaking capital in the world.
    (C) Montreal has the second highest number of French-speaking people among the world's capitals.
    (D) The capitals of the world include French-speaking people in Paris and Montreal.

READING COMPREHENSION AND VOCABULARY PRACTICE TEST C
Time—65 Minutes

This test is designed to measure your ability to understand various kinds of reading materials, as well as your ability to understand the meaning and use of words. There are two types of questions in this section, with special directions for each type.

Directions: In questions 1–45 each sentence has a word or phrase underlined. Below each sentence are four other words or phrases, marked (A), (B), (C), and (D). You are to choose the *one* word or phrase that *best keeps the meaning* of the original sentence if it is substituted for the underlined word or phrase. Then, on your answer sheet, find the number of the question and blacken the space that corresponds to the letter you have chosen so that the letter inside the oval cannot be seen.

Example:
He talked so fast that I couldn't <u>comprehend</u> what he said.
(A) hear
(B) translate
(C) understand
(D) repeat

The best answer is (C), *understand,* because logically you would not understand fast speech. You could *hear* him. No mention is made of his speaking in a foreign language, so *translate* is not a likely answer. *Repeat* is out of the question in this context.
When you understand the directions, begin work on the vocabulary problems.

1. The cure for alcoholism is complete <u>abstinence</u> from alcohol.
(A) absence
(B) avoidance
(C) sickness
(D) prescription

2. Savage hordes swept across Europe and <u>ruthlessly</u> killed all in their path.
(A) without stopping
(B) without weapons
(C) without warning
(D) without pity

3. Many of the <u>habitats</u> of birds and plants have been destroyed by man's pollution.
(A) nests
(B) forests
(C) natural homes
(D) grounds

4. Children have a <u>jargon</u> of their own that their elders frequently don't understand.
   (A) unintelligible talk   (C) strange gait
   (B) exercise plan   (D) sign language

5. The UN delegates lived in <u>temporary</u> housing until their apartment house was constructed.
   (A) timely   (C) limited time
   (B) temperate   (D) temporizing

6. Chinese <u>cuisine</u> specializes in rice dishes.
   (A) delicacies   (C) chefs
   (B) cooking   (D) gourmets

7. It was <u>inevitable</u> that women would be sent into space along with men.
   (A) unlikely   (C) influential
   (B) fantastic   (D) unavoidable

8. One of the <u>superstitions</u> related to weddings is that the bride should wear something blue.
   (A) rules of conduct   (C) nuptials
   (B) irrational beliefs   (D) religious ceremonies

9. The Industrial Revolution <u>effected</u> a drastic change in the British standard of living in the 18th century.
   (A) caused   (C) prevented
   (B) eliminated   (D) denied

10. The colonists made a <u>vehement</u> protest against taxation without representation.
    (A) veiled   (C) violent
    (B) verified   (D) voracious

11. Whenever I have to make a speech, the minute I stand up on the <u>dais</u> I forget every word.
    (A) front   (C) soap box
    (B) feet   (D) platform

12. Food manufacturers must <u>label</u> their products with content information.
    (A) sell   (C) brand
    (B) describe   (D) stick on

13. After camping in the wilderness for two weeks, he was so <u>unkempt</u> that his wife was horrified.
    (A) untidy   (C) ferocious
    (B) ugly   (D) undone

14. Two small toy manufacturers <u>consolidated</u> to form a new business.
    (A) advertised   (C) divided
    (B) united   (D) met

15. His wife's <u>extravagant</u> tastes put him in debt.
   (A) excessive
   (B) extraordinary
   (C) exclusive
   (D) exciting

16. After her husband's death, Mrs. Brown spent several <u>melancholy</u> years alone in their apartment.
   (A) tired
   (B) lonely
   (C) brief
   (D) sad

17. Because he swam too fast at the beginning of the race, he lost his <u>stamina</u> early.
   (A) vigor
   (B) place
   (C) stand
   (D) stroke

18. If you stay on this diet, <u>ultimately</u> you will lost weight.
   (A) formerly
   (B) finally
   (C) unlikely
   (D) possibly

19. He studied so <u>zealously</u> that he graduated from college first in his class.
   (A) lazily
   (B) ardently
   (C) happily
   (D) dispassionately

20. His physical condition was no <u>impediment</u> to his career as a violinist.
   (A) help
   (B) impatience
   (C) hindrance
   (D) impossibility

21. You <u>ought</u> to read the directions carefully before you begin the problems.
   (A) may
   (B) might
   (C) should
   (D) can

22. An author in the <u>throes</u> of creation hates to be interrupted.
   (A) struggle
   (B) study
   (C) wake
   (D) theater

23. A diabetic has to <u>forswear</u> sugar in his diet.
   (A) renounce
   (B) foresee
   (C) inject
   (D) curse

24. Chicago became <u>notorious</u> for crime and corruption during the days of Prohibition.
   (A) disrupted
   (B) evil
   (C) known
   (D) criminal

25. The course of studies is <u>geared</u> to an urban population.
   (A) driven
   (B) adjusted
   (C) apparent
   (D) tried

26. Physical infirmity often makes people <u>querulous</u> and hard to live with.
   (A) fretful
   (B) weak
   (C) indignant
   (D) poor

27. A French restaurant is a favorite <u>rendezvous</u> for lovers.
   (A) hidden retreat
   (B) hiding place
   (C) meeting place
   (D) dining room

28. The ship <u>foundered</u> on the rocks during the hurricane.
   (A) established
   (B) struck
   (C) failed
   (D) sank

29. The Salk vaccine has had a <u>potent</u> effect upon the incidence of polio.
   (A) potential
   (B) powerful
   (C) praiseworthy
   (D) priceless

30. At the age of ninety, she had <u>regressed</u> to infancy.
   (A) remembered
   (B) alluded
   (C) returned
   (D) progressed

31. Americans were <u>appalled</u> by the latest statistics regarding unemployment.
   (A) surprised
   (B) informed
   (C) dismayed
   (D) pleased

32. John blamed his poor grades this semester upon his having participated in too many <u>extracurricular</u> activities.
   (A) frivolous and additional
   (B) athletic and vigorous
   (C) outside the curriculum
   (D) inattentive to studies

33. <u>Furthermore</u>, I feel that his behavior is upsetting the entire classroom.
   (A) Nevertheless
   (B) However
   (C) In spite of this
   (D) In addition

34. I <u>infer</u> from his statements that he has no intention of paying the bill.
   (A) conclude
   (B) intrude
   (C) imply
   (D) hear

35. <u>Toxic</u> waste from nuclear plants is hazardous to the environment.
   (A) troublesome
   (B) poisonous
   (C) grievous
   (D) panic

36. As she aged, she became more <u>garrulous</u>.
   (A) talkative
   (B) gracious
   (C) sickly
   (D) grey

37. Obviously Helen's <u>forte</u> is chemistry.
   (A) fortitude
   (B) talent
   (C) weakness
   (D) fixation

38. That the government ought to develop a jobs program seemed to Congress an <u>indisputable</u> fact.
   (A) indefinite
   (B) indispensable
   (C) unquestionable
   (D) undefinable

39. The electrician was <u>scrupulous</u> about grounding all the wires in the factory.
   (A) afraid
   (B) employed
   (C) careful
   (D) infamous

40. The <u>interment</u> took place last Friday.
    (A) festivity
    (B) installation
    (C) launching
    (D) burial

41. We all have <u>pecadillos</u> that our intimate friends tolerate.
    (A) small faults
    (B) bad habits
    (C) minorities
    (D) foul language

42. Her disapproval was <u>implicit</u> in her response to his behavior.
    (A) implicated
    (B) important
    (C) implied
    (D) impious

43. All of the President's efforts to <u>rescind</u> the law were unavailing.
    (A) revive
    (B) change
    (C) repeal
    (D) rescue

44. Years of deprivation only made the rebels more <u>vindictive</u>.
    (A) vindicated
    (B) troublesome
    (C) weak
    (D) revengeful

45. In the <u>interim</u> between performances, the famous actress toured Europe.
    (A) interval
    (B) interception
    (C) interaction
    (D) insertion

Directions: The rest of this test is based on a variety of reading material (single sentences, paragraphs, and the like). In questions 46–90, you are to choose the *one* best answer, (A), (B), (C), or (D), to each question. Then, on your answer sheet, find the number of the question and blacken the space that corresponds to the letter of the answer you have chosen.

Answer all questions following a passage on the basis of what is *stated* or *implied* in that passage.

Read the following passage.

The shares of the apartment corporation are offered under this plan only to individuals over 18 years of age. Non-individual tenants in occupancy of apartments on the date of presentation of the plan may designate an individual to purchase the shares allocated to such apartment, provided that such individual proposes to purchase the shares for his own account and not as a nominee of any corporation, partnership, association, trust, estate, or foreign government.

Example 1:
To what does this passage refer?
(A) employment wanted
(B) apartment to share
(C) a real estate partnership
(D) sale of an apartment to a non-tenant

You should choose answer (D), because the passage says tenants in occupancy may designate an individual to purchase the shares allocated to the apartment.

Example 2:
The passage says the apartment may not be sold to
(A) a corporation
(B) a person under 18
(C) the British Embassy
(D) all of the above

You should choose (D), because the passage prohibits sale to foreign governments (the British Embassy, for example) and (A) and (B) as well.

Questions 46–48 are related to this passage.

Three years ago a group of women began a legal fight with the New York City Fire Department. They contended that a physical examination required to make them eligible to be firefighters was unfair. The test stressed strength, speed, and agility. The test has been revised. Prospective firewomen have to show they can drag an 80-pound hose, climb ladders and stairs, lift a 145-pound dummy, and excel in similar activities.

46. You can infer that women firefighters
    (A) have lost their legal battle
    (B) have to be in top physical condition
    (C) are not equal to men firefighters
    (D) revised the test

47. The author implies that the new test
    (A) is less difficult to pass than the old test
    (B) is probably as difficult to pass as the old test
    (C) does not test women's abilities at all
    (D) will probably be discontinued

48. The women candidates probably thought the test unfair because
    (A) they didn't want to take it
    (B) they believe in women's liberation
    (C) it was impossible for them to pass it
    (D) speed, agility, and strength are attributes of men only

Questions 49–54 are related to this passage.

Sloths are bizarre little beasts that are, above all, slothful. Prone to sleep ten to twenty hours a day, a sloth settles in for its daily rest at the top of a leafy tree, far from any famished predators on the ground. There the sloth makes his home, furnished with branches both for clinging and eating. A voracious vegetarian, this wild animal weighs in at about twenty pounds if it has three toes and at about ten pounds if it has two toes. There are only two genera of sloth, but each has characteristics other than the number of its toes to distinguish it from the other. The three-toed variety refuses to exist away from the wild, whereas the two-toed type has been resident in zoos and has thrived. The three-toed sloth is so slow and sleepy that it won't even take the trouble to defend itself. The two-toed fellow will attack with its hook and teeth if threatened. Both types, by definition, move so slowly as they drag their bellies along the ground that they make a tortoise look like Jesse Owens in comparison.

49. You may infer that the meaning of the word *slothful* is
    (A) vegetarian   (C) lazy
    (B) wild   (D) tree dwelling

50. A sloth's diet consists of
    (A) other sloths   (C) a variety of things
    (B) predators   (D) leaves

51. The sloth drags its belly on the ground, you can infer, because it
    (A) is too tired to do otherwise
    (B) is hunting for insects to eat
    (C) is concealing itself from other animals
    (D) has few toes

52. A three-toed sloth, when attacked,
    (A) fights back viciously
    (B) puts up a weak defense
    (C) ignores the opponent
    (D) acts like a tortoise

53. Of the two types of sloth, the two-toed variety is
    (A) more vicious
    (B) sleepier
    (C) bigger
    (D) hungrier

54. The author's purpose in comparing a tortoise to Jesse Owens, an Olympic runner who won four gold medals, is to
    (A) show how fast Owens was
    (B) show how slow a turtle is
    (C) show how slow a sloth is
    (D) compare the speeds of a tortoise, a man, and a wild animal

Questions 55–56 relate to this passage.
The Independence National Historical Park is a perennial favorite of Americans in search of their roots. Here in Philadelphia they pay homage to that resolute conclave of colonists who collaborated to declare their nation independent.

55. The reason Americans go to Independence National Historical Park is that
    (A) Philadelphia is an interesting city
    (B) here the United States began
    (C) Americans fought the Revolution here
    (D) they want to declare their independence

56. Philadelphia is a landmark because
    (A) colonists met to declare independence here
    (B) a group of men rejected Britain rule
    (C) it is a perennial favorite of Americans
    (D) all of the above

Questions 57–60 relate to this passage.
It is a measure of how far the Keynesian revolution has proceeded that the central thesis of the "General Theory" now sounds rather commonplace. Until it appeared, economists had assumed that the economy, if left to itself, would find its equilibrium at full employment. Increases or decreases in wages and interest rates would occur as necessary to bring about this pleasant result. If people were unemployed, their wages would fall in relation to prices. With lower wages and wider margins, it would be profitable to employ those from whose toil an adequate return could not previously have been made. It followed that steps to keep wages at artificially high levels, such as might result from the ill-considered efforts by unions, would cause unemployment. Such efforts were deemed to be the principal cause of unemployment.

57. The author's purpose in this passage is to
    (A) describe the Keynesian revolution
    (B) say what the central thesis of the "General Theory" is
    (C) give the theory economists had before Keynes
    (D) explain causes of unemployment

58. You can infer that the Keynesian revolution was
    (A) an armed conflict
    (B) a complete change in economic theory
    (C) a new way of government
    (D) an upheaval in labor and management

59. Before Keynes, economists believed that decreases in interest rates and wages would result in
    (A) unemployment
    (B) a depression
    (C) higher prices for goods
    (D) total employment

60. Before Keynes, economists believed in
    (A) letting the economy develop without interference
    (B) providing welfare for the unemployed
    (C) preventing unions from demanding high wages
    (D) increasing wages to get better profits

Questions 61–64 are related to this passage.

The Educational Testing Service claims that the Scholastic Aptitude Test is not a measurement of students' accomplishments in mathematics and language. It is a test of students' aptitude for learning. Educators disagree and have devised a new program for preparing students to take the SAT.

The program covers the basic high school curriculum with workbooks, videotapes, and a computer program. Whether or not the program is sold to prepare students for college entrance exams or to add to their subject matter achievement is beside the point. Every student should master the skills emphasized in the program.

61. You can infer that the teachers who devised the new program think the SAT
    (A) measures students' aptitude for learning
    (B) measures students' grasp of mathematical and verbal skills
    (C) measures students' mastery of subject matter
    (D) all of the above

62. The author feels that this program
    (A) will not help students do well on the SAT
    (B) will be outdated shortly
    (C) cannot fail to help students, whatever they do
    (D) cannot teach aptitude for intellectual pursuits

63. This program would probably be bought by
    (A) colleges
    (B) individuals
    (C) professors
    (D) high schools

64. This new study program is supported by
    (A) students
    (B) teachers
    (C) the Educational Testing Service
    (D) the high school curriculum

Questions 65–69 are related to this passage.

Statistics regarding cigarette smoking are anything but encouraging. The Federal Trade Commission recently announced that in 1980 Americans purchased 628.2 billion cigarettes, an appallingly greater number than ever before. The average smoker consumed 11,633 cigarettes, of which 44.8 percent were low-tar cigarettes containing less than 15 milligrams of tar. In 1968 the average tar content was 22 milligrams.

Despite the fact that every cigarette pack has a printed warning from the Surgeon General, those who still smoke are smoking more heavily. Many people have forsworn smoking in fear of lung cancer. The American Cancer Society reports that death rates from lung cancer have escalated, whereas those for other major cancers have leveled off or declined. Last year 111,000 Americans died of lung cancer, while it is estimated that 117,000 will succumb this year. Lung cancer heads the list in killing 35 percent of males who die from cancer. Lung cancer accounts for 17 percent of women's cancer deaths. An estimated 440,000 deaths from cancer will occur this year, 9,000 more than the previous year. Lung cancer accounts for two thirds of the increase. Although many cancer patients have survived the disease, the prognosis for lung cancer patients is most disheartening. Ninety-one percent of all diagnosed cases of lung cancer do not survive.

65. You may infer that low-tar cigarettes
    (A) reduce the dangers of smoking
    (B) appeal to a majority of smokers
    (C) cause lung cancer
    (D) have the Surgeon General's approval

66. Statistics show average smokers smoke
    (A) less than they did in the past
    (B) more than they did in the past
    (C) the same as they did in the past
    (D) none of the above

67. It is predicted that the number of deaths from lung cancer this year will be
    (A) reduced from the number last year
    (B) the same as the number last year
    (C) 6,000 more than last year
    (D) 111,000

68. The percentage of women's lung cancer deaths is
    (A) equal to that of men's lung cancer deaths
    (B) rising annually
    (C) about half the percentage of men's cancer deaths
    (D) an indication that women are not susceptible to lung cancer

69. You may infer from the passage that lung cancer
    (A) can be treated effectively
    (B) is always related to smoking
    (C) will cause cigarettes to be taken off the market
    (D) currently has no infallible cure

Questions 70–72 are related to this passage.

The Agricultural Bank of North Orange received an extortion note demanding that $50,000 be placed in a garbage can at the rear of the building at 4 P.M. the following day. Advocating compliance with their demands lest "a fatal accident" ensue, the robbers warned the bank not to call in the police. The note was signed "The Rattlesnakes."

To the profound surprise of the members of the police surveillance team, at exactly 4 o'clock the next day three children roller-skated up the alley behind the bank and opened the garbage pail. The three children, two of whom were eight years old and one eleven, took the police to their leader, an eleven-year-old boy who was convinced that his plot would succeed. It nearly had. The police indisputably had taken the note seriously and had expected a gang of innovative robbers or terrorists. Punishment for the plotters was left to their parents' discretion. The "brains" of the mob was confined to his home and forbidden to watch television until the end of the summer.

70. The police believed that the extortion note was
    (A) written by a child   (C) genuine
    (B) a joke   (D) ridiculous

71. The boy who planned the robbery
    (A) didn't think it would succeed
    (B) thought his friends would get in trouble
    (C) was put in jail
    (D) thought he would get the $50,000

72. You may infer that the idea for the robbery came from
    (A) the boy's father   (C) television
    (B) the boy's companions   (D) a terrorist's diary

Questions 73–77 relate to this passage.

Scientists claim that air pollution causes a decline in the world's average air temperature. In order to prove that theory, ecologists have turned to historical data in relation to especially huge volcanic eruptions. They suspect that volcanoes effect weather changes that are similar to air pollution.

One source of information is the effect of the eruption of Tambora, a volcano in Sumbawa, the Dutch East Indies, in April 1815. The largest recorded volcanic eruption, Tambora threw 150 million tons of fine ash into the stratosphere. The ash from a volcano spreads worldwide in a few days and remains in the air for years. Its effect is to turn incoming solar radiation into space and thus cool the earth. For example, records of weather in England show that between April and November 1815, the average temperature had fallen 4.5°F. During the next twenty-four months, England suffered one of the coldest periods of its history. Farmers' records from April 1815 to December 1818 indicate frost throughout the spring and summer and sharp decreases in crop and livestock markets. Since there was a time lag of several years between cause and effect, by the time the world agricultural commodity community had deteriorated, no one realized the cause.

Ecologists today warn that we face a twofold menace. The ever-present possibility of volcanic eruptions, such as that of Mt. St. Helens in Washington, added to man's pollution of the atmosphere with oil, gas, coal, and other polluting substances, may bring us increasingly colder weather.

73. It is believed that the earth gets colder when
    (A) volcanoes erupt
    (B) the air is polluted by modern man
    (C) the rays of the sun are turned into space
    (D) all of the above

74. The effects of Tambora's eruption were
    (A) felt mainly in the Dutch East Indies
    (B) of several days' duration worldwide
    (C) evidence of pollution's cooling the earth
    (D) immediately evident to the world's scientists

75. The cause of cold weather in England from 1815 to 1818 was
    (A) decreased crop and livestock production
    (B) volcanic ash in the atmosphere
    (C) pollution caused by the Industrial Revolution
    (D) its proximity to the North Sea

76. No one realized the cause of the deterioration of the world agricultural commodity market because
    (A) there was a long delay between cause and effect
    (B) the weather is beyond our comprehension
    (C) weather forecasts were inaccurate
    (D) ecologists didn't exist until modern times

77. If, as some scientists predict, the world ends in ice, what might be the cause?
    (A) modern man's pollution of the air
    (B) volcanic eruptions
    (C) obliteration of solar radiation
    (D) all of the above

Questions 78–82 relate to this passage.

The veterinarian and the psychologist have joined forces to redress the behavioral ills of dogs. Subject to the same emotional problems as their owners, dogs have increasingly developed neuroses formerly attributable to humans.

Dog owners frequently reveal their own egos in their choice of a pet. Haven't you seen many a huge dog taking a small person for a walk? The dog fits in with its owner's own frustrated feelings of aggression and power. Many lonely people find a dog a source of comfort—reliable, affectionate, and willing to listen. Child psychologists have turned to dogs for help. The child who rejects his or her peers or parents will treasure a dog and can be influenced by the psychologist who talks about the dog. Childless couples frequently select baby-sized dogs upon whom they lavish parental affection.

What happens to dogs that are burdened with owners who treat them like people? They behave like spoiled children. A dog whose owner feeds him on her lap refuses to eat from a bowl on the floor. A dog belonging to a childless couple for several years developed paralysis in its hind legs when they produced a real baby.

Endless are the examples of human neuroses suffered by our canine friends. The veterinarian/psychologist advises us to follow the advice of our child psychologist: Bring up our dogs with the same patience, love, and discipline we extend to our children.

78. Dogs resemble people in their inability to
    (A) work together
    (B) develop neuroses
    (C) live in confined spaces
    (D) cope with emotional changes

79. Dog owners reflect their own egos by selecting a dog that
    (A) is temperamentally similar to them
    (B) has characteristics they lack
    (C) will guard their property
    (D) resembles them in appearance

80. Child psychologists use dogs
    (A) as a means of establishing a rapport with a withdrawn child
    (B) as objects for experiments in human psychology
    (C) to train as they would train children
    (D) to make doctor visits more pleasant for children

81. You can infer that the dog that developed paralysis when its owners had a child was
    (A) struck by a disease of the nerves
    (B) affectionate toward the new baby
    (C) hit by a truck
    (D) neurotically jealous

82. The author suggests that the best way to bring up a dog is to
    (A) treat it like an animal
    (B) overindulge it
    (C) follow the rules of discipline
    (D) act as though it's a child

Questions 83–88 are related to this passage.

Botulism is a form of poisoning produced by a microorganism called *Clostridium botulinum*. The word *botulism* originated from the Latin word *botulus* for sausage, in which botulism was first identified. The spores created by *C. botulinum* are not harmful, as they grow in the soil and are consumed by us regularly when we eat vegetables and fruits. However, once the spores are put in airtight containers, the spores germinate and produce botulin, a deadly poison. Foods in cans and glass or plastic jars provide the environment botulin needs to grow. The spores are averse to low temperatures and will not develop in frozen food. Furthermore, they do not thrive in acidic, salty, sweet, or dry foods.

How can consumers protect themselves against botulism? Any can that is swollen at the top may be so because of pressure from gases produced by germinating spores. When opened, if the food sprays out of the can, the contents should be thrown out immediately. You should not taste it, since the tiniest bit could kill you. "If in doubt, throw it out" is the slogan to follow.

83. Botulism is a form of poisoning that
    (A) needs low temperatures to grow
    (B) is relatively harmless
    (C) is often fatal
    (D) is common

84. Botulism does *not* develop in
    (A) airtight containers
    (B) fresh vegetables
    (C) sausage
    (D) plastic jars

85. An indication of the presence of botulism may be
    (A) signs of food deterioration
    (B) a bad smell
    (C) a deformed can
    (D) an unpleasant taste

86. Which of the following foods may contain botulism?
    (A) dried beans
    (B) chocolate cookies
    (C) canned stringbeans
    (D) frozen hamburger

87. What should a consumer do with a can that has a raised top?
    (A) open it and taste the ingredients
    (B) put it in the garbage
    (C) take it back to the store where it was purchased
    (D) feed it to the cat

88. The name of this form of food poisoning comes from
    (A) germinating spores
    (B) airtight food containers
    (C) poisoned sausage
    (D) a warning slogan

Questions 89–90. For each of these questions, choose the answer that is *closest in meaning* to the original sentence. Note that several of the choices may be factually correct, but you should choose the one that is the *closest restatement of the given sentence.*

89. Deliberately causing small quakes in a fault area could release the pressure needed to cause a severe earthquake.
    (A) A severe earthquake builds up great pressure and deliberately causes small quakes in a fault area.
    (B) Small quakes in a fault area cause great pressure and a severe earthquake.
    (C) If man could create small quakes in a fault area, he could prevent a severe earthquake.
    (D) Small quakes in a fault area release pressure, so earthquakes are severe.

90. The history of wine coincides with the history of Western civilization.
    (A) The history of wine collided with Western civilization.
    (B) Western civilization relied on wine in history.
    (C) Wine and Western civilization developed together.
    (D) Without wine, Western civilization would not have developed.

WORD LIST

The following is a complete list of the vocabulary that is practiced in this book. The number after each word indicates the page number where the word first appears in an exercise. When you have finished the book, consult this list to verify that you have grasped all of the vocabulary.

abstinence, 37
absurd, 21
abuse, 106
access, 71
acclaim, 133
accompaniment, 79
accoutrements, 148
accrue, 29
accurate, 167
acquire, 106
acute, 44
adage, 6
adapt, 39
ad infinitum, 90
adjacent, 167
adjustment, 35
administer, 176
admonish, 122
adolescent, 111
adopt, 39
advent, 29
adverse, 39
advocate, 168
affable, 76
affinity, 73
affluent, 62
affront, 132
ailment, 76
alliance, 33
allot, 137
allusion, 39
alumna, alumnus, 90
ameliorate, 110
amenities, 62
amicable, 157
amiss, 148
amoral, 29
amphibian, 163
antagonist, 176

antedate, 29
anticipate, 76
antipathy, 29
apathy, 62
appall, 132
appease, 141
appendage, 99
aptitude, 89
ardent, 65
aromatic, 43
ascendancy, 156
assets, 75
atmospheric, 34
attract, 29
attribute, 143
audible, 6
augment, 86
augur, 172
aura, 44
autonomy, 155
averse, 39
aviary, 33
avid, 95
aware, 22
awkward, 99

bauble, 133
beautify, 34
bedroom, 22
beguile, 94
behave, 167
beset, 110
bête noire, 90
betray, 99
binoculars, 59
bipartisan, 59
bisect, 59
blizzard, 6
boom, 151

bounce, 120
boundary, 166
bountiful, 49
boycott, 132
brief, 78
bright, 113
brilliant, 95
brink, 37

cajole, 149
calculate, 167
callous, 136
capitulate, 133
captious, 100
carping, 100
carry on, 36
carte blanche, 90
catastrophic, 151
cede, 137
celebrate, 76
censorious, 100
centennial, 59
cessation, 84
chagrin, 62
chaos, 148
charlatan, 41
cheap, 123
chiropodist, 114
chivalrous, 148
chore, 84
chronology, 145
circumnavigate, 29
circumvent, 76
citrus, 108
clarify, 24
classified, 21
claustrophobia, 120
cliché, 90
clientele, 59

coalesce, 136
coin, 108
collaborate, 64
collate, 29
colossal, 148
combat, 81
comfortable, 35
commend, 72
commonwealth, 22
commuter, 120
compare, 106
compatible, 21
compete, 62
complacence, 33
complement, 40
complexity, 34
compliant, 29
compliment, 40
component, 81
comprehend, 34
concentrate, 81
concise, 81
conclave, 81
conclusively, 38
concoction, 81
concur, 81
conducive, 29
confer, 81
confide, 81
congenital, 81
connoisseur, 90
consensus, 84
consequent, 123
conservationist, 35
conservative, 58
consistent, 123
consolidate, 45
consternation, 130
consume, 45

224

contentment, 34
contrary, 29
controversy, 115
convivial, 43
coquette, 90
corpulent, 123
corrosion, 61
coterie, 59
council, 40
counsel, 40
coup de grace, 90
covenant, 133
cozy, 43
create, 167
crestfallen, 22
critical, 100
crucial, 175
cuisine, 43
culminate, 140
currently, 95
cynical, 100

dais, 110
damage, 106
dauntless, 89
deadlock, 22
debonair, 28
debris, 173
decade, 59
deceased, 71
deed, 71
default, 76
deficiency, 108
delete, 29
deliberately, 144
delusion, 39
demise, 163
dependent, 113
deplorable, 133
deprivation, 152
deputize, 72
dermatologist, 114
descend, 29
despite, 120
despondent, 152
detrimental, 117
destroy, 171
devastating, 166
devise, 94
diabolical, 136
dichotomy, 59
diet, 108

dilate, 29
dilemma, 28
dilettante, 90
diligent, 100
direct, 76
disaster, 166
disconcert, 54
disgruntled, 141
dispense with, 143
disperse, 29
disposal, 168
disreputable, 55
dissension, 176
dissolve, 37
distraught, 36
do the trick, 117
docile, 141
donate, 76
dormant, 175
double entendre, 90
drag, 99
dubious, 117
duet, 59

easygoing, 22
economical, 98
effect, 143
efficient, 61
elapse, 163
elderly, 22
electrify, 35
elicit, 29
eliminate, 123
élite, 90
embellish, 72
embryonic, 152
emigrate, 40
employer, 35
encroach, 171
enhance, 44
enigma, 95
ennui, 90
ensue, 64
entice, 99
environmentalist, 171
envisage, 176
epoch, 89
equitable, 76
escalate, 176
especially, 166
evasive, 101
evict, 137

exceed, 106
exclude, 22
exhilaration, 76
exit, 29
exotic, 43
expel, 79
expendable, 33
explicit, 40
express, 171
extracurricular, 29
extravagant, 49

fad, 123
fanatic, 15
fare, 76
faux pas, 90
feat, 89
fee, 21
felon, 117
ferocious, 38
fervor, 96
fiasco, 176
fierce, 79
fire, 37
fitness, 123
flamboyant, 59
flirtatious, 36
footloose, 22
foresee, 167
form, 167
formerly, 113
forswear, 37
forte, 90
forthcoming, 171
fossil, 162
founder, 37
frequently, 6
frivolity, 28
frugal, 100
furnace, 22
furthermore, 22
futility, 5

gap, 167
garrulous, 100
gauche, 26
geared, 53
glib, 28
godparent, 22
gourmand, 115
gourmet, 90
gracious, 34

grandparent, 22
grievous, 99
grudging, 100
gynecologist, 114

habitat, 86
halt, 127
handcuff, 22
havoc, 65
hazardous, 123
herald, 152
hexagon, 59
horrendous, 166
horticulture, 73
houseboat, 22
humble, 108
hyperactive, 29
hypertension, 29

idealist, 35
illicit, 29
illiterate, 6
illusion, 39
immigrate, 40
immobile, 121
immodest, 121
impartial, 75
impasse, 121
impediment, 89
imperfect, 121
imperious, 100
impetuous, 100
impetus, 140
impinge, 132
implement, 95
implicit, 40
imply, 40
impolite, 121
impossible, 29
impotent, 121
impoverished, 152
impractical, 121
improbable, 121
improper, 121
imprudent, 54
inability, 121
inactive, 121
inadequate, 122
incalculable, 55
incapable, 121
incentive, 126
incessantly, 55
incoherent, 54

incompetent, 121
incongruous, 54
incontrovertible, 121
incur, 71
indicative, 64
indiscreet, 55
indisputable, 121
inept, 55
inequitable, 121
ineradicable, 121
inevitable, 28
inexorable, 55
infallible, 55
infamy, 141
infectious, 35
infer, 40
inflexible, 55
infringe, 136
infuriate, 141
ingenious, 40
ingenuous, 40
initiate, 113
innovation, 62
inoculate, 120
insert, 76
insidious, 49
instability, 166
insubordinate, 57
insurgent, 140
intend, 106
interact, 120
interim, 73
interment, 72
interrupt, 29
intimate, 43
intimidate, 76
intramural, 29
intravenously, 113
intricate, 95
introduction, 29
inundated, 148
invincible, 100
irate, 169
irksome, 96
irreparable, 29
irresistible, 44

jargon, 95
jettison, 141
join, 123
jolt, 144
judicious, 110

keystone, 22

label, 108
lack, 113
laconic, 101
laden, 44
landlord, 22
landmark, 22
latitude, 161
laud, 89
lease, 21
legislate, 76
lenient, 35
lethal, 166
levity, 117
listless, 101
litigation, 76
lobster, 49
longevity, 15
longitude, 161
loquacious, 100
lucrative, 6
luxurious, 98

macabre, 90
magnum opus, 90
maiden, 148
maim, 137
make dough, 6
malediction, 29
marked, 164
market, 110
mastermind, 22
mature, 113
mean, 161
meander, 86
measure, 167
mediocre, 95
meek, 101
melancholy, 71
memorize, 35
menace, 166
mercenary, 83
militant, 155
minute, 96
misanthrope, 90
misdiagnose, 119
misogynist, 90
molten, 167
monitor, 110
monosyllable, 59
monotheist, 59

mountains of, 117
multilingual, 59
muster, 149
muted, 43

nanny, 78
negate, 45
negligent, 176
nevertheless, 22
newspaper, 22
nonagenarian, 59
nonchalant, 101
non sequitor, 90
notorious, 117
nouveau riche, 90
nuptials, 79

obituary, 71
object, 76
obnoxious, 100
observe, 167
obstetrician, 114
obstruct, 170
occur, 167
octagon, 59
oculist, 114
onerous, 152
opthalmologist, 114
optometrist, 114
orbit, 89
orthodontist, 114
ostensibly, 117
ostentacious, 63
ought, 24
overdo, 123
overgrown, 163
overt, 47

pace, 53
paean, 86
palatial, 79
pamper, 36
panacea, 76
par excellence, 90
paramount, 64
participant, 72
parvenu, 90
passive, 101
pastime, 123
pathetic, 45
peccadillo, 90
pediatrician, 114

peer, 13
penniless, 34
pentagon, 59
perimeter, 29
permeate, 29
personable, 99
pertinent, 64
petulant, 100
phlegmatic, 101
pilfer, 86
pioneer, 53
placidly, 84
poach, 84
polytheist, 59
postoperative, 29
potency, 33
potential, 166
potpourri, 90
precedent, 29
predecessor, 29
predicament, 75
predict, 167
pride, 99
principal, 5
process, 25
profound, 132
prohibit, 106
prolific, 84
prone, 167
proponent, 29
propose, 29
protagonist, 100
proviso, 153
provocation, 33
psychiatrist, 34
pugnacious, 100
punch, 49
pusillanimous, 101
put foot in mouth, 6

quack, 28
quadrangle, 59
qualify, 22
qualm, 89
quatrain, 60
querulous, 148
quintuplet, 59

raise a rumpus, 117
rapport, 90
ravage, 171
reasonable, 43

receive, 98
recognize, 171
recommend, 106
refer, 167
refuse, 106
regime, 45
regress, 113
reimbursement, 22
rejuvenate, 28
relegate, 133
relentless, 100
rendezvous, 89
reparations, 152
reply, 106
reprisal, 141
repudiate, 171
require, 106
requisite, 143
rescind, 137
resilient, 100
revolution, 161
reverberate, 151
review, 29
rigor, 53
rookie, 89
roommate, 22
roots, 53
rotation, 161
rudimentary, 86
ruthless, 113

sage, 170
sanity, 35
sardonic, 100
savoir faire, 90
savory, 43
scolding, 100
scope, 132
screwdriver, 22

scrupulous, 175
segregate, 6
select, 76
semblance, 120
semicolon, 29
senseless, 35
separate, 167
septennial, 59
sextet, 59
share, 78
shipyard, 22
shrew, 100
skeptical, 100
skyrocketing, 127
slippage, 166
soaring, 126
sojourn, 89
solidify, 176
sometimes, 22
spacecraft, 22
spice of life, 117
squeak, 77
stabilize, 34
stamina, 137
stealthy, 136
stereotype, 62
stir, 99
stratagem, 28
strenuous, 123
strip, 169
suave, 90
submarine, 29
submissive, 113
subtle, 47
subway, 120
succumb, 64
suffice, 95
sundry, 89
superficial, 6

superstition, 79
supervisor, 29
supplant, 143
survive, 5
syndrome, 119
synopsis, 5

taint, 132
tempestuous, 137
temporary, 123
tenacious, 100
tenant, 22
therapeutic, 108
throes, 151
timid, 101
tolerate, 6
toxic, 171
traditional, 33
transplant, 127
transport, 29
trappings, 58
treat, 106
tremble, 167
tremendous, 22
tricycle, 59
trilingual, 59
triplet, 60
turbulence, 35
tycoon, 148
tyro, 90

ultimately, 123
uncompromising, 100
underground, 120
undertaker, 72
unerring, 100
unfortunately, 123
unilateral, 59
unkempt, 54

unlikely, 29
unscathed, 54
urban, 53
urbane, 100
use, 106
usher, 151

vague, 101
vapid, 101
vast, 62
vehement, 141
versatility, 95
vestige, 137
villa, 49
vindictive, 100
virtuoso, 90
vocalist, 80
vogue, 59
volatile, 100

warn, 167
weekend, 22
welcome, 98
whet, 73
wholesome, 43
widespread, 22
wield, 59
wildlife, 22
woe, 38
wonders, 49
worker, 34
worry, 38
worth its salt, 117
worthwhile, 22
wrangle, 76
wrath, 14

zeal, 72
zenith, 28

ANSWER KEY

Part I. Developing Reading Comprehension Skills

Page 13—Reading 1. Lefties

The main idea is that left-handed people suffer more from stress than right-handed people.

Page 13—Reading 2. Choking

Main idea: You should know how to help a person who is choking. Supporting details:
(A) Stand behind the victim and put your arms around his or her waist.
(B) Make a fist and place the thumb side against the person's stomach.
(C) Grasp your fist with your other hand and press into the abdomen with a quick upward thrust.
(D) Repeat if necessary.

Page 14—Reading 3. Delivering Bad News

1. C   2. B   3. D

Page 15—Reading 4. Yogurt

1. D
2. B

Page 15—Questions on Readings 1 and 2

Reading 1	Reading 2
1. C	1. B
2. C	2. C
3. C	

Page 16—Reading 5. Death of a Spouse

1. C
2. C

Page 17—Reading 6. News Items

A. Who: Mexican conservationists
   What: trying to get rid of piranhas
   Where: in a lake near Puebla
   When: yesterday
   Why: killers

B. Who: The Commodities Futures Trading Commission
   What: designated four commodities exchanges
   Where: information not given
   When: today
   Why: to trade options on futures contracts

C. Who: workers
   What: put down their tools
   Where: in the Baltic seaport of Gdansk
   When: on October 14
   Why: to protest against poor working conditions

Page 17—Reading 7. Classified Ads

Page 18—Abbreviations

building	month
executive	year
terrace	including utilities
lease	near
large	separate
room	air conditioning
kitchen	beautiful(ly)
available	furnished

Page 19—A. Comprehension Check

1. D	7. In Elizabeth
2. C	8. They all have
3. Separate kitch-	four bedrooms.
en, beautifully	9. D
furnished,	10. D
$600/month	11. B
4. C	12. A
5. D	13. C
6. C	14. D

Page 21—B. Vocabulary Work

1. C	4. A	6. A
2. C	5. B	7. D
3. D		

Page 21—C. Vocabulary Building

1. land/lord	22. god/parent
2. week/end	23. long/time
3. screw/driver	24. key/stone
4. never/the/less	25. grand/parent
5. further/more	26. wide/spread
6. some/times	27. easy/going
7. room/mate	28. drug/store
8. news/paper	29. no/where
9. bed/room	30. wild/life
10. air/port	31. earth/quake
11. Thanks/giving	32. worth/while
12. some/thing	33. class/room
13. some/one	34. fire/place
14. birth/day	35. bath/room
15. ship/yard	36. type/writer
16. house/boat	37. door/man
17. moon/shine	38. common/wealth
18. crest/fallen	39. hand/cuff
19. master/mind	40. foot/loose
20. hill/top	41. dead/lock
21. space/craft	42. land/mark

Page 22—Reading 8. Letter to the Editor

Page 23—A. Detailed Comprehension

1. C
2. D

3. (A) Tenant must be 62 or older.
   (B) Tenant must live in a rent-controlled or rent-stabilized dwelling.
   (C) Tenant must pay more than one-third of his or her income for rent.
   (D) Tenant must have a yearly income of $8,000 or less.
4. True
5. A
6. A
7. C
8. C
9. D
10. B
11. D
12. C
13. C

Page 24—B. Vocabulary Work

1. B	4. D	7. C
2. B	5. C	8. A
3. C	6. B	

Page 25—Reading 9. Your Horoscope

Page 26—A. Detailed Comprehension

1. D	5. B	8. D
2. D	6. D	9. C
3. B	7. A	10. B
4. D		

Page 28—B. Vocabulary Work

1. C	5. B	8. C
2. D	6. D	9. C
3. B	7. B	10. A
4. A		

Page 29—C. Vocabulary Building

1. transport	6. predecessor
2. semicolon	7. dispersed
3. postoperative	8. antedated
4. exit	9. contrary
5. circumnavigated	10. antipathy

11. permeates
12. extracurricular
13. interrupted
14. impossible
15. submarine
16. supervisor
17. precedence
18. proponents
19. benefit
20. collate
21. review
22. abduct
23. intramural
24. perimeter
25. attracts

Page 31—Reading 10. Car Problems

Page 32—A. Detailed Comprehension

1. B
2. D
3. C
4. (A) Make sure you have gasoline.
   (B) Check the valves.
   (C) See if the engine is getting spark. Check the spark plugs.
   (D) Find out if the carburetor is feeding enough air and gas to the engine.
5. B
6. D
7. D
8. C
9. B
10. C
11. A
12. C
13. B
14. C
15. No. The author assumes that the reader knows something about a car's mechanism.

Page 33—B. Vocabulary Building

1. penniless
2. potency
3. contentment
4. comprehendible
5. gracious
6. traditional
7. alliance
8. aviary
9. expendable
10. atmospheric
11. psychiatrist
12. worker
13. complexity
14. provocation
15. stabilize
16. complacence
17. beautify

Page 35

1. employer
2. conservationist
3. sanity
4. comfortable
5. infectious
6. adjustment
7. senseless
8. idealist/idealistic
9. leniency
10. memorize
11. turbulence
12. electrify

Page 35—Reading 11. Advice Column

Page 36—A. Detailed Comprehension

1. C
2. C
3. A
4. D
5. A
6. C
7. (A) House with a pool
   (B) Lovely suburban development
   (C) Wife doesn't go out to work
8. "I don't go out to work because I think children need their mother."
9. So that they wouldn't see her "carrying on" with "Distraught's" husband.
10. D
11. C

Page 37—B. Detailed Comprehension

| 1. B | 3. D | 5. False |
| 2. B | 4. D | 6. A |

Page 38—C. Vocabulary Work

1. C	5. B	8. D
2. B	6. D	9. D
3. C	7. A	10. A
4. C		

Page 39—D. Vocabulary Building

1. A. adopt
   B. adapt
2. A. adverse
   B. averse
3. A. delusion
   B. allusions
   C. illusion

4. A. compliment
    B. complement
5. A. council
    B. counsel
6. A. elicit
    B. illicit
7. A. explicit
    B. implicit

8. A. ingenious
    B. ingenuous
9. A. infer
    B. imply
10. A. emigrate
    B. immigrate

Page 41—Quiz 1

1. studio
2. tenant
3. elderly
4. reimbursement
5. furnace
6. imply
7. stratagem
8. quack
9. zenith
10. submarine
11. perimeter
12. idealist
13. woes
14. allusion
15. council

Page 41—Reading 12. Dining Out Guide

Page 42—A. Detailed Comprehension

1. B
2. C
3. The Boathouse
4. Little Old San Juan
5. Little Old San Juan
6. The Banyan Tree
7. The Boathouse
8. Little Old San Juan
9. Cafe Henri
10. A

Page 43—B. Vocabulary Work

1. C
2. A
3. B
4. C
5. B
6. C
7. A
8. D
9. A
10. B
11. C
12. C
13. B
14. C
15. D

Page 44—C. Vocabulary Building

1. 2/1
2. 2/1
3. 2/1
4. 1/2
5. 1/2
6. 2/1
7. 3/1/2
8. 2/1
9. 2/1
10. 1/2

Page 47—Reading 13. Jaguar Ad

Page 47

Individual answers.

Page 48—Reading 14. Jamaica Ad

Page 48—A. General Comprehension

1. C
2. D
3. pleasure

Page 49—B. Vocabulary Work (Answers will vary.)

1. spoil
2. very expensive
3. reasonable
4. many beautiful things
5. large shellfish, delicious for eating
6. private house; country estate
7. drink made with fruit juices and rum

Page 50—Reading 15. Health Club Ad

Page 51—A. General Comprehension

1. C
2. C
3. D
4. B
5. D

Page 51—B. Vocabulary Work (Answers will vary.)

1. (Nautilus) equipment
2. dance
3. calisthenics
4. tennis
5. swimming pools

All the words have the connotation of action, activity, exercise.

Page 52—Reading 16. University Ad

232 / *TOEFL Reading Comprehension & Vocabulary*

Page 53—A. Detailed Comprehension

1. C
2. (A) Small classes to give you the chance to get to know your professors
   (B) An educational environment designed to take you away from daily rigors (a relaxed atmosphere)
   (C) A staff schooled (trained) in the importance of the individual
3. B
4. B
5. C
6. D

Page 53—B. Vocabulary Work (Answers will vary.)

1. speed
2. adapted, adjusted
3. origins, foundations
4. not situated in a city
5. pressures, strains
6. trained, educated
7. began the early development of
8. someone who helps people in need
9. offer, provide
10. to have a certain level of knowledge or ability, to be eligible

Page 54—C. Vocabulary Building

All of these prefixes—*un, in, im, ir, il, non,* and *dis*—mean "not."

1. C	6. A	11. D
2. D	7. C	12. A
3. A	8. B	13. C
4. C	9. D	14. C
5. D	10. B	15. D

Page 55—Synonyms

a. 6	f. 11	k. 8
b. 12	g. 3	l. 4
c. 13	h. 15	m. 7
d. 1	i. 9	n. 10
e. 2	j. 5	o. 14

Page 56—Quiz 2

1. C	6. B	11. A
2. B	7. A	12. A
3. C	8. B	13. D
4. A	9. D	14. A
5. B	10. B	15. C

Page 57—Reading 17. Tennis Wear

Page 58—A. General Comprehension

1. B	3. B	5. A
2. C	4. B	

Page 59—B. Vocabulary Work

1. C	4. B	7. D
2. C	5. A	8. C
3. D	6. C	

Page 59—C. Vocabulary Building

1. trilingual	9. binoculars
2. monosyllables	10. bipartisan
3. duet	11. decade
4. hexagon	12. nonagenarians
5. pentagon	13. triplets
6. tricycle	14. unilateral
7. polytheist/ monotheist	15. bicentennial
8. quatrain	

Page 61—Reading 18. The Automobile Industry

Page 61—A. Detailed Comprehension

1. A	4. A	7. B
2. D	5. C	8. C
3. C	6. B	

Page 62—B. Vocabulary Work

1. innovation	3. stereotype
2. Affluent	4. lucrative

5. vast
6. compete
7. rejuvenated

8. chagrin
9. amenities
10. apathy

Page 63—Synonyms

1. C
2. B
3. B
4. A
5. B
6. B
7. C

8. B
9. A
10. C
11. D
12. B
13. C
14. B

15. B
16. C
17. C
18. B
19. B
20. C

Page 65—Quiz 3

1. D
2. A
3. C
4. B
5. B

6. C
7. C
8. D
9. D
10. B

11. A
12. C
13. D
14. C
15. D

Page 66—Crossword Puzzle

¹P	O	²T	³E	N	⁴T		⁵A	⁶D	⁷A	⁸P	⁹T		¹⁰A	R	¹¹D	E	N	¹²T	¹³
O		¹⁴E	X		¹⁵R	E	C	O	M	M	E	¹⁶N	D		U		¹⁷O	R	I
¹⁸S	¹⁹O	R	T		I		U		O	²⁰N	O	V		²¹E	R			R	I
²²T	H	R	E	E		²³I	T		²⁴R	²⁵I		²⁶T	E	N	T		²⁷P	L	
	²⁸I	N			²⁹N	E	³⁰G	A	T	E	³¹R		R			³²T	R	I	
³³S	M	B	D	R	M	³⁴M			³⁵I	L		³⁶N	O	³⁷S		³⁸L	I	O	N
A		L			R		³⁹O	N				V	E		⁴⁰A	D			G
⁴¹N	⁴²E	E	⁴³D	Y			I		⁴⁴H		⁴⁵B	E			⁴⁶D	E			U
⁴⁷I	T		E		⁴⁸C	⁴⁹O	L	L	A	⁵⁰B	O	R	A	⁵¹T	E		⁵²M	A	
T		⁵³S	A	V	O	R	Y			⁵⁴V	A	S	T		⁵⁵A	N		⁵⁶E	L
⁵⁷Y	O	U	R		N				⁵⁸D	O	C	S		⁵⁹D	I		⁶⁰A	T	
		P		⁶¹A	S		⁶²S	O	C	K			⁶³T	E	N		⁶⁴N	R	
⁶⁵W	O	E	⁶⁶S		U		T	E				⁶⁷E	N	T		⁶⁸I	C	E	
I		⁶⁹R	E	I	M	B	U	R	⁷⁰S	⁷¹E		⁷²L	Y		⁷³N	E	S	T	
⁷⁴N	O		E		B		⁷⁵S	T		L									

Part II. How Thoughts Are Related

Page 70—Reading 1. A Death in the Family

Page 70—A. General Comprehension

1. C
2. B
3. A
4. D
5. The person in charge of the funeral should prepare a death notice for the newspapers. (It is stated.)
6. (A) Information should include date of death.
   (B) Information should include names of the family members.
   (C) Information should include time and place of the interment.

Page 71—B. Vocabulary Work

1. B	5. C	8. A
2. D	6. D	9. C
3. C	7. C	10. B
4. B		

Page 72—Reading 2. Central Park Conservancy

Page 72—Vocabulary Work

1. B	5. D	8. D
2. C	6. C	9. B
3. D	7. B	10. D
4. B		

Page 73—Reading 3. Divorce Settlements

Page 74—A. Detailed Comprehension

1. False/implied
2. True/implied
3. False/stated
4. True/stated
5. False/implied
6. False/stated
7. False/stated
8. No information given
9. True/stated
10. True/implied

Page 74—B. Restating

1. A	3. A	5. B
2. D	4. C	

Page 75—C. Vocabulary Work

a. 6	d. 1	g. 2
b. 7	e. 5	h. 8
c. 4	f. 9	i. 3

Page 76—D. Vocabulary Building

1. legislation	6. selection
2. anticipation	7. anticipates
3. litigation	8. insert
4. object	9. donation
5. celebrate	10. participate

Page 77—Reading 4. Royal Baptism

Page 77—A. General Comprehension

1. False (brief)
2. False (affably responded—only a squeak or two)
3. False (they sang "Happy Birthday") to the prince's great-grandmother
4. True
5. False (first worn by Edward VII in 1841)
6. True
7. False (top layer of Prince Charles and Princess Diana's wedding cake)
8. True
9. True
10. False (not a superstition—part of the ceremony)

Page 78—B. Vocabulary Work

1. B	5. D	8. B
2. D	6. A	9. C
3. B	7. C	10. B
4. A		

Page 79—Reading 5. Wedding Announcement

Page 80—A. Detailed Comprehension

1. C	5. C	8. A
2. B	6. D	9. B
3. A	7. C	10. D
4. C		

Page 81—B. Vocabulary Work

1. unknown	6. enemy
2. single	7. from
3. far	8. visitor (guest)
4. new (recent)	9. take away
5. worst	10. followed

Page 81—C. Vocabulary Building

Use your dictionary to check your answers.

Page 82

1. collaborating	9. compatible
2. congestion	10. conclave
3. concurred	11. confer
4. congenital	12. concise
5. concentrate	13. complement
6. component	14. compete
7. concoction	15. confided
8. combat	

Page 83—Quiz 4

1. A	6. A	11. B
2. C	7. C	12. A
3. B	8. A	13. C
4. C	9. B	14. A
5. D	10. D	15. D

Page 84—Reading 6. Audubon Camp

Page 85—A. Detailed Comprehension

1. Yes. The passage mentions several kinds of birds: terns, gulls, and cormorants.

2. C
3. A
4. B
5. Muscongus Bay
6. The puffin eggs were pilferred by poachers.
7. The Audubon Society had very little luck until 1981, when the puffins brought from Newfoundland began to produce young.
8. True
9. False
10. B
11. D
12. B

Page 86—B. Vocabulary Work

Synonyms

a. 8	e. 7	h. 3
b. 1	f. 2	i. 9
c. 6	g. 4	j. 5
d. 10		

Page 86—Sentence Completion

1. meander	6. complement
2. rudimentary	7. elicit
3. habitats	8. pilferred
4. stereotype	9. amenity
5. augment	10. paean

Page 87—Prefixes and Suffixes

(Answers will vary—check your dictionary.)

1. prolific—producing many young/specific—determined
2. innumerable—many/insight—understanding
3. amenity—convenience/majority—most
4. innumerable—many
5. poachers—people who catch or shoot animals, birds, etc., illegally/campers—people who camp/dwellers—inhabitants
6. sanctuary—an area where birds and animals are protected
7. compatible—able to live together in harmony
8. outdoors—in the open air
9. overhung—hanging over/overlooking—giving a view from above

10. enliven—to make lively/encompasses—includes
11. exploration—trip into a place for the purpose of discovery/cessation—stop or pause

Page 87—Reading 7. Women in Space

Page 88—A. Detailed Comprehension

1. False /A   5. D   8. False /A
2. C   6. True /A   9. C
3. B   7. B   10. C
4. A

Page 89—B. Vocabulary Work

1. A   4. dauntless
2. C   5. impediment
3. B   6. feat
4. D   7. adage
5. C   8. qualm
1. unscathed 9. rendezvous
2. aptitude   10. sundry
3. sojourn

Page 90—C. Vocabulary Building

Use your dictionary to check your definitions.

Page 91—Fill-ins

1. gourmet   11. connoisseur
2. nouveau riche   12. magnum opus
3. coquette   13. bête noire
4. dilettante   14. Rapport
5. misogynist   15. pecadillo
6. misanthrope   16. Ad infinitum
7. virtuoso   17. forte
8. tyro   18. faux pas
9. alumnus   19. potpourri
10. alumna   20. cliché

Page 92—Reading 8. Computers in School

Page 93—A. Detailed Comprehension

1. C   6. B   10. C
2. A   7. C   11. A
3. B   8. C   12. C
4. B   9. C   13. B
5. C

Page 94—B. Vocabulary Work

1. A   7. A   13. C
2. C   8. C   14. D
3. A   9. B   15. B
4. B   10. C   16. D
5. D   11. A   17. C
6. C   12. D   18. A

Page 96—Reading 9. Arabella Trefoil

Page 97—Questions

1. the Trefoils
2. Mr. Morton took a cart for the luggage.
3. Arabella Trefoil and Lady Augustus
4. Arabella Trefoil and Lady Augustus
5. her own maid
6. hair (part of her hair)
7. her complexion
8. her complexion
9. never to allow an awkward movement to escape from her
10. upon her horse

Page 97—A. Detailed Comprehension

1. B   6. D
2. C   7. B
3. B   8. C
4. False   9. B
5. They said her   10. C
   brilliant com-   11. C
   plexion was due 12. D
   to paint (make-
   up).

Page 98—B. Vocabulary Work

1. B   5. C   9. A
2. C   6. A   10. D
3. A   7. A   11. A
4. B   8. B

Page 99—C. Vocabulary Building

(Use your dictionary to check definitions.)

Words that describe Arabella Trefoil

2. <u>charlatan</u>
4. <u>enticing</u>
5. <u>frivolous</u>
7. <u>superficial</u>

Page 100—Individual definitions

Page 101—Synonyms

a.	6	e.	1	h.	10
b.	9	f.	4	i.	5
c.	8	g.	2	j.	3
d.	7				

Page 101—Quiz 5

1.	C	6.	A	11.	C
2.	B	7.	C	12.	D
3.	D	8.	B	13.	C
4.	B	9.	B	14.	A
5.	C	10.	D	15.	D

Page 103—Crossword Puzzle

Across:
1. REVIEWS
4. EMBELLISH
10. OCT
11. DEPUTIZED
13. COLLABORATE
16. MID
18. SIX
20. NODS
22. HAVOC
24. APTITUDE
26. AFFABLE
27. ENNUI
28. ABDUCT
30. YOUR
31. RAISE
33. CIRCUMVENT
36. SAT
39. ASSETS
40. INTIMIDATION

Part III. Understanding Contemporary Reading Passages

Page 105—Reading 1. Drug Abuse

Page 105—A. Detailed Comprehension

1. A   3. C   5. B
2. C   4. True

Page 106—B. Vocabulary Building

1. recommenda-tion   9. exceed
2. excessive   10. damage
3. comparison   11. Prohibition
4. refusal   12. acquisition
5. requirements   13. use
6. abuse   14. reply
7. intention   15. questionable
8. question

Page 107—Reading 2. Vitamins

Page 108—A. Detailed Comprehension

1. False
2. Meat and vegetables
3. An Englishman
4. Milk, eggs, butter, vegetables (Ans indiv)
5. True

Page 108—B. Vocabulary Work

a. 4   e. 5   h. 6
b. 10   f. 1   i. 3
c. 2   g. 8   j. 9
d. 7

Page 108—Reading 3. Propranolol

Page 109—A. Review

1. "Stage fright disconcerts even experienced performers" (It is stated.)

2. "(Propranolol) relieves the anxiety of performers." (It is stated.)
3. "Propranolol . . . must be employed judiciously." (It is stated.)
4. (A) Experiments with students were conducted.
   (B) Subjects gave solo performances.
   (C) Subjects' hearts were monitored by an electrocardiograph and their blood pressure was taken.
   (D) Symptoms of stage fright were ameliorated.
   (E) Their heart rates were relatively normal and their critics pleased by their performances.
5. (A) Propranolol is used to control high blood pressure and angina.
   (B) It is used to help prevent heart attacks.
   (C) The drug is dangerous for sufferers of asthma, hay fever, and various types of diabetes and heart conditions.
   (D) Scrupulous care must be taken to limit the sale of the drug.

Page 109—B. Detailed Comprehension

1. B   7. hyperactive, hypersensitive, hypercritical, etc.
2. False
3. D
4. A   8. D
5. D   9. A
6. B   10. C

Page 110—C. Vocabulary Work

a. 10   d. 6   g. 5
b. 3   e. 9   h. 11
c. 1   f. 4   i. 2

Page 111—Reading 4. Anorexia Nervosa

Page 111—A. Review

1. A
2. B
3. C

4. (A) Joan refuses to eat to rebel against the pressures imposed upon her by her environment.
   (B) Family members require her to achieve more than they have.
   (C) School unites with her family to push her forward.
   (D) She holds back her physical growth by self-imposed starvation.
   (E) She regresses to childhood when no one expected much from her and she was dependent upon adults who gave her love without demanding anything from her in return.

5. Before Joan developed anorexia nervosa, she was a bright student who weighed 110 pounds; now she weighs 81 pounds and is in the hospital, where she is undergoing psychiatric treatment and being fed intravenously.

Page 112—B. Detailed Comprehension

1. Anorexia nervosa is a disease common among adolescent girls characterized by loss of appetite because of a desire to avoid growing into a mature woman.
2. C
3. B
4. D
5. intramural, intravascular, etc.
6. self-educated, self-controlled, self-governing, etc.
7. underground, undercoat, undercurrent, underlying, etc.
8. True
9. True/B
10. School and family
11. C
12. B

Page 113—C. Vocabulary Work

1. C	5. B	8. B
2. A	6. A	9. B
3. D	7. A	10. C
4. A		

Page 113—D. Vocabulary Building

1. feet	6. eyes
2. skin	7. eyes
3. women	8. teeth
4. pregnant women	9. children
5. eyes	10. mind

Page 114—Fill-ins

1. orthodontist	4. psychiatrists
2. pediatrician	5. chiropodist
3. oculist, ophthalmologist, optometrist	6. dermatologist
	7. obstetrician

Page 114—Reading 5. Salt

Page 115—A. Detailed Comprehension

1. B		7. False	
2. B		8. B	
3. A		9. Information not given	
4. C			
5. False			
6. D		10. B	

Page 116—B. Vocabulary Work

(Answers to (B) will vary; therefore, only the answers to (A) are given.)

1. ruthless/endless	4. harmful
2. campaigners/ manufacturers/ salters	5. overuse
	6. hypertension
3. anti-salt	7. exposed
	8. notorious(ly)/dubious

Page 116—Synonyms

1. B	5. C	9. C
2. A	6. A	10. C
3. B	7. B	11. B
4. C	8. D	

Page 117—C. Vocabulary Building

1. do the trick
2. the salt of life
3. mountains of
4. worth his/her salt
5. raise a rumpus

Page 118—Reading 6. Subway Syndrome

Page 118—A. Review

1. A new ailment has developed among subway users. It is stated in the first sentence.
2. (A) New ailment called subway syndrome.
   (B) Causes people to turn pale and cold and even to faint.
   (C) Commuters rush to the hospital, thinking they are having a heart attack.
3. Various and sundry things make people sick on subways. It is stated.
4. (A) Dizziness is caused by not having eaten a proper breakfast.
   (B) The overcrowding causes claustrophobia, which brings on stress and anxiety.
   (C) People are afraid of mechanical failure, fire, and/or crime, so they panic.
   (D) Men show panic by having chest pains, women by becoming hysterical.
   (E) Overcrowding of both sexes, continual increase in the number of passengers, and people's inability to avoid interacting with strangers contribute to stress.
5. There are measures commuters can take to protect themselves from subway syndrome.
6. (A) Eat a good breakfast.
   (B) Concentrate on pleasant thoughts.
   (C) Bounce a bit on your toes.
   (D) Roll your head

Page 119—B. Detailed Comprehension

1. True
2. wrong
3. misconceived, mistaken, etc.
4. C
5. False
6. True
7. B

8. international, interplanetary, etc.
9. B
10. under
11. subterranean, submarine, etc.
12. D
13. D
14. B
15. C

Page 120—C. Vocabulary Work

a. 8	e. 2	h. 11
b. 3	f. 10	i. 12
c. 5	g. 4	j. 7
d. 1		

Page 121—D. Vocabulary Building

1. inactive	16. indisputable
2. inadequate	17. indiscreet
3. incapable	18. ineradicable
4. inability	19. impolite
5. incompetent	20. impractical
6. injudicious	21. incalculable
7. imprudent	22. incessant
8. insecure	23. incoherent
9. immodest	24. incontrovertible
10. improper	25. inequitable
11. inaccurate	26. inflexible
12. impossible	27. insubordinate
13. immobile	28. impasse
14. imperfect	29. improbable
15. impartial	30. impotent

Page 121—Reading 7. Physical Fitness

Page 121—A. General Comprehension

1. B	3. A	5. D
2. A	4. B	

Page 122—B. Restating

1. D	2. C	3. D

Page 123—C. Vocabulary Work

a.	10	f.	4	j.	6
b.	7	g.	3	k.	12
c.	13	h.	1	l.	5
d.	9	i.	2	m.	11
e.	8				

Page 123—Synonyms

1.	D	3.	A	5.	D
2.	C	4.	B		

Page 124—D. Inferring and Finding Specific Information

1.	True/A	4.	True/B
2.	False/B	5.	True/B
3.	True/A	6.	True/B

Page 124—Reading 8. Health Care

Page 125—A. Scanning

1.	85%	9.	4
2.	8.9%	10.	$118 billion
3.	15.1%	11.	$54.8 billion
4.	$1225	12.	three times or 300%
5.	$287 billion	13.	$24.2 billion
6.	75%	14.	4
7.	$133	15.	$73 billion
8.	$250		

Page 126—B. Cause and Effect

           cause   **effect**
1. With [soaring medical costs,] [inflation is difficult to control.]

           cause
2. [Manufacturers are paying so much for employees' health insurance] that [prices for
           effect
their products are increasing.]

           cause
3. [New construction of hospital facilities is
           effect
very expensive,] and so [medical expenses have risen.]

           cause
4. With [no incentive to cut medical expenses,]
           effect
there has been [no effort expended to cut costs.]

           cause
5. Since [a large percentage of Americans have health insurance that pays about 75% of
           effect
their health care bills,] [medical costs have continued to rise.]

           cause
6. [Modern technology and more sophisticated
           effect
equipment] [have increased medical costs.]

           cause
7. Because [insurance companies are paying
           effect
their bills,] [people are taking advantage of the high-quality medical services available.]

8. Patients with serious illnesses that formerly
           effect
would have killed them [are now kept alive]
           cause
as a result of [organ transplants.]

           cause
9. [Equipping a new intensive care unit] [adds
           effect
million of dollars to the cost of medical services.]

           cause   **effect**
10. [Escalating construction costs] [raise medical costs.]

Page 126—C. Vocabulary Work

1.	B	3.	A	5.	D
2.	D	4.	D		

Page 127—Quiz 6

1. A	6. B	11. C
2. C	7. A	12. B
3. D	8. C	13. B
4. B	9. A	14. C
5. D	10. D	15. A

Page 129—Crossword Puzzle

```
  I   D       A           D U B I O U S
  I N C A L C U L A B L E     O           T
  S   I   O           I       Y     A
  C U I S I N E       S U B M I S S I V E
  B   S   S           E       E     L
  B O U N C E     P   C       A     O     M       R
  R         Q U E S T I O N A B L E       I       E
  D     M   U       E   R           I     N       C
  M I N U T E     R O O K I E     E       T O O    O
  A N   L   N           R         U               M
  P A R T I C I P A N T     T     A               M
    T   I   E   A       O     R A I S E           E
  F E D       T E M P O R A R Y                   N
  A   E       A     A         O                   D
  D E F I C I E N C Y     R U T H L E S S
```

Across answers: DUBIOUS, INCALCULABLE, CUISINE, SUBMISSIVE, BOUNCE, QUESTIONABLE, MINUTE, ROOKIE, TOO, PARTICIPANT, RAISE, FED, TEMPORARY, DEFICIENCY, RUTHLESS

Part IV. Tactics for Reading from History Textbooks

Page 130—Reading 1. Olympic Games

Page 130—A. Scanning Practice

1. 776 B.C.—Olympic Games originated
2. 394 A.D.—Games were banned by Emperor Theodosius
3. 1896—Modern Olympic Games began
4. 1936—Hitler refused to congratulate Jesse Owens
5. 1972—Eleven Israeli athletes were murdered by Arab terrorists
6. 1976—Games held in Montreal boycotted by African nations and Taiwan withdrew
7. 1980—Sixty-two nations refused to participate in Games following Soviet invasion of Afghanistan

Page 131—B. Detailed Comprehension

1. C	4. D	7. A
2. A	5. B	8. D
3. C	6. D	

Page 132—C. Vocabulary Work

1. B	5. A	8. B
2. A	6. D	9. D
3. C	7. C	10. A
4. B		

Page 133—Getting the Meaning from Context

1. initiative	4. deplorable
2. Currently	5. detrimental
3. epoch	

Page 133—Reading 2. American Indians

Page 134—A. Detailed Comprehension

1. D	5. B	8. D
2. B	6. B	9. B
3. C	7. A	10. C
4. C		

Page 135—B. Restating

B

Page 135—C. Vocabulary Work

1. settlers, adventurers; er—one who
2. encroachment, unemployment; ment—result, state
3. callous, treacherous; ous—full of
4. capitulation; tion—action
5. ruthlessly; less—without
6. extend; ex—out
7. evicted; e—out
8. amity/mortality; ity—condition
9. sub-standard; sub—under
10. deprived; de—from, down
11. unemployment; un—not
12. superficial; super—above

Page 136—Synonyms

1. D	10. C	18. A
2. B	11. A	19. D
3. A	12. C	20. B
4. B	13. A	21. A
5. D	14. B	22. D
6. B	15. D	23. B
7. C	16. D	24. C
8. B	17. C	25. A
9. D		

Page 138—Reading 3. American Revolution

Page 138—A. Detailed Comprehension

1. C   5. B   8. B
2. B   6. C   9. D
3. C   7. D   10. D
4. B

Page 140—B. Restating

B

Page 140—C. Vocabulary Work

1. B   6. D   11. A
2. C   7. D   12. C
3. A   8. B   13. C
4. D   9. D   14. B
5. B   10. C   15. A

Page 141—Synonyms

a. 4   c. 6   e. 1
b. 5   d. 2   f. 3

Page 142—Reading 4. Industrial Revolution

Page 142—A. Cause and Effect

cause
1. [A vigorous commercial economy, expand-
    ing trade, and a population boom] were the
                                        effect
    conditions requisite for [making Britain the
    first industrial nation.]
            effect
2. [The population boom] is attributed to
                cause
    [good harvests, the end of the plague,
    youthful marriages, and greater opportuni-
    ties for work.]
            effect
3. [The plague ended] after [water supplies
                cause
    were improved and soap became more
    readily available.]

                cause
4. [With the drop in the death rate and the
    increase in the birth rate,] [more labor was
            effect
    available for industry.]
                cause
5. [Industry's need for fuel] sparked [expan-
            effect
    sion in coal mining.]
            effect   cause
6. [Production of iron] depended upon [coal.]
            effect
7. [The iron industry moved to the Midlands
                    cause
    and the North] for [coal.]
                            cause
8. Following [the invention of the steam en-
                    effect
    gine,] [water power was supplanted by
    steam power.]
            effect   cause
9. [Steam power] required [access to coal
    fields.]
                    cause   effect
10. [Labor-saving machinery] [dispensed with
    water power.]
                    cause
11. [The flying shuttle] made it possible [to
            effect
    widen cloth and double production.]
                    cause
12. [The spinning jenny and the power loom]
            effect
    [rejuvenated the cotton and wool indus-
    tries.]
                    cause   effect
13. [The need for coal] [pushed the textile
    industry north.]
                    cause
14. [Cheap transportation] was needed [to
            effect
    complement industrialization.]
                    cause   effect
15. [The canal system] [reduced coal prices.]

Page 143—B. Restating

C

Page 143—C. Vocabulary Work

a. 7   e. 1   h. 2
b. 6   f. 10   i. 5
c. 3   g. 4   j. 8
d. 9

Page 144—Reading 5. The Titanic

Page 145—A. Chronology

1. April 10, 1912
2. April 14, 1912
3. 11:40 P.M.
4. 12:05 A.M.
5. 12:15 A.M.
6. 12:45 A.M.
7. 1:40 A.M.
8. 2:05 A.M.
9. 2:10 A.M.
10. April 15, 1912
11. 2:20 A.M.
12. 4:10 A.M.
13. 5:40 A.M.

Page 145—B. Statistics

1. 46,328 tons
2. 882 feet
3. 25 knots an hour
4. 2,207
5. 5
6. 300 feet
7. $250 million
8. 1,178
9. 20
10. 10 miles away
11. 58 miles away
12. 705
13. 18
14. 139
15. 78
16. 98
17. 1
18. 53

Page 146—C. Detailed Comprehension

1. C
2. D
3. B
4. A
5. A
6. C
7. C
8. False/A
9. C
10. B

Page 147—D. Restating

D

Page 148—E. Vocabulary Work

1. B
2. C
3. A
4. B
5. D
6. A
7. C
8. D
9. B
10. C
11. C
12. B
13. C
14. B
15. D

Page 149—Reading 6. Depression

Page 150—A. Detailed Comprehension

1. D
2. A
3. D
4. C
5. B
6. C
7. D
8. C
9. D
10. C

Page 151—B. Restating

A

Page 151—C. Vocabulary Work

1. C
2. C
3. B
4. B
5. A
6. D
7. D
8. C
9. A
10. B
11. C
12. A
13. A
14. D
15. D

Page 152—Reading 7. Vietnam

Page 153—A. Dates and Numbers

1. September 2, 1945
2. 1946
3. 1954
4. 1947
5. 1961
6. February 8, 1965
7. May 1968
8. January 27, 1973
9. December 1972
10. billions of dollars
11. over a half million
12. 30
13. April 30, 1975

Page 154—B. Detailed Comprehension

1. B
2. A
3. B
4. D
5. A
6. D
7. C
8. C
9. B
10. C

Page 155—C. Vocabulary Work

1. D
2. A
3. D
4. B
5. B
6. B
7. D

Page 156—Crossword Puzzle

C	E	D	E		K			S			A			A	R	D	E	N	T		T
A		E		M	I	L	I	T	A	N	T			C							A
L	O	T		A	T		N		N	O	T			C		A	N	T	I		I
L		R		I			D		T		R			O		C			N		T
O			I	M	M	O	B	I	L	E			B	E	T	W	E	E	N	
U		M		S			S				B	E	T	W	E	E	N	S		
S	E	E	N		I	N	C	U	R		U		R		S	O				
	N		S				R		I		T	R	E	A	S	U	R	E		
A	P	T	I	T	U	D	E		S	E	E		M						X	
P		A		E			E		E		E			A			P			
P	A	L		M	E	E	T	I	N	G		N	O	R	M	A	L		I
E		I				F				B		T		O				I		
A	D	M	O	N	I	S	H		A	M	I	S	S		U			C	
S		N	A			E			E		E		N				I		
E	N	C	E		A	U	R	A		D	E	P	E	N	D	E	N	T

Page 157—Quiz 7

1.	D	6.	D	11.	B
2.	C	7.	B	12.	D
3.	A	8.	D	13.	B
4.	B	9.	A	14.	A
5.	C	10.	C	15.	D

Part V. Interpretation of Scientific Reading Materials

Page 159—Reading 1. The Moon

Page 159—Prequestions

1. A   2. C   3. B

Page 160—A. Note Taking

1. 27 days, 7 hours, and 43.2 minutes
2. 29 days, 12 hours, and 44.05 minutes
3. 238,857 miles
4. 2,160 miles
5. 3,963 miles
6. 1,080 miles
7. 216,420 miles
8. 1959

Page 160—B. Detailed Comprehension

1. Sidereal period is the time it takes for the moon to go around the earth.
2. Synodical period is the period from one new moon to the next.
3. average
4. False
5. B
6. A
7. B
8. True
9. True
10. We measure from the center of the earth to the center of the moon.
11. One time is the time the moon takes to go around the earth, and the other time is the period from one new moon to the other.
12. Photographs taken by Soviet and United States spaceships
13. The moon's path is elliptical, not circular.
14. Latitude is the distance north or south of the equator. Longitude is the position on the earth east or west of a meridian.
15. B

Page 162—Reading 2. Life on Earth

Page 162—Prequestions

1. C
2. Devonian period/ Mesozoic Era/ Cenozoic Era/ An era is longer

Page 162—A. Detailed Comprehension

1.	C	11.	B
2.	three billion years	12.	life
3.	jawless fish	13.	D
4.	vegetation	14.	D
5.	False	15.	C
6.	True	16.	A
7.	False	17.	B
8.	C	18.	C
9.	C	19.	B
10.	B	20.	D

Page 164—Reading 3. Earthquakes

Page 164—Prequestions

1. 5   3. 5   5. 1
2. 4   4. 1

Page 165—A. Detailed Comprehension

1. B   5. C   8. B
2. A   6. B   9. A
3. A   7. A   10. B
4. A

Page 166—B. Vocabulary Work

1. lethal   9. menace
2. slippage   10. disaster
3. devastating   11. foreseen
4. instability   12. accurately
5. potential   13. molten
6. horrendous   14. adjacent
7. especially   15. gaps
8. boundaries   16. prone

Page 167—C. Vocabulary Building

1. predict/prediction
2. separation/separate
3. tremble/tremors
4. devastate/devastation
5. warn/warning
6. observe/observations
7. calculate/calculations
8. creation/create
9. refer/reference
10. form/formation
11. occur/occurrence
12. behavior/behave
13. measure/measurements

Page 168—Reading 4. Strip-mining

Page 169—A. General Comprehension

1. B	5. A	9. B
2. C	6. C	10. A
3. B	7. B	11. C
4. C	8. C	

Page 170—B. Vocabulary Work

1. B	4. B	6. A
2. C	5. B	7. C
3. B		

Page 171—C. Prefix and Suffix Review

1. D	3. C	4. B
2. D		

Page 171—D. Vocabulary Building

a. 3	e. 8	h. 4
b. 9	f. 11	i. 13
c. 6	g. 2	j. 5
d. 1		

Page 172—E. Restating

1. B	3. A	5. C
2. A	4. B	

Page 172—Reading 5. Nuclear Power

Page 172—Prequestions

Answers to 1 and 2 will vary.
3. catastrophe/chaos
   failure/disaster/debacle
   dilemma

Page 174—A. Detailed Comprehension

1. D	5. B	8. B
2. D	6. B	9. C
3. A	7. C	10. C
4. D		

Page 175—B. Vocabulary Work

1. A	9. B
2. D	10. C
3. D	11. escalate
4. B	12. beset
5. C	13. administer
6. B	14. appease
7. A	15. solidify
8. C	16. envisage

Page 177—Crossword Puzzle

```
S C R U P U L O U S . D O R M A N T . . T
A . E . A . I . . O . . E A T . . . O . N
G A P . L . S . M A L . . . A . . R . . E
E L E M E N T A R Y . . . . T . . E . . G
. . A . . . S T S . I . . . T . . C . . L
L A T E N T . O . . I N F R I N G E . . I
A T . X . H I M . . E . A . . . O I N G .
U . . T . R . . T O X I C . . . . V . . E
D E A R . O . . E . P . T . . . B E E N .
A . . A . W R A N G L E S . . . U . . . T
B A G . . . A . . . I . . . . E S T . . .
L . R . A V I D . C O A X . . . . . F E E
E P O C H . A . . I F . . U S A . . . . X
. . U . . G R E A T . . A . S . R . . . I
A P P E A S E D . . . . A D J A C E N T .
```

Page 178—Quiz 8

1. C	6. D	11. A
2. C	7. A	12. A
3. C	8. D	13. B
4. D	9. B	14. C
5. B	10. D	15. A

Page 185. Practice Test A

1. B	9. A	17. B	25. A	33. D	41. B
2. D	10. C	18. B	26. D	34. A	42. D
3. B	11. B	19. A	27. A	35. B	43. A
4. A	12. D	20. C	28. C	36. B	44. B
5. D	13. B	21. A	29. B	37. D	45. C
6. A	14. D	22. D	30. D	38. D	46. B
7. B	15. A	23. B	31. C	39. C	47. D
8. A	16. C	24. D	32. D	40. C	48. A

49.	C	56.	C	63.	A	70.	C	77.	A	84.	D
50.	C	57.	D	64.	A	71.	A	78.	A	85.	D
51.	D	58.	D	65.	C	72.	B	79.	D	86.	B
52.	C	59.	C	66.	C	73.	C	80.	C	87.	C
53.	B	60.	C	67.	D	74.	B	81.	C	88.	D
54.	C	61.	B	68.	C	75.	D	82.	B	89.	A
55.	C	62.	B	69.	D	76.	B	83.	C	90.	C

Page 198. Practice Test B

1.	D	16.	B	31.	A	46.	A	61.	C	76.	B
2.	B	17.	C	32.	B	47.	D	62.	C	77.	B
3.	D	18.	A	33.	D	48.	C	63.	C	78.	B
4.	D	19.	B	34.	A	49.	D	64.	D	79.	D
5.	B	20.	D	35.	A	50.	C	65.	C	80.	C
6.	B	21.	C	36.	C	51.	D	66.	B	81.	C
7.	C	22.	B	37.	A	52.	C	67.	A	82.	D
8.	B	23.	D	38.	C	53.	C	68.	B	83.	D
9.	A	24.	A	39.	C	54.	B	69.	A	84.	A
10.	B	25.	D	40.	D	55.	D	70.	D	85.	B
11.	C	26.	C	41.	A	56.	D	71.	C	86.	C
12.	C	27.	B	42.	B	57.	C	72.	A	87.	B
13.	A	28.	B	43.	C	58.	D	73.	D	88.	D
14.	B	29.	C	44.	D	59.	B	74.	A	89.	B
15.	C	30.	A	45.	D	60.	D	75.	A	90.	C

Page 211. Practice Test C

1.	B	16.	D	31.	C	46.	B	61.	B	76.	A
2.	D	17.	A	32.	C	47.	A	62.	C	77.	D
3.	C	18.	B	33.	D	48.	C	63.	D	78.	D
4.	A	19.	B	34.	A	49.	C	64.	B	79.	B
5.	C	20.	C	35.	B	50.	D	65.	C	80.	A
6.	B	21.	C	36.	A	51.	A	66.	B	81.	D
7.	D	22.	A	37.	B	52.	C	67.	C	82.	D
8.	B	23.	A	38.	C	53.	A	68.	C	83.	C
9.	A	24.	C	39.	C	54.	C	69.	D	84.	B
10.	C	25.	B	40.	D	55.	B	70.	C	85.	C
11.	D	26.	A	41.	A	56.	D	71.	D	86.	C
12.	B	27.	C	42.	C	57.	C	72.	C	87.	B
13.	A	28.	D	43.	C	58.	B	73.	D	88.	C
14.	B	29.	B	44.	D	59.	D	74.	C	89.	C
15.	A	30.	C	45.	A	60.	A	75.	B	90.	C